Forgotten Warriors

The Amphibious March Across the
Pacific During World War II

D. Ralph Young, with patriotic poetry
by shipmate Timothy D. Churchill

© 2016 D. Ralph Young
All Rights Reserved.

No part of this publication may be reproduced, stored in a retrieval system, or transmitted, in any form or by any means, electronic, mechanical, photocopying, recording, or otherwise, without the written permission of the author.

First published by Dog Ear Publishing
4011 Vincennes Road
Indianapolis, IN 46268
www.dogearpublishing.net

ISBN: 978-1-4575-4591-7

This book is printed on acid free paper.
Printed in the United States of America

CONTENTS

AKNOWLEGMENTS vii

INTRODUCTION ix

PREFACE: WHY I WROTE THIS BOOK xi

PART I: OBSERVATIONS AND REFLECTIONS
ON THE WAR 1
    WHY WAS THERE A WAR IN THE PACIFIC? 6
    PEARL HARBOR, DECEMBER 7, 1941 10

PART II: WORLD WAR II LEADERSHIP IN THE
PACIFIC THEATER OF WAR 25
    ADMIRAL CHESTER W. NIMITZ 25
    GENERAL DOUGLAS MACARTHUR 27
    ADMIRAL WILLIAM HALSEY JR. 28
    ADMIRAL RAYMOND SPRUANCE 31

PART III: THE BATTLES 34
    THE ALEUTIAN ISLANDS CAMPAIGN 34
    THE SOLOMON ISLANDS CAMPAIGN 41
    THE BATTLE OF GUADALCANAL 44
    THE BATTLE OF BOUGAINVILLE 53
    THE BATTLE OF THE CORAL SEA 59
    THE BATTLE OF MIDWAY 64
    THE BATTLE OF TARAWA 73

THE BATTLE OF KWAJALEIN AND
   ROI-NAMUR IN THE MARSHALL ISLANDS ..82

THE BATTLE OF ENIWETOK 87

THE BATTLE OF THE PHILIPPINE SEA 90

THE BATTLE OF SAIPAN 94

THE BATTLE OF TINIAN 103

THE BATTLES OF GUAM 109

THE BATTLE OF LEYTE 115

THE BATTLE OF LUZON................................133

THE BATTLE OF PELELIU..............................168

THE BATTLE OF IWO JIMA..........................175

THE BATTLE OF OKINAWA 203

PART IV: THE USS *J. FRANKLIN BELL,* AND
HER HISTORY AND DEMISE 229

PART V: THE OTHER FORGOTTEN WARRIORS 244

US WOMEN OF WORLD WAR II 244

THE UNITED STATES SUBMARINE SERVICE .248

THE US COAST GUARD 252

THE US SEABEES NAVAL
   CONSTRUCTION BATALLIONS 255

CONGRESSIONAL MEDAL OF HONOR
   HEROES OF THE PACIFIC...........................262

   THE BATTLE OF BUNA...........................262

   THE BATTLE FOR NEW GUINEA 263

    THE BATTLE FOR NEW GEORGIA 270
    THE BATTLE OF SAVO ISLAND 273
    HEROES OF THE PACIFIC NOT INCLUDED IN ANY OF THE ABOVE BATTLES 276
    ACE FIGHTER PILOTS 291

PART VI: SUMMARY OF WORLD WAR II 297
    THE COST 297
    OTHER FACTS 300

PART VIII: SHIPMATE REUNIONS—COMMENTARY ON FIVE REUNIONS, WITH POETRY BY TIMOTHY CHURCHILL 304
    CANTON, OHIO (1997) 304
    LEXINGTON, KENTUCKY (2005) 304
    GOLD CANYON, ARIZONA (2007) 306
    DANVILLE, KENTUCKY (2008) 307
    TYLER, TEXAS (2009) 309

PART IX: CONCLUSION AND FINAL THOUGHTS 311

APPENDIX A: REFERENCES 317

APPENDIX B: ORIGINAL CREW ASSIGNED TO USS *J. FRANKLIN BELL*, APRIL 2, 1942 319

APPENDIX C: SURVIVING USS *J. FRANKLIN BELL* SHIPMATES AND/OR SPOUSES IN 2009 332

APPENDIX D: DECEASED SHIPMATES AS OF 2009 . 338

APPENDIX E: USS J. FRANKLIN BELL
ASSOCIATION MEMBERS AS OF 2009 339

APPENDIX F: LISTING OF PICTURES, MAPS
AND TABLES 343
    PHOTOGRAPHS 343
    MAPS 344
    TABLES 345

APPENDIX G: POETRY BY TIMOTHY D. CHURCHILL 347

AKNOWLEGMENTS

Writing this book at ninety years of age has not been easy, particularly with the coming of Windows 10 at a crucial stage, but writing has been rewarding in bringing back so many memories of when I was a teenager. I have several people to thank for reading portions and giving me their comments—including Bill Chadwell, Caroline and Bill Lancaster, Helen Hume, and Angela and Jess Correll.

It was a thrill to have my grandson Chad Young design my book cover. Feedback about the cover has been excellent.

Also, thanks to Neil Chethik for his comments at a recent writer's conference at the Carnegie Center in Lexington, Kentucky, and thanks to Julia Young for allowing me to start writing my book in the privacy of her lake house, where the isolation was perfect for thought and reflection on the past.

I thank all my shipmates for their input but give a special thanks to Tim Churchill for allowing me to use his patriotic poetry about World War II and about our many shipmates' reunions and for being my shipmate for several years in the vast Pacific Ocean.

Above all, I want to thank my beautiful and talented wife Janice Louise Young. Without her knowledge of Windows 10, overall support and encouragement, I would never have been able to complete this book.

INTRODUCTION

Part I of this book will cover why there was a war in the Pacific, described the attack on Pearl Harbor, and explained the role that my ship, the USS *J. Franklin Bell*, played in the Pacific Theatre.

Part II describes the four main leaders in the battles in the Pacific Theatre and gives some details into their leadership styles.

In Part III, I list all the major battles that occurred in the Pacific as well as the numbers of troop, ship, and aircraft casualties in each battle. I've also listed all Medals of Honor awarded in the Pacific Theatre. This is my effort to see that they are not forgotten.

Part IV deals with the final stages of the USS *J. Franklin Bell* and lists her various captains and the awards that various crew members and the ship received during her numerous battles.

In Part V, I review the other warriors in the Pacific Theater during WWII, and on the home front: women of the United States, the Coast Guard, the Seabees, the Submariners, and other Congressional Medal of Honor heroes of the Pacific.

Part VI examines some other interesting facts about WWII.

Part VII lists the number of total casualties in WWII and compares the numbers with other wars.

Part VIII reports on a few of the numerous reunions of the shipmates of the *J. Franklin Bell*: Canton, Ohio; Lexington, Kentucky; Gold Canyon, Arizona; Danville, Kentucky; and Tyler, Texas. Also included is poetry written by Timothy Churchill during each of the reunions.

Part IX includes my conclusion and final thoughts.

Finally, the appendices provide a list of references used, a complete listing of the first crew assigned to the USS J. Franklin Bell in 1942, when she was taken over by the Navy; a listing of the Bell roster as of 9/22/2009; a listing of the J. Franklin Bell Roll of Honor(Deceased) as of 9/22/2009; a listing of the members of J. Franklin Bell Association as of 9/22/2009; a listing of pictures, maps, and tables found throughout the book; and a listing of the poems written by Timothy Churchill that are included in this book.

PREFACE: WHY I WROTE THIS BOOK

World War II began on December 7, 1941, a day to be remembered. I recall the date vividly and can still hear the announcer on the radio saying that the Japanese had attacked Pearl Harbor. Bill Scheuer, my best friend, and I were hitchhiking home from attending a movie in Stanford, Kentucky. The driver of the car was listening to the radio and told us that the Japanese had just bombed Pearl Harbor.

I was sixteen years old at the time. Everything pointed toward a long war, and there was little doubt that the military draft would be lowered from twenty-one to eighteen. I just knew I would be off to the war at eighteen years of age.

Initially, I want to be a pilot. I can still remember walking to the backfields on our farm to bring the cows up for milking and watching the planes flying over our farm. I could visualize myself at the control of a powerful plane, wearing a leather helmet, my scarf flying in the wind.

A good friend of mine, Glen Faulkner, had researched aviation and talked about flying all the time. The fact that I did not have enough education to become a pilot was a problem, however, and therefore necessitated a reality check on my part about my future in the war effort.

At that time, one did not get to select a particular branch of service if he waited to be drafted; the government put draftees where they were most needed. With all this in mind, when I became seventeen, I convinced my mother that I should enlist in the Navy because I would then be allowed to finish high school. I therefore enlisted when I was seventeen but did not have to report for duty until I was eighteen, just after high school graduation, and my boot camp training was at Great Lakes, Illinois.

This book is not meant to be about me, however. (About me is a book titled *The Power of a Mother's Prayer*.) This book is about all those Marines, soldiers, and sailors (which includes me) who fought in the Pacific and now, in my opinion, have been forgotten.

It seems that we celebrate the invasion of Normandy, the Battle of the Bulge, and the European Theatre of war every year, but missing from such recognitions are the invasions in Peleliu, Tarawa, and Tinian and so forth. Often we hear about VE Day but seldom hear about VJ Day. This indifference is further illustrated in the World War II Museum in New Orleans. Although the museum was founded in the year 2000, only now in 2015 has it started an exhibit entitled the Road to Tokyo, though an exhibit entitled the Road to Berlin has already been completed. Have those in charge forgotten who attacked us at Pearl Harbor? However, this museum is great to have and especially since it is dedicated to the memory of World War II veterans. I did make the financial contribution requested to bring the Pacific Theatre up to equal status with the European Theatre. In addition, the museum is fast becoming number one for World War II history.

Since there are hundreds and hundreds of books that analyze World War II very well, this book is meant to summarize some of the major battles in the Pacific and to briefly answer the questions of what, where, when, and why. It is not intended to provide an in-depth analysis of every battle across the Pacific during World War II but rather to discuss only those major battles and the ones that applied to my ship, the USS *J. Franklin Bell* and me.

What kind of enemy did our Pacific Theater troops face? In the book *War in the Pacific,* Edwin P. Hoyt describes the Japanese code produced by Hideki Tojo in a pamphlet called "Senjinkum" for the Japanese soldier.

The new army held that the emperor was divine, being above men, and that the lives of everyone in the Japanese empire had to be dedicated to imperial service: Don't stay alive in dishonor; don't die in such a way as to leave a bad name behind you. This philosophy led to the shooting of Allied medical corpsmen while attending the wounded, the murdering of Allied chaplains while administering the last rites, and the bayoneting of Allied soldiers because they were too weak to walk. The

Japanese were a medieval enemy with a barbarian philosophy. A Japanese slogan used by the army in the early 1940s said, "To die for the emperor is to live forever."

I do not mean to imply that all my comrades were saints. In the heat of battle, we did some things that were not very pretty, like cutting off someone's ear and attaching it to your belt, but these were isolated cases and not standard operating procedures as they were with the Japanese soldiers.

If you want further proof of the vicious training the Japanese military received, read about the Rape of Nanking or consider the words of China's Chiang Kai-Shek about the 250,000 Chinese executed because of the Doolittle raid on the Japanese for allowing the B-25 bombers to land at Chinese airports. In contrast, the German and Italian soldiers were tough fighters but were more humane, not barbarians.

Another example of the breed of enemy we fought in the Pacific is the survival rate for prisoners of war (POWs). For those captured by the Germans and Italians, the death rate was just over 1 percent. For those under Japanese control, the death rate was over 40 percent. The fanatical attitude of the Japanese soldiers is readily explained by the killed-to-wounded ratio. This ratio was about three (3) wounded for each one (1) killed for the US military during World War II, but for the Japanese it was about eighteen (18) killed for each one (1) wounded because Japanese soldiers refused to surrender. This suicidal philosophy of the Japanese in the Pacific is evident in the numbers listed in the table below which shows a comparison between the Pacific and European campaigns. This information was taken from *The Pacific Online Encyclopedia*.

Table 1. Comparison of Average Casualty rates for ground Combat Units

	Pacific Amphibious Campaigns	European Protracted Campaign
Killed in Action	1.78	0.36
Wounded in Action	5.50	1.74
Missing in Action	0.17	0.08

This means that in the Pacific Theatre, compared to the European Theatre, a US soldier was nearly five times more likely to be killed; more than three times likely to be wounded and more than two times likely to be missing in action. But, regardless of the theatre of war the American soldiers fought with pride, commitment, and moral integrity throughout World War II. I know I speak for all the veterans of World War II when I say we were proud and honored to have served our country.

Compare all of the above with what Timothy Churchill says about the American Veteran:

The American Veteran

America's veterans, young and old
Have made our nation proud;
We salute you for your service now,
And sing your praise aloud.

We know the sacrifices you've made,
To serve and face the foe;
And save the freedom for our land,
That all the world should know.

America's veterans, always first,
And always in our prayers;
As you march to war, in any war,
America always cares.

And just as surely, we can share,
Our patriotic dream,
That peace returns, when you return,
With victory to redeem.

The ones who marched in former time,
Some gone, but honored still,
And those who wave the flag today,
Salute, as veterans will.

And so we take this time to say,
Our "thanks" to one and all;
For those who serve our nation's cause.
Salute, you're standing tall.

I have yet another reason for writing this book: I am proud to have served on the USS *J. Franklin Bell*. It did not have the prestige of a battleship or cruiser, nor the beautiful lines and swagger of a destroyer, but as an attack transport (APA) ship they were always in the middle of the action and served our nation well. The role of all APAs during WWII was to pick up troops, carry them to the island selected, and then land them on the beaches together with equipment, armament, and supplies. To aid in the unloading, each APA ship would supply a beach party that exited the ship and traveled to the beach with the troops to aid in flow of troops and battle supplies. The beach party also maintained the guns and landing craft if problems occurred. This is why I ended upon the beach at Saipan and Tinian.

The USS *J. Franklin Bell* received six battle stars for her contribution as she moved across the Pacific Theater of War toward Japan during World War II.

Also, note that the vast majority of the rungs in the ladder in our climb from Guadalcanal toward the mainland of Japan were not won by the battleships', cruisers', and destroyers' bombardments of beaches but by putting soldiers, marines, and naval personnel *on the beaches*. The final victory proves a *great joint effort*.

PART I: OBSERVATIONS AND REFLECTIONS ON THE WAR

The deafening sound of battle was everywhere when the Marine commander said, "We have a wounded comrade on the front line of battle and I need a stretcher detail of four men to go to the front and bring him back here."

Among the four volunteers, was Richard Kraus, an eighteen-year-old Marine from Minneapolis, Minnesota, seeing his first battle on the Island of Peleliu in 1944. As the volunteers advanced toward the front lines, the machine-gun fire and hand grenades launched became so intense that they had to take cover in a foxhole. Suddenly, they saw two men approaching their foxhole and demanded a password. Instead of a password, the four mariners received a hand grenade tossed into their group. Richard Kraus threw his body onto the grenade, absorbing the full impact of the explosion, thereby giving his life to save the lives of his three comrades, and subsequently for this action received the Medal of Honor.

Other than his family, how many people would remember Richard Kraus? Even fewer would remember that there was a battle on the island of Peleliu. This is why I feel compelled to write about the war in the Pacific and all those unforgotten battles and soldiers.

It seems that we celebrate Normandy every year, but not Peleliu, where we had 3201 more casualties during the invasion than the D-Day invasion of Normandy.

While critics might question the comparison, the fact remains that *everyone* remembers Normandy and *nobody* remembers Peleliu. This statement is based on asking people this question during the two-year period of writing this book. This book in no way intends to degrade any of the many sacrifices made by our troops at Normandy. They deserve all the attention and respect they have received; however, the forces at Peleliu and other battles in the Pacific Theatre call for comparable notice as well.

I believe the troops who fought in the Pacific are mostly forgotten by the present generation. Others believe the same as I do, as illustrated in an article in *Naval History* titled "Peleliu: The Forgotten Battle," by Maj. Henry Donigan, who fought there and lived to write and publish the story in September 1994. He wrote, " Fifty years ago, in a forgotten backwater of the Central Pacific, Marines, soldiers and sailors fought the Japanese in one of the most savage and costly battles in World War II. The assault on the island of Peleliu compares to the most famous battles in American history in terms of ferocity and valor. Yet this battle has been all but forgotten except by a few historians and the valiant men who fought there."

All of these soldiers of World War II were a generation called the Greatest Generation by many (including Journalist Tom Brokaw). They were from all walks of life and trusted our government and loved our country with a love so deep that they were willing to die for our nation and for our country's freedoms. They never asked our government for anything other than "Where and when do you want me to start defending my country?"

Timothy Churchill, my shipmate on the USS *J. Franklin Bell*, in his poem "A Celebration of Our Forces," put all of the above eloquently:

A Celebration of Our Forces

You heard your country's call to arms,
Once more to take a stand,
Your brave response was loud and clear,
"Keep freedom in your land."

You marched away with fearless stride,
You fought on foreign soil;
With courage, calm, and sacrifice,
You challenged war's turmoil.

You came from every walk of life,
To heed our nation's call;
You're American's Forces, Guard, Reserve
You are our heroes all.

Your stand is to defend the right,
You are our country's pride;
You bravely march into harm's way,
Your cause is justified.

So march today, you honored vets,
With banner, standing tall.
May God bless each and every one,
We thank you one and all.

My children joke about the many letters I write to newspaper editors on subjects that concern me. The fact is, I have written twice as many as they know about, because after getting my opinions off my chest, I often toss the letters in the wastebasket—but for this book, I will finish the course for all my comrades and shipmates who fought and died in that vast, intimidating, and unimaginable but sometimes beautiful Pacific Ocean. In addition, this book is also written for those who are still alive, with my thoughts and prayers in their honor on every page.

When I first started to think about writing this book, I checked the Internet to research World War II in the Pacific. It was during this early stage of research that I came upon a picture of young Richard Kraus, whom I mentioned in the opening paragraphs. I was inspired to research and write this book by the youthful looking Richard and the millions of us just like him with the thought that we had to engage in combat with the vicious and cruel Japanese.

The records show that the Pacific Theater of War had about 50 percent of the total casualties in World War II, or about 36 million. If total sacrifices are the criteria, why not give the Pacific equal billing? I just want to have parity in the press and museums for veterans of the Pacific Theater of World War II.

Richard Kraus at eighteen   D. Ralph Young at eighteen, on board the USS *J. Franklin Bell*

Yes, we were very young back in those days, and when I look at a picture of Richard, I feel guilty for being over ninety years of age after Richard died so young. Young men like Richard should not have had to die in wars between nations. I just wish that the leaders of all nations could experience for a few days the front lines of battle and have to contend with the smell of human flesh decaying right before their eyes, in the hot temperatures of the Pacific Theater. It is a smell you will never forget regardless of your age. I think this would go a long way toward creating permanent peace in the world.

Other than my own experience and those of a few shipmates, all of my information has come from the sources listed in the bibliography at the end of this book. My target is for a quick reference describing each major battle that will identify casualties and loss of ships and aircraft and will identify the Medals of Honor awarded.

WHY WAS THERE A WAR IN THE PACIFIC?

The country of Japan, with a population of nearly 100 million people, allowed itself to be governed by its military, which numbered around 12,000 in the late 1930s. There were two factions within the military: one that wanted to expand north and another that wanted to expand south. Those who wanted to expand north won the internal battle and began the expansion but suffered defeat every time they met the Russians. This brought a pause whereby the south supporters convinced all the military that an advance toward Malay and Dutch East Indies would be easier if the US Navy could be defeated or neutralized. The Japanese at that time had enough reserves of oil and other resources to last about one year. Malay's tin and rubber and the East Indies' oil made a south adventure very attractive.

Peace between Japan and the United States did not appear possible for two reasons: first, the United States had cut off oil shipments to Japan, which infuriated the Japanese, and second, a condition that the United States insisted upon—Japanese's withdrawal from China—would never be accepted.

Another factor influencing Japan's action in the Pacific Theater was the Japanese's feeling of inferiority to white people. In an attempt to overcome that inferiority and to prove their superiority, they often took up all of the sidewalk to force a foreign person into the streets. The Japanese were intent on driving the Americans, British, and Dutch from Asia. This in all probability had a great influence on the Japanese being accepted so readily in Burma, Thailand, Indochina, Indonesia, and other areas of the Pacific.

Japanese historians concluded that the year 1940 was the 2600th anniversary of their nation. As a result, the emperor scheduled a large celebration resulting in a high wave of enthusiasm for the nation. On January 1, 1941, all the political leaders of Japan vowed to give up their rights and to join the cause as set forth by the army leaders. This meant that an adventure in some direction was a foregone conclusion. In fact, Japanese Admiral Isoroku Yamamoto announced, "The goal of our nation is that all eight corners of the world would be under one roof." To achieve success in Asia, the Japanese knew that they had to neutralize the US Navy, so the attack on Pearl Harbor was developed. In fact, most of 1941 was used by the Japanese Navy to prepare for the attack. Kagoshima on the southern tip of Kyushu, where a model of Pearl Harbor had been set up for training using torpedoes specially designed for the shallow waters to be encountered at Pearl Harbor.

Throughout my book I have tried to reflect, on some of the happenings and events in that period of time, to give the reader an opportunity to visualize the mood of the American people during World War II. Also, the information is valuable to me and my comrades because we were off fighting a war at that time.

During 1941, Americans in the United States were busy following the war in Europe, which was dominating world affairs. Attention was given to events like the completion of Mt. Rushmore featuring US Presidents by Gutzon Borglum and the development of the United Service Organization (USO), which would be providing coffee, donuts, and entertainment to US military members being drafted at the age of 21.

Americans at home were more concerned during this period, with the cost of living: an average new home cost $4,075.00, a gallon of gasoline cost $0.12, a new car was $850.00, and a house rented for $32.00 per month. Additionally, on their minds, was the war in Europe and Land Lease Act President Roosevelt signed, providing military aid to the Allies. Other focuses were the Willys jeep, introduced for use by the US Army; Glen Miller's recording, "Chattanooga Choo Choo;" and the Andrew Sister's melody, "I'll Be with You in Apple Blossom Time" were the hit recordings.

In charge of the Japanese attack on Pearl Harbor was Admiral Yamamoto. His plan was to inflict enough damage to the US fleet so that it would not be able to interfere with the Japanese invasion of all of Southeast Asia. Yamamoto was willing to commit six aircraft carriers to the surprise attack, which did not go over well with the battleship commanders because they considered this too much of a risk and exposure of their naval aircraft and resources, but Yamamoto felt that risk was necessary in time of war.

On November 10, 1941, the Japanese began their journey to an island in the Kuriles where they assembled to stock up on oil and supplies previously stashed for this purpose. On December 2, 1941, they departed for the surprise attack on Pearl Harbor. During this same period of time in early December two Japanese ambassadors were meeting with Secretary of State Hull in Washington, DC, talking peace.

PEARL HARBOR, DECEMBER 7, 1941

The mindless rejoicing at home is appalling; it makes me fear that the first blow against Tokyo will make them wilt at once. ... I only wish that [the Americans] had also had three carriers at Hawaii. —Admiral Isoroku Yamamoto, Commander in Chief of the Japanese Navy

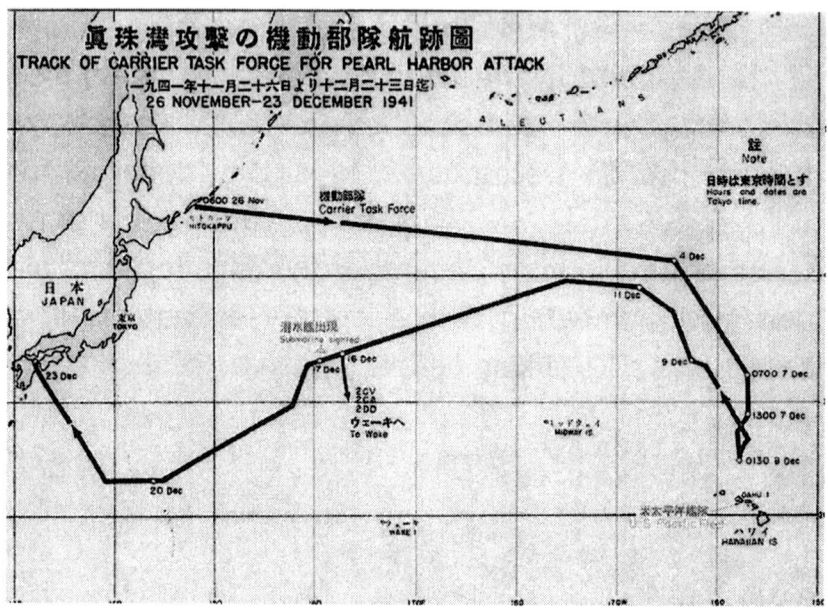

The routes taken by the Japanese for their attack on Pearl Harbor and return to Japan (Courtesy Wikimedia- Public Domain)

A Navy launch approaches the blazing USS West Virginia to rescue a sailor (Courtesy U.S. Navy Photograph – Public Domain)

The surprise attack on Pearl Harbor occurred at 7:48 AM Hawaiian time (12:48 PM Eastern) on December 7, 1941. There were similar (but not simultaneous, because of time zone differences) attacks on the Philippines, Malaya, Singapore, and Hong Kong, which brought the Netherlands and England into the war in the Pacific along with the United States. The attack came as a shock to the American people, and the United States declared war on Japan the following day, December 8, 1941. Germany and Italy declared war on the United States on December 11, 1941, and the United States responded with declarations of war on them on the same day.

The Japanese had chosen a weekend for the attack because they had noted that the US battleship commanders had always made an effort to get their crews in port for weekend shore leave. They also considered this a weakness in the Americans and felt that their own soldiers were far superior. In addition, at that time, the most prestigious ship in any navy was the battleship.

The Battle Ship USS Pennsylvania in the background with the Destroyers Downes and Cassin damaged and sinking in the foreground (Courtesy U. S. Navy photograph - Public Domain)

Ford Island photograph taken by the Japanese during the surprise attack. (Courtesy U.S. Navy photograph -Public Domain)

They also had hoped that our aircraft carriers would be in port, but the carriers were out at sea and the Japanese did not know where they were. This, in all probability, caused the Japanese to cut short the complete destruction of Pearl Harbor; they left the area without doing any damage to the navy yard, the above ground oil tank farms, or the submarine base. Another thought held by many is that the Japanese *underestimated* the will and determination of the American people and expected a short war with the United States.

Being in Pearl Harbor had to be a frightening experience for those awakening to the sounds of bombs exploding, the general quarters alarm, and loud gunfire. Many people dressed on their way to their general quarters stations. The defenders were totally unprepared, with no ammunition, their ammunition lockers locked, and aircraft parked close together for the purpose of protecting from sabotage.

A total of 353 Japanese planes made up the two waves of attacks. Torpedo bombers led the first wave of 152 planes, with their target being the battleships. Then the dive-bombers came with their attack on the air bases across Oahu. The second wave of 171 planes concentrated its attack on Bellows Field and Ford Island. Ninety minutes after it began, the attack was over. Table 2 below lists the killed and wounded. Nearly half of the US fatalities were caused by the forward magazine explosion of the battleship *Arizona*.

The following poem reflects what Timothy Churchill had to say about our country and the attack on Pearl Harbor.

The Day the Music Died

The music from the radio,
Died so suddenly;
I caught my breath and
dropped a dish,
That day of infamy.

Remembering "Pearl Harbor,"
As a day in time for some;
A day's event to change the world,
And shape what was to come.

Pearl Harbor now a
peaceful place,
Where havoc was in store;
That day so many years ago,
When aircraft bombed our shore.

America woke to bombs and fire,
That turned our peaceful tide,
No more would life
go on the same,
That day the music died.

For those who still recall that day,
Their minds remember well,
And live again just
where they were,
And wept for those who fell.

The history of our nation's plight,
Brings honor, then as now.
Our brave American response,
Kept "victory" as our vow.

Remembering "Pearl
Harbor Event,"
As source of pride;
Salute our nation's gallantry,
Our Forces, far and wide.

The courage of our fighting men,
Reflects the honor due,
To all of those who
passed before,
And those we never knew.

Salute our nation's gallantry,
Our Forces, far and wide.
The courage of our fighting men,
Reflects the honor due,
To all of those who
passed before,
And those we never knew.

I have never been overly impressed with the memorial for the *Arizona* at Pearl Harbor maybe because it did not say anything to me and looked odd. My research tells me that the designer, Alfred Preis, meant to convey a sagging center with the ends being strong and vigorous, meaning initial defeat and ultimate victory. Maybe it will look different to me the next time I visit.

The Memorial for the USS Arizona sitting over the sunken battleship at Pearl Harbor (Courtesy U.S. Navy Photograph – Public Domain)

The Japanese planners had decided to select a location where their troubled planes unable to return to their carriers could land for rescue. They chose the Island of Niihau. A Zero flown by Petty Officer Shigenori Nishikaichi was damaged during the attack on Wheeler Air Force Base and again on landing. A native Hawaiian who was aware of tensions between the United States and Japan helped the officer from the wreckage. He took the Japanese pilot's maps and other documents.

The local inhabitants had no telephone or radio contacts so were completely unaware of the attack by the Japanese. The Japanese officer enlisted the support of three Japanese American residents in an attempt to recover his documents. A struggle followed, the Japanese officer was killed and a civilian was wounded. One of the three Japanese Americans committed suicide and his wife and the other Japanese American were sent to prison. The thought of our putting 110,000 Japanese Americans in internment camps sounds awful, but, the above incident probably played a key role in that decision.

The war with Japan created some bizarre events, such as a two-day battle against no one. The Los Angeles Times reported that on February 24 and 25, 1942, unexplained lights in the sky were thought to be Japanese planes, but they were actually lost weather balloons and were mistaken as enemy aircraft. The result was the sky being pummeled for two nights with round after round of ammunition. Every base involved thought Japanese bombers were attacking the other. Shortly after February 25, Secretary of the Navy Frank Knox admitted it was a false alarm.

After Pearl Harbor, the Japanese quickly took control over a large area of the Pacific. Included were the Aleutian Islands, the Solomon Islands, Indonesia, Thailand, Burma, Singapore, and the Philippines.

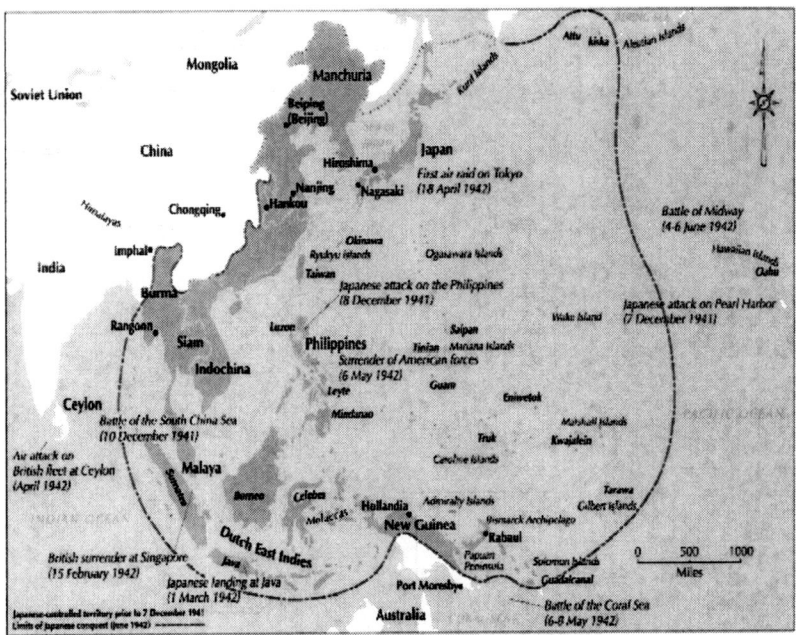

The area shaded dark shows the Japanese Empire in early 1942. (Courtesy Jacqueline Goins UK Cartography Lab)

During World War II, the Medal of Honor was awarded to 464 recipients, with 266 awarded posthumously. The criteria for being awarded the Medal of Honor are "for conspicuous gallantry and intrepidity at the risk of life, above and beyond the call of duty," and the medal is authorized by Congress and awarded by the President.

I have elected to write a short description about those awarded the Medal of Honor throughout the Pacific Campaign. By my account, there were 197. A total of fifteen were awarded for the attack on Pearl Harbor, though by all accounts that I have read, there should have been sixteen, but Doris "Dorie" Miller was denied the award because he was of the "wrong" race—African American. I have included him in the following list and have tried to describe his actions during the bombing and strafing by enemy aircraft.

Table 2 shows the following troop, ship and, aircraft casualties occurred at Pearl Harbor.

Table 2. Pearl Harbor casualties

	USA	JAPAN		USA		JAPAN	
				Destroyed	Damaged	Destroyed	Damaged
Killed	2403*	64	Battleships	4			
Wounded	1178*		Cruisers	3			
Captured		1	Destroyers	3			
			Other types	5	4		
			Midget Subs			4	1
			Aircraft	188	158	29	

*USA Civilian Casualties: an additional 68 killed and 35 wounded.

Below are descriptive accounts of the fifteen Medal of Honor recipients and Dorie Miller for the Pearl Harbor attack. All of the Medal of Honor descriptions throughout this book are condensed versions of the original public domain citation issued by the United States Government and other sources noted in the References.

MARVYN BENNION, Captain, U.S. Navy, born May 5, 1887, in Vemon, UT. Captain Bennion, commanding officer of the USS *West Virginia,* with extraordinary courage beyond the call of duty during the attack on Pearl Harbor on December 7, 1941, after being mortally wounded in fighting to save his ship, strongly protested being carried from his bridge by Dorie Miller and other crew members. Using one arm to hold his wound closed, he bled to death while still commanding his crew.

JOHN WILLIAM FINN, Lieutenant, U.S. Navy, born July 15, 1909, in Los Angeles, CA. Although painfully wounded many times, he continued to man his 50-caliber machine gun and to return enemy fire vigorously with telling effect and complete disregard for his own personal safety. Only by specific orders was he persuaded to leave his post to seek medical treatment. He returned to the squadron area and actively supervised the rearming of returning planes.

FRANCIS C. FLAHERTY, Ensign, U.S. Navy Reserve, born March 15, 1919, in Charlotte, MI. When the USS *Oklahoma* was about to capsize and orders were given to abandon ship, Ensign Flaherty remained in a turret, holding a flashlight so the remainder of the turret crew could escape, thereby sacrificing his own life.

SAMUEL GLENN FUQUA, Captain, U.S. Navy, born October 15, 1899, in Laddonia, MO. Despite being knocked unconscious by an enemy bomb, he recovered to lead in fighting a fire that was spreading throughout the ship. His amazingly calm and cool manner and excellent judgment inspired all those who saw him and resulted in the saving of many lives.

EDWIN JOSEPH HILL, Chief Boatswain, U.S. Navy, born October 4, 1894, in Philadelphia, PA. During the strafing and bombing at Pearl Harbor, he led his men of the line handling to the quays that tied the ship to the dock. He cast off the lines and swam back to the ship. While attempting to release the anchors, he was killed by the explosion of several bombs.

HERBERT CHARPOIT JONES, Ensign, U.S. Navy Reserve, born December 1, 1918, in Los Angeles, CA. Ensign Jones organized and led a party to supply ammunition to the antiaircraft battery on the USS *California* after the mechanical hoist was put out of action. He was fatally wounded, and when two men attempted to take him away, he refused to leave, saying, "Leave me alone! I am done for. Get out before the magazines go off."

ISAAC CAMPBELL KIDD, Rear Admiral, U.S. Navy, born March 26, 1884, in Cleveland, OH. Rear Admiral Kidd immediately went to the bridge, and as Commander, Battleship Division One, he courageously discharged his duties as Senior Officer Afloat until the USS *Arizona*, his flagship, blew up from a magazine explosion and a direct bomb hit on the bridge resulted in his death.

JACKSON CHARLES PHARRIS, Lieutenant, U.S. Navy, born June 26, 1912, in Columbus, GA. Lieutenant Pharris was stunned and severely injured by the concussion of the first torpedo. He recovered quickly and acted on his own to set up a hand-to-hand supply for the antiaircraft guns. Twice rendered unconscious by the nauseous fumes, he persisted in his desperate effort to speed up the supply of ammunition. He risked his life several times to enter flooding compartments to drag unconscious shipmates to safety. He was largely responsible for keeping the *California* in action during the attack.

THOMAS JAMES REEVES, Radio Electrician (Warrant Officer), U.S. Navy, born December 9, 1895, in Thomaston, CT. After the mechanized hoists were put out of action on the USS *California*, Reeves on his own initiative, in a burning passageway, assisted in the maintenance of ammunition supply by hand to the antiaircraft guns until he was overcome by smoke and fire, which resulted in his death.

DONALD KIRBY ROSS, Machinist Mate, U.S. Navy, born December 8, 1910, in Beverly, KA. Machinist Mate Ross forced his men to leave the USS *Nevada* forward dynamo room because of smoke, steam, and heat. He continued doing all the duties until he became unconscious and was rescued and resuscitated. He returned to secure the forward dynamo room and then proceeded to the aft dynamo room, where he was again rendered unconscious, by exhaustion. Again recovering consciousness, he returned to his station on the USS *Nevada*.

ROBERT R. SCOTT, Machinist Mate First Class, U.S. Navy, born July 13, 1915, in Massillon, OH. The air compressor compartment in the USS *California* to which Scott was assigned as his battle station was flooded as result of a torpedo hit. The remainder of the personnel evacuated that compartment, but Scott refused to leave, saying, "This is my station and I will stay and give air as long as the guns are going."

PETER TOMICH, Chief Watertender, U.S. Navy, born June 3, 1893, in Prolog, Austria. Although realizing that the ship was capsizing as a result of enemy bombing and torpedoing, Tomich remained at his post in the engineering plant of the USS *Utah* until he saw that all boilers were secure and all fireroom personnel had left their stations. By doing so, he lost his life.

FRANKLIN VAN VALKENBURGH, Captain, U.S. Navy, born April 5, 1888, in Minneapolis, MN. As commanding officer of the USS *Arizona*, he gallantly fought from his ship until the ammunition magazine exploded and a direct bomb hit to the bridge resulted in his death.

JAMES RICHARD WARD, Seaman First Class, U.S. Navy, born September 10, 1921, in Springfield, OH. When it was seen that the USS *Oklahoma* was going to capsize and the order was given to abandon ship. Ward remained in a turret holding a flashlight so the remainder of the turret crew could see to escape, thereby sacrificing his own life in a similar fashion as Francis C. Flaherty.

CASSIN YOUNG, Commander, U.S. Navy, born March 6, 1894, in Washington, DC. Commander Young's ship, the USS *Vestal,* moored alongside the *Arizona*. When the ammunition magazine exploded, it blew him off the ship. He managed to swim back to his ship through oil and fire to take command of his ship and move away from the *Arizona*. He eventually beached his ship to keep it from sinking.

DORIS "DORIE" MILLER, Messman Third Class awarded the Navy Cross, born October 12, 1919, in Waco, TX. When torpedoes hit the battleship *West Virginia* at 7:57 AM, Miller headed for his general quarters station, only to find it destroyed by the torpedo. He then reported for duty to a central station. He was asked to go with the communications officer to the bridge to assist in removing the ship's captain, who had a gaping wound in the abdomen. The captain refused to leave. Miller assisted in moving him to a part of the bridge that had some shelter. Miller then helped two officers load the 50-caliber machine guns. One of the officers noted that when he looked back, Miller was firing the machine gun, a gun he was not at all familiar with and had not had any training on. Miller then assisted in moving injured sailors through oil, water, and fire to the quarterdeck, thereby unquestionably saving the lives of a number of shipmates—all of this under heavy bombing and strafing and without concern for his own life. Miller was recognized as one of the first heroes of World War II. He then did a brief war bond tour in the United States. Then he was assigned to the escort carrier *Liscome Bay,* which was torpedoed on November 24, 1943, in the Battle of Makin. The torpedo resulted in the aircraft bomb magazine exploding. The result was that only 272 from a crew of more than 900 survived. Dorie Miller was among the missing.

After Pearl Harbor, the Japanese quickly gained control over a huge area of the Pacific - from the Philippines to Burma to the Aleutians to the Solomon Islands. It appeared that the Japanese misjudged the will and determination of the American people and as a result overextended themselves. By occupying such a large area and with any substantial losses, they would not have the resources to replace their losses. This became evident during the naval Battles of the Coral Sea and Midway, with the advances of the Japanese checked at the Coral Sea and, a month later, the United States going on the offensive at Midway and continuing that aggression until victory was complete.

PART II: WORLD WAR II LEADERSHIP IN THE PACIFIC THEATER OF WAR

A military man can scarcely pride himself on having smitten a sleeping enemy; it is more a matter of shame, simply for the one smitten. — Admiral Isoroku Yamamoto, Commander in Chief of the Japanese Navy (about Pearl Harbor, 1942)

When this war is over, the Japanese language will be spoken only in hell. — Admiral Bill Halsey (December 7, 1941)

ADMIRAL CHESTER W. NIMITZ

Chester W. Nimitz, fleet admiral of the United States Navy, was born on February 24, 1885, and died on February 20, 1966. He played a major role in the naval history of WWII as commander in chief of the United States Pacific fleet. He was also the leading US Navy authority on submarines and was a key factor in the building of the first nuclear-powered submarine, the USS *Nautilus*.

Admiral Nimitz's father died six months prior to his birth, and the future admiral was heavily influenced by his grandfather, who had been a German Merchant Marine. The lesson he learned from his grandfather was that the sea—like life itself—is a stern taskmaster and the best way to get along with either is to learn all you can, then do your best and don't worry—especially about things over which you have no control.

Originally, Nimitz applied for West Point, but no appointments were available. He was told by Congressman James L. Slayden that he had one appointment available for the Navy and that he would award it to the best candidate available. Nimitz thought that this was his only opportunity for advanced education and applied himself to win the award. He graduated seventh of a class of 114 on January 30, 1905, from the Naval Academy.

In early 1942, the US Joint Chiefs of Staff divided the Pacific Theater into three regions: The Southwest Pacific under General MacArthur, and the Pacific Ocean Areas and the Southeast Pacific under Admiral Chester W. Nimitz, with the responsibility for all land, air, and sea operations in his areas. On September 2, 1945, Admiral Nimitz signed for the United States when Japan formally surrendered onboard the USS *Missouri* in Tokyo Bay.

Admiral Nimitz suffered a stroke in late 1965 and died on February 20, 1966. He was buried with full military honors at the Golden Gate National Cemetery in San Bruno, California, and lies alongside his wife and longtime friends Admiral Raymond A. Spruance, Admiral Richmond K. Turner, and Admiral Charles A. Lockwood, an arrangement they made while living.

GENERAL DOUGLAS MACARTHUR

Douglas MacArthur was born on January 26, 1880, and died on April 5, 1964. Raised in a military family in the old west, he attended the United States Military Academy at West Point, where he graduated first in his class of 1903. His tour of duty included superintendent of West Point after his assignment in Europe, where he became a brigadier general. In World War I, he was nominated for the Medal of Honor and was awarded the Distinguished Service Cross twice and the Silver Star seven times.

General MacArthur retired from the military in 1937 and became military advisor for the Philippine government. He accepted a recall to active duty in 1941 and was given command of the Army Forces in the Far East.

On the night of March 12, 1942, MacArthur and a select group directed by President Roosevelt were relocated to Australia. A PT boat took him and his family to Mindanao, where they boarded a B-17 and flew to Australia. It was at this time he made the speech saying, "I came through and I shall return." When asked by Washington to change the "I" to a "we," he ignored the request, which was typical of MacArthur.

In July 1944, President Roosevelt summoned both MacArthur and Nimitz to meet him in Hawaii "to determine the next phase of action against Japan." Nimitz made a case for attacking Formosa, but MacArthur convinced Roosevelt that there was an obligation to liberate the Philippines. The road to Japan was therefore going to be through the Philippines with the attack on the beaches of Leyte on October 20, 1944.

On August 29, 1945, MacArthur took charge of the rebuilding of the Japanese government. By 1946, he had developed a new Japanese constitution that instituted a parliamentary system of government under which the emperor acted only on the advice of his ministers.

ADMIRAL WILLIAM HALSEY JR.

William Halsey Jr. was born on October 30, 1882, in Elizabeth, New Jersey, and died on August 16, 1959, while holidaying on Fishers Island, New York.

Early in life, after waiting two years for an appointment to the United States Naval Academy, he decided to study medicine at the University of Virginia. After his first year there, he received the appointment to the Naval Academy and entered in the fall of 1900. Initially, he served on the battleship *Missouri,* but torpedoes and torpedo boats became his specialties.

In 1934, Admiral Ernest King offered Halsey command of the aircraft carrier USS *Saratoga,* contingent upon Halsey completing a course about air observation.

Captain Halsey elected to enroll as a cadet for the full twelve-week naval aviator course, which caused his wife to say to their daughter, "What do you think that the old fool is doing now? He is learning to fly! "On May 15, 1935, at the age of fifty-two, Halsey got his wings. He was the oldest man in US Naval history to accomplish this feat.

Navy intelligence thought that the war with Japanese would start with a surprise attack on Wake Island. Admiral Halsey received orders to use the USS *Enterprise* to ferry aircraft to Wake to reinforce the Marines. Halsey gave orders to sink any ship sighted and to shoot down any aircraft sighted. When protest occurred about this decision, Halsey said, "We will shoot first and argue afterwards."

The *Enterprise* was delayed in its return to Pearl Harbor on December 6, 1941 by a storm. The ship was still 200 miles out to sea when word of the Pearl Harbor attack arrived. Admiral Halsey and the USS *Enterprise* searched to the south and west for the Japanese fleet, but it had departed to the north and west.

In early 1942, Admiral Halsey contracted a chronic skin condition so serious that a cruiser sent him to San Francisco for treatment. This prohibited him from being a part of the Battle of Midway. He said to a group of midshipman while in the USA, "Missing the Battle of Midway has been the greatest disappointment of my career, but I am going back to the Pacific, where I intend personally to have a crack at those yellow-bellied sons of bitches and their carriers."

Upon Admiral Halsey's return to the Pacific by air to Noumea, New Caledonia, he received a sealed envelope containing a message from Admiral Nimitz saying, "You will take command of the South Pacific area and South Pacific Forces immediately." Two days after taking command, Admiral Halsey ordered all naval officers to dispense from wearing neckties. This order given to conform to Army practice, but mostly for comfort in the tropics.

With Admiral Halsey in command, the war in the Solomon's went on the offensive. Halsey's willingness to place at risk two of his fast battleships for a night engagement around Guadalcanal paid off, with the Navy winning the battle. These battles with the Japanese checked the Japanese offensive, drained their naval forces of carrier aircraft and experienced pilots. By this time in the war, the US Navy was doing things the Japanese never thought possible, such as neutralizing the Japanese land-based planes and dominating whatever area the fleet was operating. Also in early 1942 in the Pacific, the overall Naval command was divided between Admirals Halsey and Spruance. Halsey dubbed his staff the Department of Dirty Tricks. The two admirals were a contrast in styles. Halsey was aggressive, a risk taker, while Spruance was cautious, professional, and calculating. Most high-ranking officers preferred to serve under Spruance, while the common sailors preferred and were proud to serve under Halsey.

Eventually, Halsey passed command of his fleet to Spruance, but in his departure after the cessation of hostilities, his aggressive nature came through in a communiqué, which said three things:

- "Cessation of hostilities"
- "The War is over"
- "But, if any Japanese planes appear, shoot them down in a friendly way."

Admiral Halsey was one of the few Navy personnel able to work with General MacArthur and expressed the greatest admiration and respect for him.

ADMIRAL RAYMOND SPRUANCE

Raymond Spruance was born in Baltimore, Maryland, on July 3, 1886. He died on December 13, 1969. He attended the Indianapolis public school system and graduated from Shortridge High School. He followed that by graduating from the Naval Academy in 1906. His first duty assignment was on the battleship USS *Iowa,* and he served on the battleship USS *Minnesota* and was commander on five destroyers before 1916, when he transferred to the battleship USS *Pennsylvania* for her commissioning until 1917. After this service, he was associated for several years with the US Naval War College.

At the beginning of WWII, Admiral Spruance commanded four heavy cruisers and support ships attached to a task force built around the aircraft carrier USS *Enterprise*. This task force was under command of Vice Admiral William F Halsey Jr. Admiral Spruance's claim to fame came by a stroke of luck: He was nearby when Admiral Halsey was stricken with a bad case of shingles and hospitalized in the US, just before the Battle of Midway. Halsey recommended Spruance to Nimitz and suggested that Spruance lean heavily on his battle-proven expert in carrier warfare, Captain Miles Browning.

The resulting battle saw the sinking of all four of the Japanese fleet carriers with only one US carrier being lost. The additional loss of aircraft and pilots by the Japanese during this battle nearly depleted their ability to fight in the air. Thus was born the kamikaze as a Japanese offensive weapon.

Admiral Spruance's coolness and patience at just the right moment caused historian Samuel E. Morison to write, "Fletcher did well but Spruance was superb: Calm. Collected. Decisive. Yet receptive to advice, keeping in his mind the picture of widely disparate forces, yet boldly seizing every opening, Raymond A. Spruance emerged from the battle one of the greatest admirals in American Naval history."

To many people, Admiral Spruance was a mystery because he never expressed his feeling, prejudices, hopes, or fears. He was very active and thought nothing of walking several miles a day. He once said, "Some people think that when I am quiet ... I am in deep important thought, but the truth is that my mind is a complete blank." He loved wearing old khakis and work shoes and spending time in his greenhouse and garden.

Admiral Spruance died in Pebble Beach, California, on December 13, 1969. He is buried alongside his wife and Fleet Admiral Chester Nimitz, Admiral Richmond K. Turner, and Admiral Charles A. Lockwood.

PART III: THE BATTLES

THE ALEUTIAN ISLANDS CAMPAIGN

In the first six to twelve months of a war with the United States and Great Britain, I will run wild and win victory upon victory. But then, if the war continues after that, I have no expectations of success. — Admiral Isoroku Yamamoto, Commander in Chief of the Japanese Navy

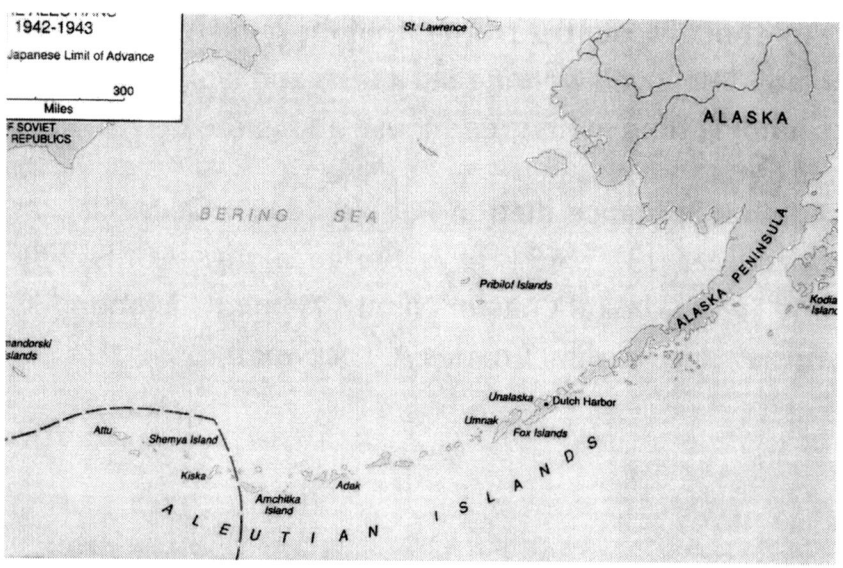

The Aleutian Islands campaign for Adak, Attu and Kiska
(Courtesy U.S. Army History- Public Domain.)

The Japanese wanted to control the Aleutian Islands to prevent a possible US attack across the northern Pacific. The United States was fearful that these islands would be used for an assault on the west coast. The battle for the Aleutians is referred to as the Forgotten Battle because it was fought at the same time as the

Guadalcanal Campaign. In both of these campaigns, a third enemy appeared: the *weather* in the Aleutians and the *jungle and swamps* in Guadalcanal.

The Aleutian Islands Campaign, in early 1943, brought my ship, the USS *J. Franklin Bell,* to its first of many campaigns in the Pacific war. (See Part IV to discover more information about the USS *J. Franklin Bell.*)

The USS *J. Franklin Bell,* with several other ships, arrived at Adak in the Aleutian Islands, with D-Day set for August 30, 1942. The occupation forces were prepared for enemy opposition, but the landing accomplished without incident. The Japanese had withdrawn from Adak.

The attack on the island of Attu was quite difficult because of a shortage of landing craft, unsuitable beaches, and equipment that failed to work in the appalling weather conditions. Intermittent shelling of the beaches by the Japanese slowed the landing of supplies, and four narrow misses by enemy torpedoes did not enhance the *Bell*'s unloading operation. Shipmate Bob Tagatz spent the first night in an LCVP (Landing Craft Vehicle Personnel) command boat and had this to say about the Aleutian campaign:

> We landed on Adak with Seabees and Alaskan Scouts, no opposition. They were to build an airfield. We landed on Attu May 11, 1943, with the Army 7th Infantry Division, Holtz Bay, and north-

ern side. Massacre Bay was the other landing, south side. We could only land four LCVPs at a time. I was engineer F1/c, Jim Weaver, Coxan. We were the control LCVP with an officer. We controlled the landing craft. Visibility: ship's length. Received motor fire from across Holtz Bay. Japanese in a cave. Landed some shots as close as twenty yards from boat. Too, close, so we kept moving around.

The destroyer *Phelps* DD498 made a couple of runs with their five-inch point blank and took care of the motor and Japanese. That evening, a Japanese sub came out of Holtz Bay and fired a torpedo at the *Bell,* which missed. The *Bell* took off, leaving us in boats to find ways to stay alive. We had about 1500 troops ashore but did not know if the Japanese would counter-attack. I believe we lost three LCVPs because of load. We could not get to the bilge strainers to be cleaned. Boat sank, but we transferred crew to another boat. We finally landed all the boats about two miles down the island. What a night: fog, rain, cold, did not know if Japanese were coming, visibility zero. After all the men and supplies unloaded, we took on wounded to return to States. To my surprise, a man from my hometown, Montello, Wisconsin, a Sergeant Phil Czeshleba, wounded, came aboard. He was wounded by shell fragments as he was bringing a squad member back to his foxhole. He got the Silver Star for this. The *J. Franklin Bell* got back to San Francisco, California, safely. Then on down to San Diego to Travis for the next landing, which would be Kiska. On August 16, 1943, we landed the Fourth Army, but the Japanese were already gone.

Two members of the crew, Buck Jordon and Leroy Holland, were wounded during the landings. Leroy Holland did not survive his wounds and was buried at sea on May 17, 1943. Very applicable to this situation is another poem written by Tim Churchill:

Another Shipmate Gone

Another shipmate passed beyond,
The veil of life on earth,
Reminding us who still remain,
To value life from birth.

The past, and all that happened then,
Just makes us whom we are;
We learn to give, and take and love,
And wish on every star.

Each failure ends one more success,
No effort is in vain,
But wins and losses teach us well,
That sunshine follows rain.

We learn to take life's ebb and flow,
Like sweet and bitter times;
Maturity means bearing pain,
When good and bad combines.

Then having learned, we share life's load,
And share the love we give,
Then honor those whom we have loved,
And value those who live.

On May 29, 1943, the last of the Japanese forces staged, without warning, one of the first and largest banzai attacks of the Pacific campaign. After furious, brutal, and often hand-to-hand bloody combat, the Japanese were virtually eliminated. Only twenty-eight had been willing to be taken alive.

The final activity in the Aleutians was the invasion of Kiska. The *J. Franklin Bell* went to San Francisco to pick up the troops that were in training for the Kiska operation in early July 1943. Then the ship proceeded to the San Diego area to practice landing with other ships of the task group. Finally, the group proceeded to the Aleutians and anchored in Kulak Bay, Adak, on August 5, 1943.

The US troops were lowered away with full equipment for a week of conditioning in the Aleutians' terrain and weather, necessitated by the lack of issuing heavy clothing during the Attu evasion. The Japanese, on the other hand, were dressed in fur-lined uniforms. (Of the 3416 wounded for the entire Aleutian Islands Campaign, 2100 were the result of exposure, trench foot, and shock.) The troops returned to the ship on August 11, 1943.

D-Day for the Kiska invasion set for August 15, 1943. The forces landed to find the island abandoned. Under the cover of favorable weather conditions and fog, the Japanese had removed their troops on July 28. US casualties still numbered 313 as result of friendly fire, booby traps, and weather conditions (Table 3). As with Attu, Kiska offered an extremely hostile environment.

While many people in the USA, in 1943, were searching their world maps to locate places like Guadalcanal and the Aleutians Islands, on the home front, the Pentagon, the world's largest office building, was being completed; the average family wage per year was $ 2000.00; The future President John F. Kennedy's PT boat 109 was sunk by a Japanese destroyer; a coca cola costs $0.05 and one could relax to Glen Miller's *In the Mood* or watch the young and not so young go crazy over the music of Frank Sinatra.

Table 3. Aleutian Islands casualties

TROOPS	USA	JAPAN	SHIPS/AIRCRAFT	USA		JAPAN	
	-	-	-	Destroyed	Damaged	Destroyed	Damaged
Killed	1481	4350	Submarines	2	-	-	-
Wounded	3416	-	Warships	-	-	7	-
Captured	8*	28	Destroyers	1	-	-	-
Missing in Action	640	-0	Cargo Ships	-	-	9	-

*US Navy

The following received the Medal of Honor for the Aleutian Campaign. (Citations for each are noted in References.)

JOE P. MARTINEZ, Private U.S. Army born July 27,1920, in Taos, NM. Over a period of several days, repeated efforts to drive the enemy from a key defensive position high in the snow-covered precipitous mountains between East Arm Holtz Bay and Chichagof Harbor had failed. On May 26, 1943, troop dispositions were readjusted and a trial coordinated attack on this position by a reinforced battalion was launched. Initially successful, the attack hesitated. In the face of severe hostile machine-gun, rifle, and mortar fire, Private Martinez, an automatic rifleman, rose to his feet and resumed his advance. Occasionally, he stopped to urge his comrades on. His example inspired others to follow. After a most difficult climb, Private Martinez eliminated resistance from part of the enemy position by BAR fire and hand grenades, thus assisting the advance of other attacking elements. This success only partially completed the action. The main Holtz–Chichagof pass rose about 150 feet higher, flanked by steep rocky ridges and reached by a snow-filled defile. Passage was barred by enemy fire from either flank and from tiers of snow trenches in front. Despite these obstacles, and knowing of their existence, Private Martinez again led the troops on and up, personally silencing several trenches with BAR fire and ultimately reaching the pass itself. Here, just below the knifelike rim of the pass, he encountered a final enemy-occupied trench, and as he was engaged in firing into it, he was mortally wounded. The pass, however, was taken, and its capture was an important preliminary to the end of organized hostile resistance on the island.

THE SOLOMON ISLANDS CAMPAIGN

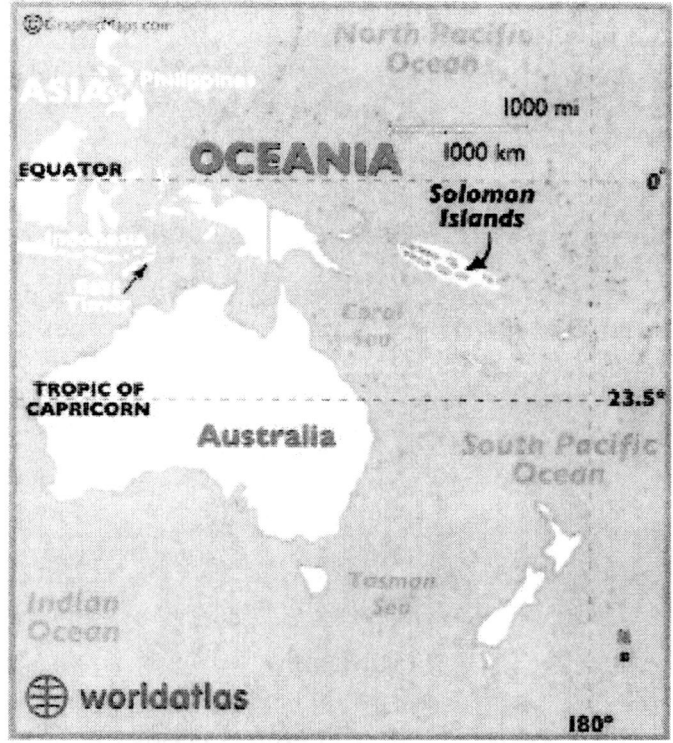

The Solomon Islands (Courtesy WorldAtlas)

The Japanese objective in the Pacific was to cut off any shipping and communications between the United States and Australia and New Zealand. As a result, the Japanese occupied the Solomon Islands and Bougainville (of New Guinea) during the first few months of 1942. Also, the Japanese needed the Solomon Islands to protect the eastern flank of their expansion into Southeast Asia. The Allies, in an effort to remove the Japanese from Solomon Islands, attacked in August 1942. The campaign was fought on land, on the sea, and in the air. The battle for the Solomon's meant that the United States had stopped being on the defensive and was on the offensive.

Some areas in the Solomon's were bypassed by the Allies, leaving the Japanese cut off from supply lines and therefore isolated. Many Japanese soldiers left in the Solomon's continued fighting after the war was over, some for as many as twenty-nine years.

Table 4 lists the overall personnel, ships, and aircraft casualties for the Solomon Islands Campaign, which included Guadalcanal and Bougainville and others. (The first two of these battles is reviewed separately because of the intensity of these battles and the need to recognize the forgotten warriors who fought under the most difficult conditions in the Pacific Theater.

The Allies, in order to defend their communication and supply lines in the South Pacific, supported a counter-offensive in New Guinea, isolated the Japanese base at Rabaul, and counterattacked the Japanese in the Solomon's with landings on Guadalcanal and small neighboring islands. The Allies wore the Japanese down, inflicting irreplaceable losses on the Japanese military assets. They also isolated and neutralized some Japanese positions, which were then bypassed.

Table 4. Solomon Islands casualties

TROOPS	USA	JAPAN	SHIPS/AIRCRAFT	USA	JAPAN
Killed	10,600	80,000	Ship Sunk	40	50
Wounded	-	-	Aircraft Destroyed	800	1500

THE BATTLE OF GUADALCANAL

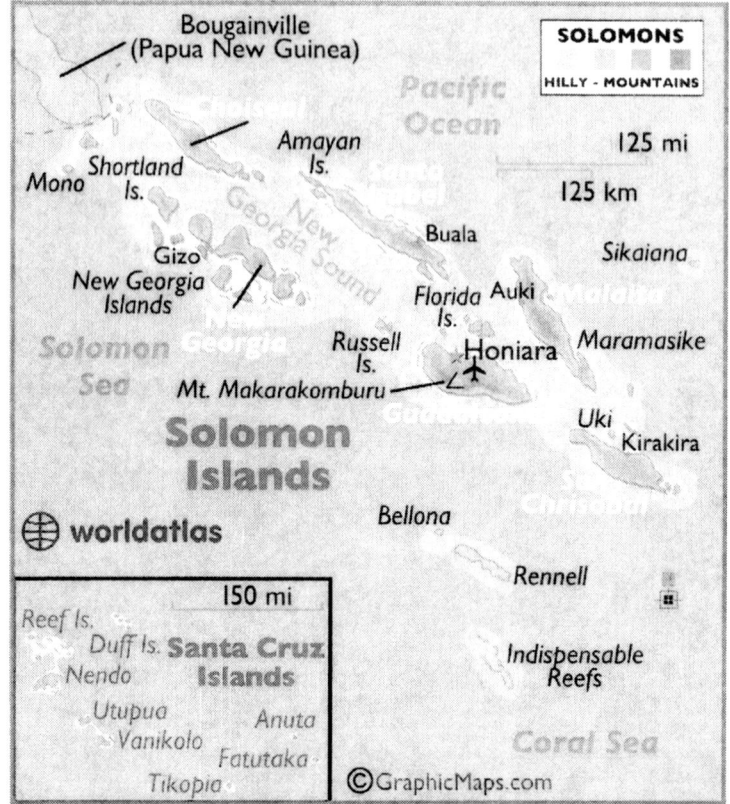

Guadalcanal, in the Solomon Islands (Courtesy WorldAtlas)

The Battle of Guadalcanal was the first major offensive by the United States in the Pacific. It was fought between August 1942 and February 1943. The reason for the delay in the Pacific offensive after the Japanese attacked Pearl Harbor, was that President Roosevelt and some military leaders were of the opinion that Germany had to be defeated first. Other military commanders pointed out that, if left unchecked, the Japanese would cut off all communication and supplies between the United States and Australia and New Zealand. Putting a stop to the Japanese advance to the east therefore meant going on the offensive in the Pacific. This resulted in the Aleutian Islands and the Solomon Islands being the beginning of the march toward Japan—the first rungs on the ladder.

The Japanese had built a large naval base at Rabaul on New Britain in the Solomon Islands, and initially, the Allies thought there was a need for the United States to capture this base. Later, the Allies decided to bypass New Britain, thereby isolating and neutralizing the base at Rabaul. It was at this time that the United States decided that it must select a long-term strategy. MacArthur was determined to keep his pledge of "I shall return" by directing the war through the Philippines while the naval commanders proposed a central Pacific route to Japan. In May of 1943, the Joint Chiefs of Staff resolved the above dispute between MacArthur and the Navy by approving a "dual drive" toward Japan. Earlier, in August of 1942, the Allied forces had surprised the Japanese by landing and capturing Tulagi and Florida as well as an airfield on Guadalcanal, named Henderson Field after a Marine pilot previously lost in combat at Midway.

The Japanese made numerous attempts to retake the airfield but were never successful. On one attempt, the first wave of Japanese soldiers attempting to breach the razor-sharp wire strung around the perimeter of the base threw themselves onto the wire so the second wave could cross over their bodies to breach the barrier.

The Battle for Guadalcanal was costly to both sides in the war. The United States suffered heavy losses in personnel during this campaign—so many that the United States refused to release the numbers to the public. Likewise, the loss to the Japanese both strategically and in manpower and materials was enormous. About 25,000 experienced Japanese ground troops were killed during the campaign, which ended Japan's attempt to blockade the shipping and communications between the United States and Australia and New Zealand.

In a bizarre event, Calvin Graham enlisted in the Navy shortly after Pearl Harbor. He was an enlisted man on the USS *South Dakota*. During a naval battle at Guadalcanal, he helped in the fire-control efforts. For his efforts during battle aboard his ship, he was awarded the Bronze Star and the Purple Heart. His mother revealed his age, however, and he was put in the brig for three months for lying about his age. When his sister threatened to go to the newspaper with his story, he was released from service with a dishonorable discharge and was stripped of his medals. He later joined the Marines and ended up breaking his back while serving. He spent the rest of his life fighting for medical benefits and cleaning up his record. After writing to Congress in 1988, he was given back all his medals except the Purple Heart. He was twelve years old when he first enlisted in the Navy.

Table 5 shows the troop casualties for the Battle of Guadalcanal Island.

Table 5. Guadalcanal casualties

TROOPS	USA	JAPAN
Killed	7,100	31,000
Wounded	1000	-
Captured	4	1,000

The following people received the Medal of Honor for their action on Guadalcanal. (Citations for each are noted in References.)

KENNETH D. BAILEY, Major, U.S. Navy born October 26, 1910, in Pawnee, OK. Major Bailey, despite a severe head wound, repeatedly led his troops in fierce hand-to-hand combat for a period of ten hours. His great personal valor while he was exposed to constant and merciless enemy fire, and his indomitable fighting spirit, inspired his troops to heights of heroic endeavor that enabled them to repulse the enemy and hold Henderson Field.

JOHN BASILONE, Sergeant, U.S. Marines born November 4, 1916, in Buffalo, NY. While the enemy was hammering at the Marines' defensive position, Sergeant Basilone, in charge of two sections of heavy machine guns, fought valiantly to check the savage and determined assault.

He repaired a gun under fire and then manned it, gallantly holding his line until replacements arrived. A little later, with ammunition critically low and supply lines cut off, Sergeant Basilone, at great risk of his own life and in face of continued enemy attack, battled his way through hostile lines with urgently needed shells for his gunners. The result was a virtual annihilation of a Japanese regiment. He is the only enlisted man to have received both the Medal of Honor and the Navy Cross.

HAROLD WILLIAM BAUER, Lieutenant Colonel, U.S. Marine Corps born November 20, 1908, in Woodruff, KA. Volunteering to pilot a fighter plane in the defense of a position on Guadalcanal, Lieutenant Colonel Bauer destroyed a Japanese bomber and four enemy fighter planes while being outnumbered two to one. He then successfully led twenty-six planes on an overwater ferry flight of more than 600 miles. While circling to land, Bauer sighted a squadron of enemy planes attacking the USS *McFarland*. Undaunted by the formidable opposition, and with valor above and beyond the call of duty, he engaged the entire squadron, and although alone and low on fuel, he fought brilliantly, which resulted in the destruction of four Japanese planes before he was forced down by lack of fuel.

ANTHONY CASAMENTO, Corporal, U.S. Marine Corps born November 16, 1920, in Brooklyn, NY. Serving as a leader of a machine gun section, Corporal Casamento directed his unit to advance along a ridge near the Matanikau River where they engaged the enemy. During the course of the engagement, all members of his crew were killed or severely wounded, and he himself suffered multiple wounds. Nonetheless, Corporal Casamento continued to provide critical supporting fire for the attack and in defense of his position. Following the loss of all effective personnel, he set up, loaded, and manned his unit's machine guns, tenaciously holding the enemy at bay.

CHARLES W. DAVIS, Major, U.S. Army born February 21, 1917, in Gordo, AL. Major Davis, executive officer of an infantry battalion, volunteered to carry instructions to the leading companies of his battalion, which had been caught in crossfire from Japanese machine guns. With complete disregard for his own safety, he made his way to trapped units, delivered the instructions, supervised the execution of those instructions, and remained overnight in this exposed position. On the following day, Major Davis volunteered to lead an assault on the Japanese position. When his rifle jammed at its first shot, he drew his pistol and, waving his men on, led the assault over the top of the hill. Electrified by his action, another body of soldiers followed and seized the hill.

MERRITT AUSTIN EDSON, Colonel, U.S. Marine Corps born April 25, 1897, in Rutland, VT. After the airfield on Guadalcanal had been seized from the enemy, Colonel

Edson, with a force of 800 men, was assigned to the occupation and defense of a ridge dominating the jungle on either side of the airport. When the enemy, in a subsequent series of violent assaults, engaged the US force in desperate hand-to-hand combat with bayonets, rifles, pistols, grenades, and knifes, Colonel Edson, although continuously exposed to fire throughout the night, personally directed defense of the reserve position against a fanatical foe of greatly superior numbers. By his astute leadership, he enabled his men to cling to their position on the ridge.

JOSEPH JACOB FOSS, Captain U.S. Marine Corps born April 17, 1915, in Sioux Falls, SD. Captain Foss was engaged in almost daily combat from October 9 to November 19 in 1942. During this period, he personally shot down twenty-eight Japanese planes and damaged others so severely that their destruction was probable. In addition, he successfully led a large number of escort missions during this period. On January 15, 1943, he added three more enemy planes to his count. Then, on January 25, 1943, he led his air crews of F4F and P-38s into action; four Japanese fighters were shot down, and the Japanese bombers turned away without dropping their bombs.

WILLIAM G. FOURNIER, Sergeant, U.S. Army born June 21, 1913, in Norwich, CT. As leader of a machine gun section charged with the protection of other battalion units, Sergeant Fournier's group was attacked by a superior number of Japanese, his gunner killed, his assistant gunner wounded, and an adjoining gun crew put out of action. When ordered to withdraw from this hazardous position, Sergeant Fournier refused to retire but rushed forward to the idle gun and, with the aid of another soldier who joined him, held up the machine gun by the tripod to increase its field of action. They opened fire and inflicted heavy casualties on the enemy. While so engaged, both gallant soldiers were killed, but their sturdy defense was a decisive factor in the success of the attacking battalion that followed.

LEWIS R HALL, Technician Fifth Class, U.S. Army born March 2, 1895, in Bloom, OH. As a leader of a machine gun squad charged with the protection of other battalion units, Hall and his group were attacked by a superior number of Japanese; his gunner killed, his assistant gunner wounded, and an adjoining gun crew put out of action. Ordered to withdraw, he refused and, with the assistance of another soldier, held up the machine gun by the tripod to be more effective, inflicting heavy losses on the Japanese. His partner had to be William G. Fournier listed above.

DOUGLAS ALBERT MUNRO, Signalman First Class U.S. Coast Guard born October 11, 1919, in Vancouver, British Columbia. Munro received this award for extraordinary heroism and conspicuous gallantry in action.

After making preliminary plans for the evacuation of nearly 500 beleaguered Marines, Petty Officer Munro, under constant strafing by enemy machine guns on the island, and at great risk of his life, daringly led five of his small craft toward the shore. As he closed the beach, he signaled the others to land, and then, to draw the enemy fire and protect the heavily laden boats, he valiantly placed his craft with its two small guns as a shield between the beach and the Japanese. When the perilous task of evacuation was nearly completed, Munro was instantly killed by enemy fire, but his crew, two of whom were wounded, carried on until the last troops had loaded and cleared the beach.

NORMAN SCOTT, Rear Admiral, U.S. Navy born August 10, 1889, in Indianapolis, IN. Scott was awarded this medal for extraordinary heroism and conspicuous intrepidity above and beyond the call of duty in action against Japanese forces both in October and November of 1942. Off Savo Island in October 1942, he intercepted a Japanese force intent on landing troops as reinforcements at Guadalcanal. He destroyed eight enemy vessels and put the others into flight. Challenged a month later by the return of the persistent and stubborn foe, he led his forces into a desperate battle against tremendous odds. He was killed in a furious bombardment by their superior firepower, but his dauntless initiative, inspiring leadership, and judicious foresight in a crisis contributed decisively to the defeat of a powerful invasion fleet.

THE BATTLE OF BOUGAINVILLE

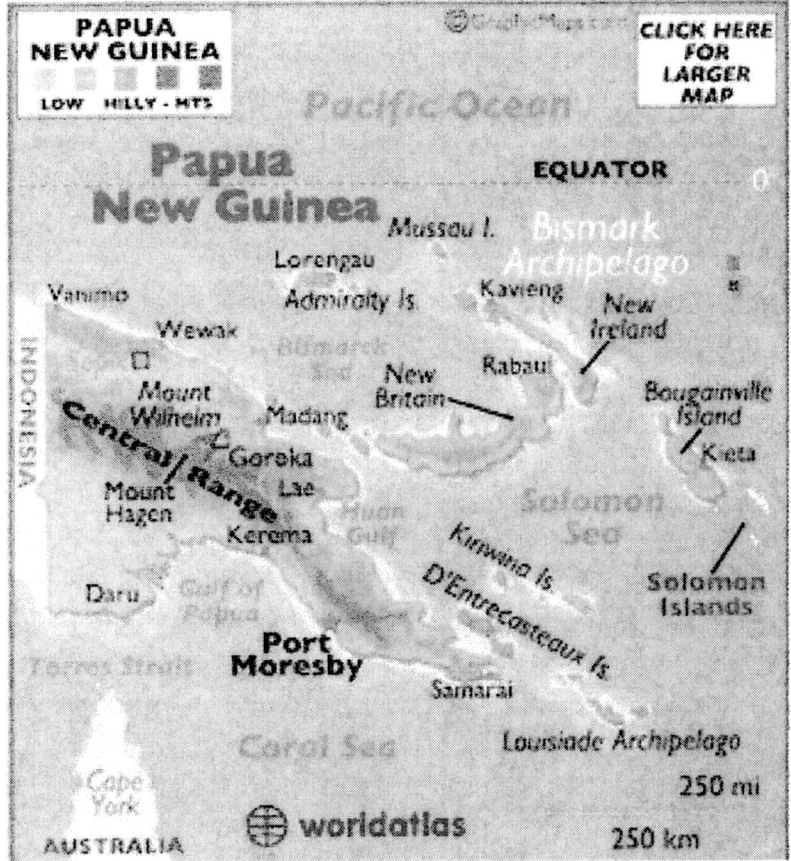

Bougainville Island, Centre right on map (Courtesy WorldAtlas)

The Battle of Bougainville started in 1943 by the Allies to retake the island, which the Japanese had occupied in 1942. The Japanese had developed naval aircraft bases in the north, east, and south of the island, in addition to airfields and naval anchorages on the adjacent islands of Treasury and Shortland. The purpose of these military facilities was to protect Rabaul, the major Japanese garrison and naval base in New Guinea, as well as on down the Solomon Islands chain to Guadalcanal.

Before the war, Bougainville administered as part of the Australian territory of New Guinea even though geographically, Bougainville is part of the Solomon Islands chain. Thus, US troops began fighting alongside the Australians.

The Royal Australian Navy had set up a remarkable means of communication as far back as 1919 using what they called Coastwatchers. The Coastwatchers were a group of individuals—missionaries, farmers, traders, and the like—that reported anything unusual along the coast. It was through this effort that, in 1939, the Australians became aware of the special interest that Japan was taking in the Solomon Islands area. As a result, Australia expanded the Coastwatchers' efforts on several Islands.

The Coastwatchers were not to confront the enemy but rather to fade into the jungle and keep reporting on a special radio frequency, which was constantly monitored. Through these people, advanced warning about air attacks came, describing the type of plane, the number of planes, and direction, thereby allowing time for antiaircraft crews to be ready for the enemy attack.

Combat operations on Bougainville ended with the surrender on August 21, 1945, of the Japanese forces, which consisted of about 23,500 Japanese troops and laborers.

Table 6 lists the troop casualties for the Bougainville Campaign.

Table 6. Bougainville casualties

TROOPS	USA	JAPAN	AUSTRALIAN
Killed	727	18,500-21,500	516
Wounded			572
Captured			

The following five troops received the Medal of Honor for their actions at Bougainville. (Citations for each are noted in References.)

JESSE R. DROWLEY, Staff Sergeant U.S. Army born September 9, 1919, in St. Charles, MI. Staff Sergeant Drowley saw three members of the assault company fall badly wounded. When intense hostile fire prevented aid from reaching the casualties, he fearlessly rushed forward to carry the wounded to cover. After rescuing two men, Staff Sergeant Drowley discovered an enemy pillbox undetected by the assaulting forces. He delegated the rescue of the third man to an assistant and ran across open terrain to one of the tanks. He boarded the tank, exchanged his weapon for a submachine gun, and then directed the tank crew toward the pillbox by using tracers loaded into the machine gun. Although he received a severe bullet wound in the chest, he refused medical treatment and remained on the tank, continuing to direct its progress until the pillbox was destroyed.

HENRY GURKE, Private First Class, U.S, Marine Corps born November 6, 1922, in Neche, ND. While his platoon was engaged in a vital road block near Empress Augusta Bay on Bougainville Island, Private First Class Gurke, in company with another Marine, was delivering a fierce stream of fire against the main vanguard of the Japanese. When a Japanese grenade dropped squarely into his foxhole, Gurke thrust his partner aside and flung his body over the missile to smother the explosion. With unswerving devotion to duty and superb valor, Private Gurke sacrificed himself in order that his comrade might live to carry on the fight.

ROBERT MURRAY HANSON, First Lieutenant U.S. Marine Corps born February 4, 1920, in Lucknow, India. On November 1, 1943, while flying cover for US landing operations at Empress Augusta Bay, Hanson dauntlessly attacked six enemy torpedo bombers, forcing them to jettison their bombs, and destroyed one Japanese plane. Then, on January 24, 1943, First Lieutenant Hanson waged a lone battle against hostile interceptors as they were orbiting to attack US bombers; striking with devastating fury, he brought down four Zeros and probably a fifth. Handling his plane superbly in both pursuit and attack measures, he was a master of individual air combat, accounting for twenty-five Japanese aircraft.

ROBERT ALLEN OWENS, Sergeant U.S. Marine Corps born September 13, 1920, in Greenville, SC. Owens received this award for conspicuous gallantry and intrepidity at the risk of his own life while serving with a Marine division at Cape Torokina, Bougainville, Solomon Islands, on November 1, 1943. Forced to pass within disastrous range of an enemy's well-camouflaged 75 mm gun, the landing units were suffering heavy losses. Having noticed the ineffectiveness of the small arms fire against the emplacement, Sergeant Owens unhesitatingly determined to charge the gun bunker. Calling on four of his comrades to provide covering fire toward other enemy pillboxes, he entered the emplacement through the fire port, driving the gun crew out of the rear door, which ensured their destruction, before he was wounded himself. Sergeant Owens silenced a powerful gun that had been of tremendous value to the Japanese. His action contributed immeasurably to the success of this operation.

HERBERT JOSEPH THOMAS, Sergeant U.S. Marine Corps born February 8, 1918, in Columbus, OH. Thomas received this award for extraordinary heroism and conspicuous gallantry while serving with the 3rd Marines in action against Japanese forces at the Koromokina River, Bougainville Island, Solomon Islands. Sergeant Thomas led his men through dense jungle undergrowth in the face of severe hostile machine-gun fire. After destroying two gun emplacements, Sergeant Thomas and his men were coordinating the attack on the third. Sergeant Thomas's men were around him, and after he threw the grenade, they were to attack, but when Thomas tossed the grenade, it hit a vine and bounced back into the group. Without hesitation, Sergeant Thomas threw himself onto the grenade to take the explosion and save his men.

What I have written about the Battles of Guadalcanal and Bougainville does not come close to describing the intensity of these battles and the terrain and conditions under which US and Australian troops had to cope while facing a fanatical enemy. Those troops that fought in the Solomon Islands were our (US) very first combat troops to fight in WWII. The officers who led them were also rookies to combat. They experienced on-the-job training in warfare in a jungle that is hard to describe: critters and insects and an enemy hell-bent on death rather than surrender.

If you ever have the opportunity to meet a soldier who served on Guadalcanal or Bougainville, look him in the eye and say, "Thank you, thank you for your service." They, along with our submarine service, should receive special recognition, and they, more than any of our troops in WWII, need your praise and thanks.

THE BATTLE OF THE CORAL SEA

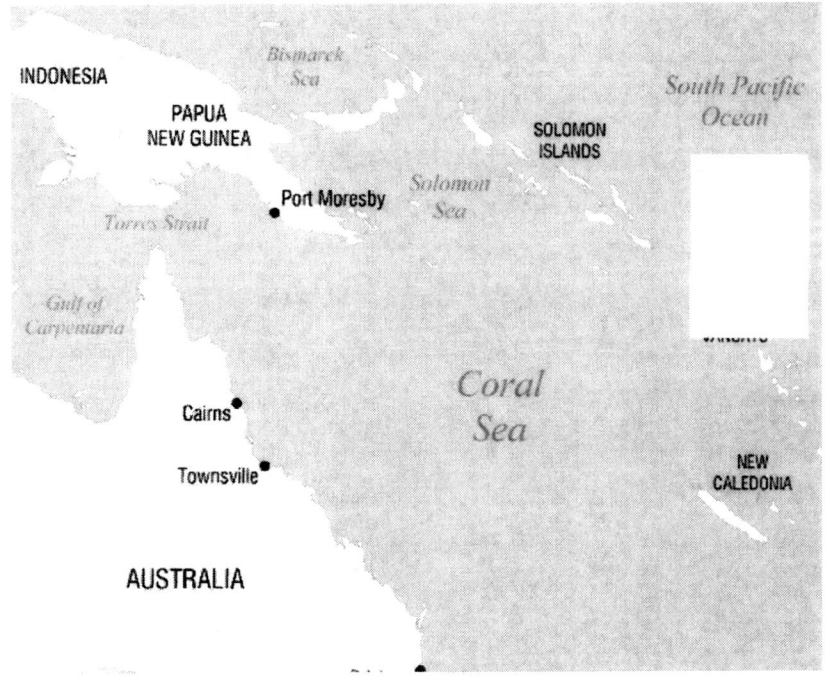

Battle of the Coral Sea (Courtesy of GNU Free Documentation License-Wikipedia)

The Battle of the Coral Sea was fought during May 1942. The Japanese, in an attempt to strengthen their defensive position for their new empire in the South Pacific, had decided that they needed to occupy Port Moresby in New Guinea and Tulagi in the southeastern Solomon Islands. The United States learned of the Japanese plan through signal intelligence and sent two carrier task forces to oppose the Japanese offensive.

Under the leadership of Navy Lieutenant Commander Joseph Rochefort, who was fluent in the Japanese language, the Japanese code was broken. This permitted Admiral Nimitz to know where the ships of the Japanese navy were located and their intentions. With knowledge of the Japanese invasions, two US Navy carrier task forces and a joint Australian–American cruiser force were sent to oppose the Japanese offensive. The Japanese were successful in the invasion of Tulagi, but many of their warships and aircraft were surprised by planes from the USS *Yorktown*. The Japanese, now aware of the US presence in the area, entered the Coral Sea with the intention of finding and destroying the Allied naval forces.

At the time, the Japanese navy was far superior to the US Navy as result of the losses at Pearl Harbor, so the United States had to pick and choose where and when to engage in battle. The information derived from breaking the Japanese code allowed this to happen.

In early May, the two carrier forces exchanged airstrikes over a period of two days. Their heavy losses of aircraft made the Japanese call off the invasion of Port Moresby for the time being.

Although a tactical victory for the Japanese in terms of ships sunk, the battle would prove to be a strategic victory for the United States for two reasons: This was the first time an expansion by the Japanese had been stopped, and two Japanese fleet carriers were out of action for the time being, one damaged, the other depleted of its aircraft and unavailable a month later for the Battle of Midway, contributing significantly to the US victory in the Battle of Midway.

Table 7 shows the troop, ship, and aircraft casualties for the Coral Sea naval battle.

Table 7. Coral Sea casualties

TROOPS	USA	JAPAN	SHIPS /AIR CRAFT	USA		JAPAN	
				Damaged	Destroyed	Damaged	Destroyed
Killed	656	966	Fleet Carrier	1	1	1	1
Wounded	-		Destroyer	-	1	-	1
Captured	-	-	War Ships	-	-	2	3
			Transport	-	-	1	-
			Oiler	-	1	-	-
			Aircraft	-	69	-	92

The following three troops received the Medal of Honor for action during the naval battle of the Coral Sea. (Citations for each are noted in References.)

WILLIAM E. HALL, Lieutenant Junior Grade U.S. Naval Reserve born October 31, 1913, in Storrs, UT. Hall received this award for extreme courage and heroism in combat above and beyond the call of duty as a pilot of a scouting plane in action against the Japanese at the Battle of the Coral Sea. In a resolute and determined attack, Lieutenant (junior grade) Hall dived his plane at an enemy aircraft carrier, contributing materially to the destruction of that vessel. The next day, while facing heavy and fierce opposition, he again displayed extraordinary skill as an aviator by effectively executing counterattacks against superior numbers of enemy planes in destroying three enemy aircraft. Though seriously wounded in this engagement, he was able to land his plane safely.

JOHN J. POWERS, Lieutenant U.S. Navy born July 13, 1912, in New York City, NY. For distinguished and conspicuous gallantry and intrepidity at the risk of his life, Lieutenant Powers participated in five engagements with Japanese forces in May 1942 in the Coral Sea area. During this engagement, an attack developed on an enemy aircraft carrier. On this occasion, Lieutenant dived in the face of heavy antiaircraft fire to an altitude well below the safety altitude, in order that he might positively obtain a hit in a vital part of the enemy ship. There were many observers of this action and of the ship soon after. That evening, Lieutenant Powers gave a lecture to the squadron on the diving technique. He advocated a low release point to improve accuracy but impressed on the men the risk of being hit by their own bomb blasts and fragments. The next morning, he led his section of dive-bombers down to the target from 18,000 feet through a wall of bursting antiaircraft shells and into the face of enemy fighter planes to an altitude that would ensure a hit on the enemy vessel. He was last seen attempting to recover from his dive at an altitude of 200 feet through smoke, flame, and debris from the stricken enemy vessel.

MILTON E. RICKETTS, Lieutenant U.S. Navy born August 5, 1913, Baltimore, MD. Rickets received the Medal of Honor for extraordinary and distinguished gallantry as officer-in-charge of the engineering repair party of the USS *Yorktown* in action against the Japanese. During the severe bombarding of the *Yorktown* by enemy forces, an aerial bomb passed through and exploded directly beneath the compartment in which Lieutenant Ricketts' battle station was located, killing, wounding, or stunning all of his men and mortally wounding him. Despite his ebbing strength, Lieutenant Ricketts promptly opened the valve of a nearby fireplug, partially led out the fire hose, and directed a heavy stream of water into the fire before dropping dead beside the hose. His courageous action undoubtedly prevented the rapid spread of fire. He gallantly gave his life for his country.

THE BATTLE OF MIDWAY

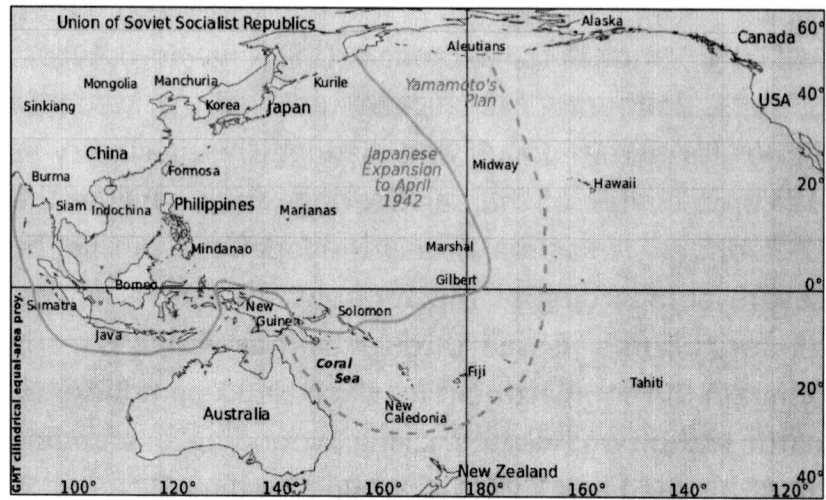

Battle of Midway, upper center of map (courtesy Wikipedia the free Encyclopedia- Public Domain.)

Note: The dashed line indicates the Japanese planned expansion if they were successful in the naval battle at Midway

Leading up to the Naval Battle of Midway was the Battle of the Java Sea, which the Japanese won handily. This caused the dissolution of the ABDA (American–British–Dutch–Australian) Command. Then there was the tactical defeat by the Japanese at the Battle of the Coral Sea just one month before the Battle at Midway. How prepared were we? This was just six months after the attack on Pearl Harbor, and US pilots were flying obsolete aircraft. Most of the pilots, like Richard E. Fleming, who had arrived at Midway ten days after Pearl Harbor, were rookies. These rookie pilots were called upon to fight a group of veteran Japanese pilots experienced in air battles and with a fighter planes, the Zeros, which were far superior to our fighter aircraft at that time.

The Japanese plan was to lure the US aircraft carriers into a trap and to occupy Midway to extend their defensive perimeter, but the US code breakers were able to determine the date and location of the attack, enabling the United States to set up an ambush of its own. The code breakers were led by Joseph Rochefort, whose group determined that the Japanese code for Midway was AF. To confirm, Captain Edwin Layton (Nimitz's chief of intelligence) asked Rochefort to send out an uncoded message that said the water plant had failed on Midway and there was a shortage of fresh water. The code group soon received a message in Japanese that said the AF was short on water. Admiral Nimitz now knew for sure the Japanese fleet was headed for Midway. The code-breaking crew was so accurate that it predicted the Japanese fleet would be within 175 miles of Midway at 6 AM on June 4 from a bearing 315° Northwest. Admiral Nimitz later commented to Captain Layton, "Well, you were only five miles, five degrees, and five minutes off."

The *Yorktown* was damaged in the Battle of the Coral Sea. It was thought that she would have to go to Puget Sound Naval Yard for several months of repair, but instead, she was taken to Pearl Harbor Naval Shipyard. After inspecting the ship and the damages, Admiral Nimitz said to the workers, "You have got three days to make the repairs." As a result, around the clock, workers in seventy-two hours put her in a battle-ready condition, and off she went to fight in the Battle of Midway.

The code breaking was used to the United States' advantage in the Battle for Midway and eventually led to the shooting down of the plane that carried the Japanese admiral responsible for all naval operations in the Pacific, Admiral Yamamoto. On April 14, 1943, intelligence experts intercepted a message revealing that Yamamoto would be flying to Bougainville four days later. On April 18, 1943, Lieutenant Thomas Lanphier shot off the right wing of the aircraft, sending it plummeting to the ground. Japanese searchers later found Admiral Yamamoto's charred body in the jungle.

During this campaign, the Japanese captured three pilots and a machinist's mate. They were interrogated and then murdered by being tied to gasoline cans filled with water and thrown overboard.

The Battle of Midway has been called the turning point of the Pacific, but the United States did not move from a state of parity to a state of supremacy until after several more months of hard combat. The Battle of Midway was the first major US victory, however, and the Japanese military went to great lengths to hide the fact from their people. For example, they put their wounded in isolation and shipped them off to other areas of combat when they recovered, without allowing them to see family or friends. It is more likely that the combined Battles of the Coral Sea and Midway were the turning point in the Pacific war.

We should never forget what this group of pilots contributed toward the defeat of the Japanese. They did it within six months after Pearl Harbor and two years and two days before the invasion of Normandy, so they did not have time to train beforehand. This was on-the-job training, in an activity that meant life or death.

Richard Fleming was one of these pilots. He had been born in St. Paul, Minnesota, and graduated from the University of Minnesota. When he finished school, he had decided to try for flight training with the Marine Corps. During his college days at the University of Minnesota he met a Peggy Crooks at the local drug store and began dating her. However, soon, he was off to Pensacola, Florida, for serious flight training.

Ten days after Pearl Harbor, Fleming led his Marine Scout bombing squadron 1,137 miles across the Pacific to build up the defenses at Midway. In late May 1942, they received sixteen SBD-2s (Dauntless Dive Bombers), which were a great improvement over the Vindicators they had been flying. Their training on the new planes was limited because the Japanese fleet was on its way to Midway. On June 4 while flying wing on Commanding Officer Major Lofton Henderson, the squadron spotted the Japanese carriers. At about the same time, Fleming shouted over the radio, "Here come the Zeros." (At this time, the Zero was the best fighter plane in the war in the Pacific, but by the time of the Battle of the Philippine Sea, the United States had developed the F6F Hellcat, which was more powerful and maneuverable than the Zero.)

One of the first planes to be hit was Henderson's; as Henderson's plane went down, Fleming took charge of the action. His gunner was wounded but continued to fight off the Zeros as Fleming flew through a hail of bullets from the Zeros as well as antiaircraft fire. For greater accuracy, he flew to just over 400 feet before dropping his bombs. When Fleming and his gunner arrived back at the base, they counted 179 holes in the aircraft. Fleming had only two minor wounds.

The next day, Fleming was back in action, this time leading a flight of six SB2U-3s (carrier- and land-based dive bombers). The target was the heavy cruiser *Mikuma*. The Japanese put up a strong defense, and Fleming, unable to use a true dive-bombing approach, decided to try a glide-bombing run starting at 4000 feet and with the sun to his back. With smoke and fire in his engines, he managed to control his plane and drop his bombs, but when he pulled out of his glide, his plane burst into flames. Neither Fleming nor his gunner, Private First Class George A. Toms, was ever seen again.

Fleming had written a letter to his girlfriend, Peggy Crooks, on May 30, 1942, which was labeled "To be opened only upon my death." The letter said, "Letters like this should not be morbid nor maudlin, and we'll let it suffice to say that I've been prepared for this rendezvous for some time. This is something that comes once to all of us and we can only bow before it." Richard E. Fleming was awarded the Medal of Honor for his actions in the Battle of Midway.

The battle was not without more heartbreaking events for the United States. For example, from the carrier *Hornet*, Lieutenant Commander John Waldron led his squadron of fifteen men in their TBD-1 Devastators (Navy fighter planes) to attack the Japanese carriers, and only one man, Lieutenant George Gay, survived. He survived the crash into the water and then again survived the Japanese by pulling a cushion over his head in the water to hide from Japanese planes and ships that were strafing everything that moved in the area. He was a witness to the sinking of three Japanese carriers and spent thirty hours in the water before being rescued by a Navy PBY plane.

After his Navy career ended, George Gay spent thirty years as a commercial pilot for TWA. When he passed away at age seventy-seven, his wife fulfilled his wishes to be cremated and spread his ashes over the area of the Battle of Midway, as he wanted to join his comrades who had not survived the battle.

In addition to the above, still more tragedies befell the United States in this battle.

1. The *Hornet* sent an additional twenty-eight planes into the battle; only ten returned.
2. The carrier *Yorktown* sent twenty-four planes into battle; only three returned.

These men who fought for our country should never be forgotten. They fought without the benefit of the best weapons, planes, and training available for later troops. Military historian John Keegan called the battle of Midway "the most stunning and decisive blow in the history of naval warfare." The Marine and Navy pilots turned defeat into victory for the United States, and because of their courage in battle, we are still speaking English rather than Japanese in our country.

Walter Lords in his 1967 book about Midway stated, "They had no right to win but they did." These warriors deserve to be elevated to a pedestal like Normandy for everyone to see, though after more than seventy years, they have also nearly fallen into the Pacific Theater forgotten warriors. I use the word *nearly* because if it had not been for John Ford, the famous Hollywood director, although wounded by shrapnel, caught most of the Midway battle on camera. Ford then produced two films

The Battle of Midway, intended for the American public at large. Without these films the battle might have been totally forgotten by 2015. He also made a special film *Torpedo Squadron* for the families of the pilots who lost their lives at Midway.

By the time of the Battle of the Philippine Sea, the Japanese had somewhat rebuilt their carrier forces in terms of numbers, but their planes were obsolescent and they had lost their veteran pilots to the war. The planes being flown by Japan were with pilots that were inexperienced and poorly trained. The Japanese ability to build additional carriers was very poor compared to that of the United States. In the time it took Japan to build three carriers, the United States had commissioned more than two dozen fleet and light fleet carriers and numerous escort carriers.

Table 8 displays the troop, ship, and aircraft casualties during the Battle of Midway.

Table 8. Midway casualties

TROOPS	USA	JAPAN	SHIP/AIR CRAFT	USA		JAPAN	
				Destroyed	Damaged	Destroyed	Grounded
Killed	307	3057	Carriers	1	-	4	-
Wounded	500	-	Destroyer	1	-	-	-
Captured	4*	-	Heavy Cruiser	-	-	1	1
			Aircraft	150	-	248	-

*Captured, interrogated, and then murdered by the Japanese

Only one Medal of Honor was awarded for action in the Battle of Midway. (Citations are noted in References.)

RICHARD E. FLEMING, Captain U.S. Marine Corps Reserve born November 2, 1917, in Saint Paul, MN. Fleming was awarded this medal for extraordinary heroism and conspicuous intrepidity during action against enemy Japanese forces when his squadron commander was shot down during the initial attack upon an enemy aircraft carrier. Captain Fleming led the remainder of the division with such fearless determination that he dived his plane to a perilously low altitude of 400 feet before releasing his bomb. Although his plane was riddled with 179 hits, he pulled out with only two minor wounds. The following day, after fewer than four hours of sleep, he led the squadron in a coordinated attack against a Japanese battleship, during which his plane was set afire, and he continued his attack to an altitude of 500 feet and scored a near miss, then crashed into the sea. (This is the official version, because there is reason to believe that Fleming could have crashed his plane into the Japanese heavy cruiser *Mikuma,* based on eyewitness accounts by a Japanese naval officer and by Fleming's wingman, but that story was never accepted by the Navy because if was lacking in absolute verification.)

THE BATTLE OF TARAWA

Casualties many; Percentage of dead not known; combat efficiency; we are winning. — Colonel David M. Shoup (Tarawa, November 21, 1943)

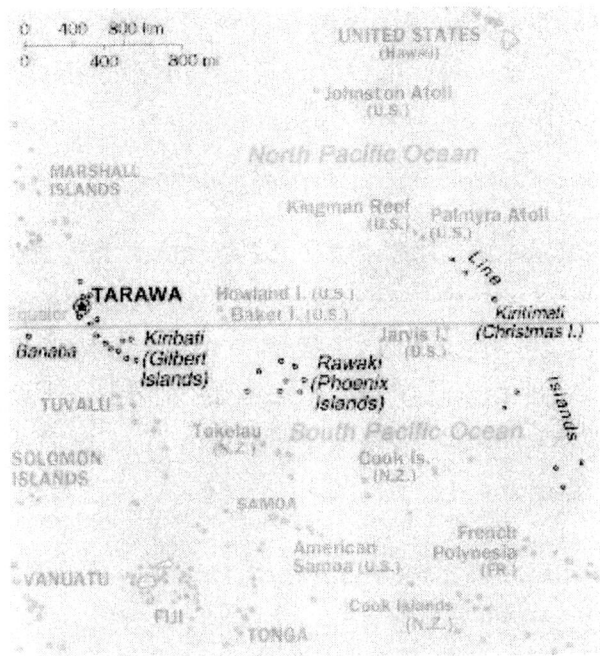

The Gilbert Islands (left center), is the island of Tarawa, (Courtesy Wikipedia the free encyclopedia- Public Domain)

The Battle for Tarawa in the Gilbert Islands was fought during the month of November 1943 and was the first amphibious landing into Japanese resistance in the march toward Japan. The previous landing in the Solomon Islands had seen little or no Japanese resistance in landing troops. It was US Navy philosophy at the time of the war with Japan that for an amphibious attack to succeed, land-based aircraft were needed to protect the invasion force as well as to weaken the existing enemy defenses. This led to a ladder philosophy, with every move across the Pacific calculated to move up the rung of the ladder a step at a time. Prior to the Battle of Tarawa, the Mariana Islands were the major goal, but to get there, a base was needed in the Marshall Islands, and to get to the Marshals, the United States had to take the air base on the tiny island of Betio in the Tarawa Atoll.

Unfortunately, the Japanese anticipated that the United States would invade this island and went to great lengths to make an invasion impossible. It was reported that the Japanese commander on the island told his troops that it would take one million men one hundred years to conquer Tarawa.

My ship, the USS *J. Franklin Bell,* on November 1, 1943, loaded 1800 officers and men of the 2nd Marine Division and departed for Efate in the New Hebrides, where several practice landings were made. After this training, the *Bell* and other ships of the task force sailed for Tarawa on November 13. The force arrived off Tarawa Atoll just after midnight on November 19.

Early on the morning of November 20, the Japanese shore batteries opened fire on the *Bell* and other ships of the task force, with a few narrow misses, so the ships in the area withdrew outside the gun range. After some delay, the H hour (time of the attack) was set for 9:00

AM. The assault troops in the amphibious tractor made it over the reef, but the LCVPs could not make it over because the Higgins boats required five feet of clearance over the coral reef and only four feet were available. It was obvious that the Marine planners had not planned for a neap tide, which occurs twice a month, when the moon is in its first or last quarter. Neap tide is a phenomenon in which the countering tug of the sun counteracts the pull of the moon and water levels deviate less. Some military observers noted that it seemed that "the water just sat there."

My nephew Earl Hutchison was among those who charged the beach. He said, after he was able to get over the reef, the water level for some distance was over his head and he had to bounce up and down to get a breath of air. In full battle dress, that became more and more difficult. He reached the point where he prayed, "Lord, you are going to have to help me." Immediately, he felt the earth solid under his feet and his mouth above water level. Earl was a machine gunner and with an assistant operated a BAR (Browning automatic rifle). He told me about the banzai charges by the Japanese and how it seemed that the more Japanese they killed, the more Japanese came. One Japanese made it to my nephew's foxhole and was killed in hand-to-hand combat. Earl himself was wounded when a bullet lodged in his head, so near the brain that physicians considered it better that he lived with a bullet rather than chance an operation. The result was occasional headaches the rest of his life. He was awarded the Purple Heart and sent back to Hawaii for rest and recuperation, then on to the Battle of Tinian, where we came within a few feet of seeing each other.

At about 5:50 PM on D-Day, November 20, the *Bell* beach party left to report to the commander of Transport Four, who was Captain McGovern, our previous ship's captain. The beach party worked all night under heavy enemy fire, salvaging stranded boats and unloading ammunition, water, and rations for the Marines. During the night, casualties started arriving from the beach and continued for several days.

Orders were received by the *Bell* on the next day, November 21, to land her troops on the island of Bairiki, which was next to the island of Betio. This action was to block the Japanese troops from crossing a sandbar on the extreme eastern end of the islet to Bairiki. The landing came under machine-gun fire, and the air force was called in to soften the defenders. The Japanese had gasoline stored in the bunker, which was ignited by the bombing and completely wiped out the bunker. The operation proceeded with little resistance. After the landing, unloading operations started and continued until late morning the following day. On November 23, the *Bell* returned to the transport area and continued to receive casualties from the ongoing battle on Betio. The military lesson learned from this battle was of tremendous value to US planning for the rest of the war in the Pacific, but it was costly, as two out of three Marines died in the assault on the beach.

Other lessons learned came about from mishaps such as transports missing the correct landing area, misjudging the depth of the tide resulting in the troops having to wade ashore under heavy enemy fire, and failure to coordinate air support, all of which proved tremendously valuable in the continued push across the Pacific.

Robert Sherrod, *Time* magazine war correspondent, wrote on December 6, 1943, "Last week some 2000 or 3000 United States Marines, most of them dead or wounded gave the nation a name to stand beside those of Concord Bridge, the Bonhomme Richard, the Alamo, Little Bighorn and Belleau Wood. That name was Tarawa." That notoriety has not happened, but it should have—just one more reason for me to write this book.

My shipmate Clyde Crammond remembered his time on the *Bell* and Tarawa:

> I was only on the *Bell* for one invasion which was Tarawa so there is not much I can tell you that the others haven't already told you. I was an RM/3C at that time so I was in the radio shack working 4 hours on and 4 hours off copying Morse code which came over in 5-letter code groups that were broadcasted by shore stations. When the *Bell* got back to Pearl Harbor I was transferred to

the 5th Amphibious Force Pacific which I stayed in the rest of my time in the Pacific.

Control communications teams were being formed to coordinate troops and supplies at landing sites and I was in the first that was formed which consisted of a Chief Radio Repairman and 4 Radiomen. We were on small vessels such as PC, PCS and the like and were 1000 yards off the landing beach. All the troops in the landing craft were on the line of departure and we gave them the signal when to proceed. The Commodore was on board and gave the signal which one of them gave to all the landing craft on the circuit. Our first test was Kwajalein followed by Eniwetok and a total of 11 before the last one which was Okinawa.

Table 9 shows the troop and carrier casualties that occurred at Tarawa.

Table 9. Tarawa casualties

TROOPS	USA	JAPAN	SHIPS/AIR CRAFT	USA		JAPAN	
				Destroyed	Damaged	Destroyed	Damaged
Killed	1,711	4690	Aircraft Carrier	1**			
Wounded	2,100	-					
Captured	-	17*					

*An Additional 129 Japanese Labors Captured (mostly Korean)

** The *Liscome Bay* (Dorie Miller's Ship) was sunk with the loss of 687 shipmates.

The following four troops were awarded the Medal of Honor for action in the Battle for Tarawa. (Citations for each are noted in References.)

ALEXANDER BONNYMAN JR., First Lieutenant U.S. Marine Corps born May 2, 1910, in Atlanta, GA. Acting on his own initiative when assault troops were pinned down at the far end of Betio Pier by overwhelming fire of Japanese shore batteries, First Lieutenant Bonnyman repeatedly defied the blasting fury of the enemy bombardment to organize and lead the besieged men over the long open pier to the beach. Then he voluntarily obtained flamethrowers and demolitions, organized his shore party into assault demolitionists, and directed the blowing of several hostile installations before the close of D-Day. On the second day, he voluntarily crawled forty yards beyond US lines to place demolitions in the entrance of a large Japanese emplacement. Withdrawing only to replenish his ammunition, he led his men on in a renewed assault, fearlessly exposing himself to the merciless slash of hostile fire. Assailed by additional Japanese after he had gained his objective, he made a heroic stand on the edge of the structure, defending his strategic position with indomitable determination in the face of the desperate enemy charge and killing three Japanese before he fell mortally wounded.

WILLIAM J. BORDELON, Staff Sergeant U.S. Marine Corps born December 25, 1920, in San Antonio, TX. Landing in the assault waves under withering enemy fire that killed all but four of the men in his tractor, Staff Sergeant Bordelon hurriedly made demolition charges and personally put two pillboxes out of action. Hit by enemy machine-gun fire just as a charge exploded in his hand while he assaulted a third position, he courageously remained in action and, although out of demolition, provided himself with a rifle and furnished fire coverage for a group of men scaling the sea wall. Disregarding his own serious condition, he unhesitatingly went to the aid of one of his demolition men who was wounded and called for help in the water. He rescued a man and another who was wounded trying to reach his comrade's call for help. Still refusing aid for himself, he again made up demolition charges and single-handedly assaulted a fourth Japanese position but was instantly killed when caught in a final burst of fire from the enemy. He gallantly gave his life for his country.

WILLIAM D. HAWKINS, First Lieutenant U.S. Marine Corps born April 19, 1914, in Fort Scott, KA. First Lieutenant Hawkins was first to disembark from the jeep lighter. He unhesitatingly moved forward under heavy enemy fire at the end of Betio Pier, neutralizing emplacements in coverage of troops assulting the main beach positions. He fearlessly led his men on to join the forces fighting desperately to gain a beachhead. He repeatedly risked his life throughout the day and night to direct and lead attacks on pillboxes and installations with grenade and demolitions. At dawn the next day, Lieutenant Hawkins resumed the dangerous mission of clearing the beachhead of Japanese resistance. Crawling forward in the face of withering fire, he boldly fired point-blank into loopholes and completed the destruction with grenades. Lieutenant Hawkins steadfastly carried the fight to the enemy. After being wounded in the chest, he destroyed three more pillboxes before being caught in a burst of Japanese shellfire and was mortally wounded. He was an inspiration to all his comrades during the most critical time of battle.

DAVID M. SHOUP, Colonel U.S. Marine Corps born December 30, 1904, in Tippecanoe, IN. Although severely shocked by an exploding enemy shell soon after landing at the pier and suffering from a serious leg wound that had become infected, Colonel Shoup fearlessly exposed himself to the terrific and relentless artillery, machine guns, and rifle fire from hostile shore emplacements. Rallying his hesitant troops by his own heroism, he gallantly led them across the reefs to charge the heavily fortified island and reinforce hard-pressed, thinly held US lines. Upon arriving on shore, he assumed command of all landed troops and, working without rest and under constant withering enemy fire during the next two days, conducted smashing attacks against unbelievably strong and fanatically defended Japanese positions despite innumerable obstacles and heavy casualties. Colonel Shoup was largely responsible for the final decisive defeat of the enemy.

THE BATTLE OF KWAJALEIN AND ROI-NAMUR IN THE MARSHALL ISLANDS

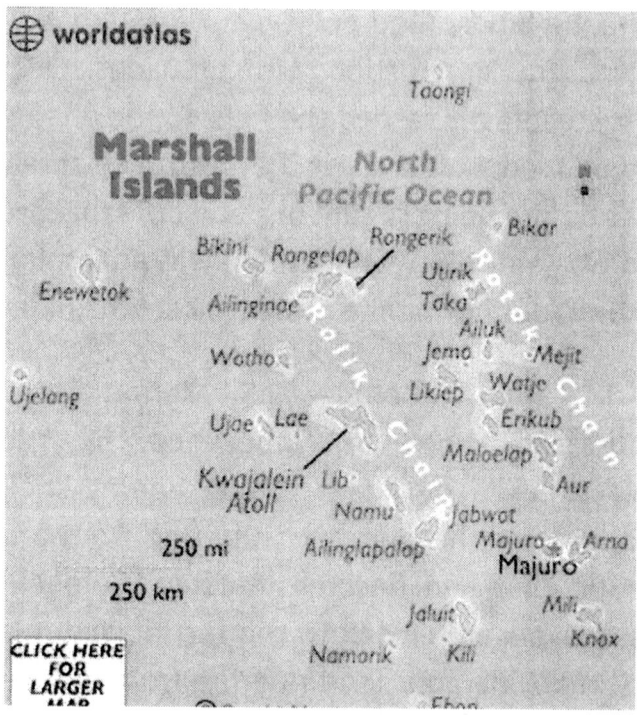

Kwajalein center of map (Courtesy of WorldAtlas)

The Battle for Kwajalein and Roi-Namur was fought during January and February 1944. It was the next step in the march up the ladder toward the Japanese homeland. This battle is significant because it was the first time the United States attacked the so-called outer ring of the Japanese Pacific sphere. This battle was also the last time the Japanese tried to stop an invasion at the beaches. After that time, the Japanese chose a strategy of putting minimum defenses at the beachheads and concentrated on setting up bunkers and heavy gun emplacements to put the American troops in crossfire.

On January 22, 1944, the USS *J. Franklin Bell* sailed with the southern task force for the invasion of Kwajalein Atoll. Training exercises were conducted in route, and the atoll was sighted at 7:00 AM on January 31. A beach reconnaissance boat of volunteers was sent to the USS *Monrovia,* where it joined three other boats from other APAs for a mission to move within a short distance of the beach so as to survey the conditions of the reef and the extent of beach defenses. Battleships moved in close and covered the group with bombardment, which demolished the beach defenses.

The troops for the first assault wave were transferred to LSTs (Landing Ship Tank) for landing the next day with amphibious tractors. On landing day, all boats were lowered and the remaining troops were sent to the beach. The *Bell* moved inside the lagoon and finished unloading supplies and equipment. Casualties were received, and the *Bell* furnished fuel and supplies to destroyers and LSTs and other small craft in the area.

I loved this location in the Pacific because later in the war, when we went into the lagoon at Kwajalein, the captain allowed us to go swimming. It was a beautiful spot surrounded by coral reefs.

For the next several months, the *Bell* was busy transporting troops back and forth between the United States and Honolulu in addition to being repaired in San Pedro, California.

Table 10 shows the troop casualties at Kwajalein and Roi-Namur.

Table 10. Kwajalein and Roi Namur casualties

Kwajalein			Roi Namur		
TROOPS	USA	JAPAN	TROOPS	USA	JAPAN
Killed	142	4,300	Killed	206	3,500
Wounded	845	-	Wounded	617	-
			Captured	181*	87

*USA 181 Missing probably from drowning

The following four troops were awarded the Medal of Honor for action in the Battle for Kwajalein. (Citations for each are noted in References.)

RICHARD B. ANDERSON, Private First Class U.S. Marine Corps born June 26, 1921, in Tacoma, WA. During action against enemy Japanese forces on Roi-Namur, Kwajalein Atoll, Marshall Islands, February 1, 1944, while entering a shell crater occupied by three other Marines, Private First Class Anderson was preparing to throw a grenade at an enemy position when it slipped from his hands and rolled toward the men at the bottom of the hole. With insufficient time to retrieve the armed weapon and throw it, Private Anderson fearlessly chose to sacrifice himself and save his companions by hurling his body upon the grenade and taking the full impact of the explosion. His personal valor and exceptional spirit of loyalty in the face of almost certain death were in keeping with the highest traditions of the US Naval Service. He gallantly gave his life for his country.

AQUILLA JAMES DYESS, Lieutenant Colonel Dyess, U.S. Marine Corps born January 11, 1909, in Augusta, GA, undaunted by severe fire from automatic Japanese weapons, launched a powerful final attack on the second day of the assault, unhesitatingly posting himself between the opposing lines to point out objectives and avenues of approach and personally leading the advancing troops. Alert, and determined to quicken the pace of the offensive against increased enemy fire, he was constantly at the head of advance units, inspiring his men to push forward until the Japanese had been driven back to a small center of resistance and victory assured. While standing on the parapet of an antitank trench, directing a group of infantry in a flanking attack against the last enemy position, Lieutenant Colonel Dyess was killed by a burst of enemy machine-gun fire.

JOHN VINCENT POWER, First Lieutenant U.S. Marine Corps Reserve born November 20, 1918, in Worcester, MA. Severely wounded in the stomach while setting a demolition charge on a Japanese pillbox, First Lieutenant Power was steadfast in his determination to remain in action. Protecting his wound with his left hand and firing with his right, he courageously advanced as another hostile position was taken under attack, fiercely charging the opening made by the explosion and emptying his carbine into the pillbox. While attempting to reload and to continue the attack, First Lieutenant Power was shot again in the stomach and head and collapsed in the doorway.

RICHARD KEITH SORENSON, Private U.S. Marine Corps Reserve born August 28, 1924, in Anoka, Minnesota. A brave defense against a particularly violent counterattack by the enemy during invasion operations, Private Sorenson and five other Marines occupying a shell hole were endangered by a Japanese grenade thrown into their midst. Unhesitatingly, and with complete disregard for his own safety, Private Sorenson hurled himself upon the deadly weapon, heroically taking the full impact of the explosion. As a result of his gallant action, he was severely wounded, but the lives of his comrades were saved.

THE BATTLE OF ENIWETOK

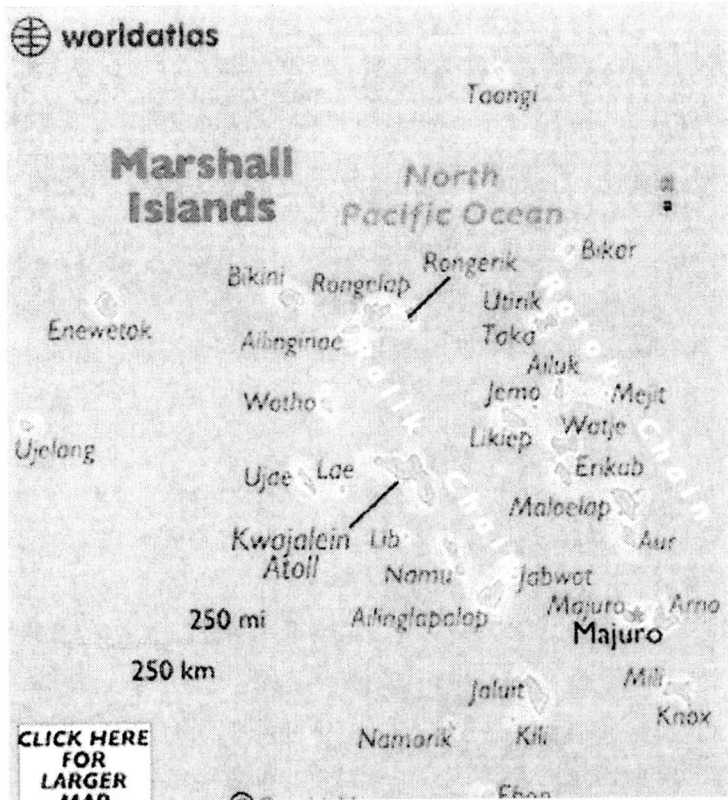

Eniwetok in upper left corner of map (Courtesy WorldAtlas)

The Battle of Eniwetok was fought during February of 1944. It followed the Battle of Kwajalein as part of the Marshall Islands Campaign to secure naval and land air bases to support the battle for the next rungs in the ladder: Saipan, Tinian, and Guam of the Mariana Islands. The Mariana Islands were important because they brought Tokyo within range of the new B-29 bombers. The Japanese knew this, which was the reason for their desperate attempt to intercept the invasion of Saipan, which resulted in the naval battle in the Philippine Sea.

In 1943, the Japanese had established a light defense at Eniwetok on the islands of Engebi and Parry. The Japanese defense on Engebi was stronger than expected, so additional bombardments were brought in for the Parry Island. The result was that the regimental commander radioed at 7:30 PM—after the landing at 9:00 AM on the same day, February 22, 1944—"I present you with the island of Parry."

Table 11 shows troop casualties for the Battle of Eniwetok.

Table 11. Eniwetok casualties

TROOPS	USA	JAPAN
Killed	313	3,380
Wounded	879	-
Captured	77*	105

*Missing – Probably from drowning

One Medal of Honor was awarded for actions during the Battle of Eniwetok. (Citation is noted in References.)

ANTHONY PETER DAMATO. Corporal U.S. Marine Corps born March 28, 1922, in Shenandoah, PA. Serving with an assault company in action against enemy Japanese forces on Engebi Island, Eniwetok Atoll, Marshall Islands, on February 19–20, 1944. Highly vulnerable to sudden attacks by small fanatical groups of Japanese still at large despite the efficient and determined efforts of our forces to clear the area, Corporal Damato lay with two comrades in a large foxhole in his company's defense perimeter, which had been dangerously thinned by the forced withdrawal of nearly half of the available men. When one of the enemy approached the foxhole undetected and threw in a hand grenade, Corporal Damato desperately groped for it in the darkness. Realizing the imminent peril to all three and fully aware of the consequences of his act, he unhesitatingly flung himself on the grenade and, although instantly killed as his body absorbed the explosion, saved the lives of his two companions.

THE BATTLE OF THE PHILIPPINE SEA

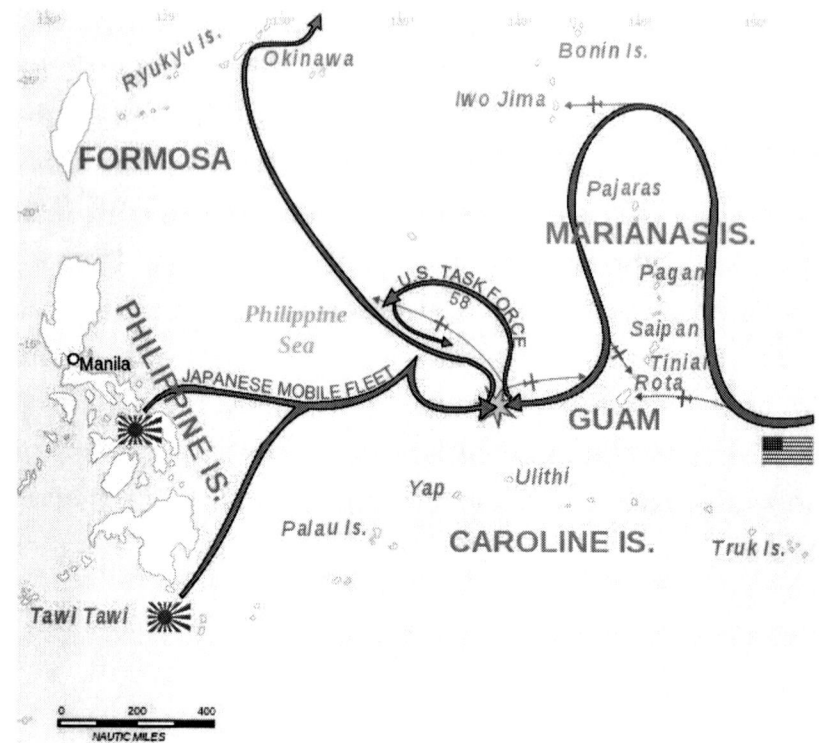

Paths taken by the naval forces during the Battle of the Philippine Sea (Courtesy Wikipedia the free Encyclopedia- Public Domain)

During the Battle of the Philippine Sea, celebrations were under way for the success of the invasion of Normandy on June 6, 1944. Meanwhile in the US prices of goods and services in the United States were modestly on the rise. Gas was priced at $0.15 per gallon; a new home cost, on average, $3,450.00. The average wage had increased to $2,400.00 per year. The average cost to rent a house per month was $50.00, and a loaf of bread cost $0.10. Sadly, Glen Miller was reported as missing in action.

The Battle of the Philippine Sea was fought in June 1944 under the leadership of Admiral Raymond Spruance and was a crushing defeat for the once proud navy of the Japanese Empire. This battle took place about 180 miles west of Saipan and came about as result of the Japanese attempt to intercept the invasion of Saipan.

The commander of the Japanese fleet was Admiral Ozawa, who launched sixty-nine planes as his first wave. The American pilots shot down forty-two of this first wave, in what has come to be known as the Great Marianas Turkey Shoot, because one of the pilots said, "It is just like a turkey shoot back home."

Ozawa's second wave, of 128 planes, followed, and again, they were met by the Americans, with seventy more planes being shot down. Twice more the Japanese launched more planes, and twice more the same results. In total, Ozawa put 373 planes in the air and only 130 returned. This number did not include about fifty land-based planes launched from Guam that were also shot down.

Of this number Lieutenant Alexander Vraciu downed six Japanese dive bombers in one mission. The Japanese Navy air arm had lost about three-fourths of its planes.

In addition to planes, the Japanese Navy lost three fleet carriers and three oilers. Another six ships were damaged.

Admiral Mitscher, with Admiral Spruance's approval, set out in pursuit of the Japanese fleet which was retreating. It was spotted late in the afternoon on June 20, 1944. Mitscher knew full well that his pilots might not make it back before dark and also that the distance was borderline with fuel capacity of the planes. Sixty-five more Japanese planes were shot down and several ships sunk or damaged. This happened at twilight, and Admiral Mitscher, at the risk of submarine attack, turned on all carriers' lights to help the returning pilots, many of whom did not make it back, landing in the ocean. For the United States, the two-day battle resulted in the loss of 130 planes and 75 pilots, but for Japan, it resulted in defeat, as it had only about thirty-five planes left of the nearly 500 they had started the battle with. This defeat meant that there was no longer any hope of rescue for the Japanese on Saipan, and the Japanese knew that the bombing of their homeland was just a matter of time, with the Marianas being an easy hop with the United States' new B-29 bombers.

Table 12 lists the troop, ship, and aircraft carrier casualties for the Battle of the Philippine Sea.

Table 12. Philippine Sea casualties

TROOPS	USA	JAPAN	SHIPS/AIR CRAFT	USA		JAPAN	
				Destroyed	Damaged	Destroyed	Damaged
Killed	75	250	Aircraft Carriers	-	-	3	-
Wounded	100	-	Aircraft	123	-	550-645	-
			Oiler Ships	-	-	2	-
			Other Ships	-	-	-	6
			Battleships	-	1	-	-

THE BATTLE OF SAIPAN

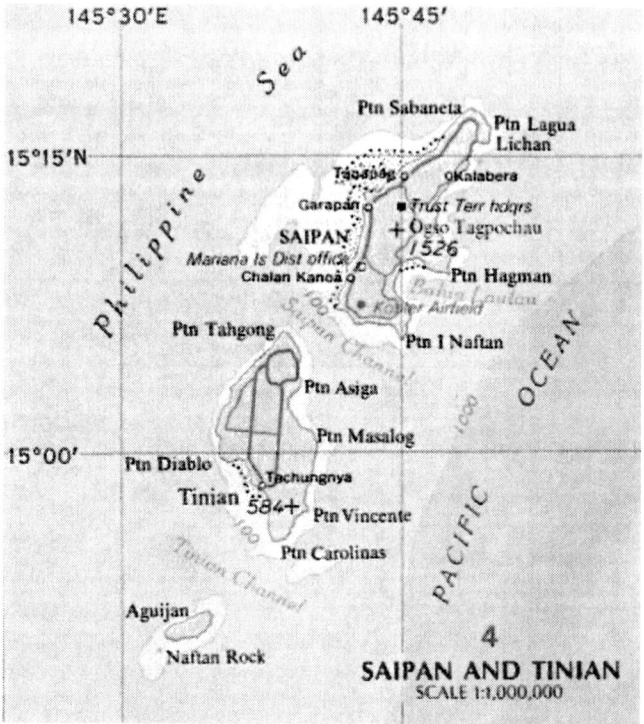

The Battle of Saipan (Courtesy Wikipedia the free Encyclopedia-Public Domain)

The Battle of Saipan, which was fought in June and July of 1944, has extra significance for me because it was the first of four battles that I experienced in the war in the Pacific. I went aboard the USS *J. Franklin Bell* in February 1944 and almost immediately went on a trip to Hawaii and then back to San Pedro, California, where the ship spent the next forty-five days in dry dock, getting repairs and alterations. I remember it well because I kept telling myself, "I came to fight a war, and all I am doing is spending my time on fire watch duty, observing welders make repairs," but the time passed quickly and by May 13, 1944, the ship had moved to Honolulu and loaded Army equipment and supplies. On May 18, Army troops came aboard and amphibious landings were practiced at Malaise Bay, Maui, and Kahoolawe. By that time, I had been selected to be a gunner's mate, which became my duty for the rest of my tour on the *Bell*.

At that point in the war, the United States had at its disposal the new long-range B-29 bomber, which was capable of operating around a radius of 1500 miles. With Japan being only 1300 miles to the northwest of Saipan, the island became an enormously important base for the air war on the Japanese. On June 15, the assault troops were landed on Saipan along with the *Bell*'s beach party, and the unloading of combat equipment was started.

After the troops and the *Bell* beach party had been sent to the beach and the unloading of equipment and supplies had started, the Task Force discovered that the Japanese fleet was about 180 miles to the southwest and headed for Saipan. Admiral Spruance, commander of the US Fifth Fleet, ordered all transports to flee to the east and await the outcome of the naval battle in the Philippine Sea. This did not allow time for the *Bell* to pick up the beach party or the LCVPs that were in action, so we, the *Bells* beach party remained on the beach for nearly two weeks, getting our supplies of food and water from what we could steal from the Army and Marines. I remember very well getting caught taking a carton of food off a sledge being pulled down the beach with a jeep. The carton contained food meant for officers, which was far above the quality of the K and C rations we enlisted men had to eat. When I explained to the soldier that we had been abandoned by our ship, he felt sorry for us and asked how many were in our group. When I responded, he said, "Take another case." I made a hit with our group because the cartons had cheese, spam, crackers, and candy bars, among other things.

Upon landing, we had been told to dig a foxhole, which we did, but not very deep. Around dusk, a Japanese plane came strafing down the beach and we all opened fire. The sky was full of red tracer bullets, which represented only about a third of all bullets because we normally loaded so every third bullet was a tracer. We did that because the tracers became a good aiming tool. We enlarged our foxholes after that close call. I can still hear the Army men adjacent to us the next morning saying, "Did you see how fast those Navy guys were expanding their foxholes after that strafing run last night?"

The invasion of Saipan completely surprised the Japanese because they had predicted the US would attack farther south. The Battle for the Philippine Sea, which resulted in great losses for the Japanese Navy, made it virtually impossible for them to resupply Saipan.

The island of Saipan had been under the control of the Spanish and then later the Germans before WWI. At the end of WWI, the League of Nations mandated the island of Saipan to Japanese; therefore, a large group of Japanese civilians—the best estimate was about 25,000—lived on the island. Emperor Hirohito was very disturbed about the risk that many of the civilians would find the treatment by the US acceptable and thus might aid the Americans in a propaganda war, so he sent out an imperial order encouraging the civilians on Saipan to commit suicide rather than surrender. They were promised that in the afterlife, they would have a spiritual life equal to that of soldiers dying in combat. Thousands of the civilians followed his advice.

At the northern tip of Saipan was a plateau about 800 feet above the rocky coral beach below. From this point the Japanese parents threw their children off the cliff and then followed, jumping to their deaths on the coral below. The Japanese troops did essentially the same thing by staging one of the most furious banzai attacks of the war in the Pacific. The troops charged with guns, grenades, bayonets, and sticks and were slaughtered by the Americans, incurring heavy Japanese losses. Machine gunners had to move their weapons higher to shoot over the pile of Japanese bodies.

Sergeant Thomas Baker provided an example of the fight put up by the Americans. He was wounded, and when his unit withdrew, he asked to be propped up by a tree and to be given a pistol. The next morning, he was found dead, but with eight Japanese bodies lying around him.

A couple of days later, as the fighting ended, 4311 Japanese bodies were counted on the beach at Tanapag on the island of Saipan. The Japanese General Saito, when all appeared lost, sat down in his cave headquarters, had a dinner of canned crabmeat and sake, and then committed suicide. Admiral Nagumo, the naval commander for Saipan, also committed suicide. The battle for Saipan was a crowning blow to the Japanese military because it left the Japanese mainland open to attacks from the American B-29 bombers.

The *Bell* returned to the area on June 25 and finished unloading equipment and supplies. On July 16, she sailed for Eniwetok, where she was replenished with fuel and supplies. We of the beach party were transferred to the USS *Cavalier* and sent back to Saipan, where we made plans for the invasion of Tinian.

It was on the *Cavalier* that we met the Hollywood actor Cesar Romero, who was part of that crew. It seemed strange to me to see him hosing down decks like an enlisted man, but it did not seem to bother him. I remember a few months later when someone posted a newspaper article on our ship's bulletin board showing Cesar with his arms around Betty Gable, with a caption saying, "He was glad to get home to see his mother."

Table 13 shows the troop casualties that occurred at Saipan.

Table 13. Saipan casualties

TROOPS	USA	JAPAN
Killed	3,426	24,000*
Wounded	13,160	-
Captured	-	921

* Additional 5,000 Japanese troops suicides
Note: An additional 22,000 Japanese civilians died (mostly suicides)

The following seven troops were awarded the Medal of Honor for their action during the Battle of Saipan. (Citations for each are noted in References.)

HAROLD CHRIST AGERHOLM. Private First Class U.S. Marine Reserve born January 25, in Racine, WI. When the enemy launched a fierce, determined counterattack against US positions and overran a neighboring artillery battalion, Private First Class Agerholm immediately volunteered to assist in the efforts to check the hostile attack and evacuate the wounded, locating and appropriating an abandoned ambulance jeep. He repeatedly made extremely perilous trips under heavy rifle and mortar fire and single-handedly loaded and evacuated approximately forty-five casualties, working tirelessly and with utter disregard for his own safety during a grueling period of more than three hours. Despite intense, persistent enemy fire, he ran out to aid two men whom he believed to be wounded Marines but was himself mortally wounded by a Japanese sniper while carrying out his hazardous mission.

THOMAS A. BAKER, Sergeant U.S. Army born June 25, 1916, in Troy, NY. Private Baker's position came under attack by a large Japanese force. Although seriously wounded early in the attack, he refused to be evacuated and continued to fight in the close-range battle until running out of ammunition. When a comrade was wounded while trying to carry him to safety, Baker insisted that he be left behind. At his request, his comrades left him propped against a tree and gave him a pistol, which had eight bullets remaining. When American forces retook the position, they found the pistol, now empty, and eight dead Japanese soldiers around Baker's body.

HAROLD G. EPPERSON, Private First Class U.S. Marine Reserve born July 14, 1923 in Akron, OH, Private First Class Epperson, part of the 2nd Marine Division, threw himself on a grenade to prevent the blast from killing members of his squad. For his bravery and sacrifice, he was posthumously awarded the Medal of Honor. His Medal of Honor was presented to his mother in a ceremony on Wednesday, July 4, 1945, in Tiger Stadium, Massillon, Ohio. The USS *Epperson* (DD-719), a Gearing-class destroyer, was named in his honor.

ROBERT H. MCCARD, born November 25, 1918, in Syracuse, NY. On June 16, 1944, when his tank was put out of action by enemy 77 mm guns. He ordered his men out of the escape hatch while he continued to throw hand grenades at the enemy. When out of hand grenades, he took one of the machine guns from the tank and continued to assault the enemy so his troops could escape. Gunnery Sergeant McCard, a Marine, killed sixteen enemies while sacrificing himself to ensure the safety of his tank crew. McCard was posthumously awarded the Medal of Honor for his actions. The USS *Robert H. McCard* (DD-822), a Gearing-class destroyer, was named in his honor.

WILLIAM O'BRIEN. Lieutenant Colonel U.S. Army born (Date of birth unknown) in Troy, NY. When his battalion came under attack from a much larger enemy force on July 7, Lieutenant Colonel O'Brien refused to leave the front lines even after being wounded, and he continued to lead his men until being overrun and killed. He was posthumously awarded the Medal of Honor on May 9, 1945, for his actions throughout the Battle of Saipan. The US Army ship USAT *Col. William J. O'Brien,* which served in the Pacific Ocean at the end of WWII, was named in his honor.

BEN L. SALOMON, Captain U.S. Army born September 1, 1914, in Milwaukee, WI. Captain Salomon, the battalion surgeon of 2nd Battalion, 105th Infantry Regiment, 27th

Infantry Division, aided the evacuation of wounded soldiers. After defending his patients from four Japanese soldiers, he manned a machine-gun post and effectively repelled numerous enemy forces to enable the evacuation of wounded personnel. When his body was recovered after the battle, ninety-eight dead Japanese soldiers were found in front of his position. For gallantry in battle, Captain Salomon was posthumously awarded the Medal of Honor in May 2002. Salomon was the third Jewish service member to be awarded the Medal of Honor during WWII.

GRANT FREDERICK TIMMERMAN. Sergeant U.S. Marine Corps born February 14, 1919, in Americus, KA. During action against enemy Japanese forces on Saipan, Marianas Islands, on July 8, 1944, Sergeant Timmerman, advancing with his tank a few yards ahead of the infantry in support of a vigorous attack on hostile positions, maintained steady fire from his antiaircraft sky-mount machine gun until progress was impeded by a series of enemy trenches and pillboxes. Observing a target of opportunity, he immediately ordered the tank stopped and, mindful of the danger from the muzzle blast, prepared to open fire with the 75 mm. He fearlessly stood up in the exposed turret and ordered the infantry to hit the deck. Quick to act as a grenade hurled by the Japanese was about to drop into the open turret hatch, Sergeant Timmerman unhesitatingly blocked the opening with his body, holding the grenade against his chest and taking the brunt of the explosion.

THE BATTLE OF TINIAN

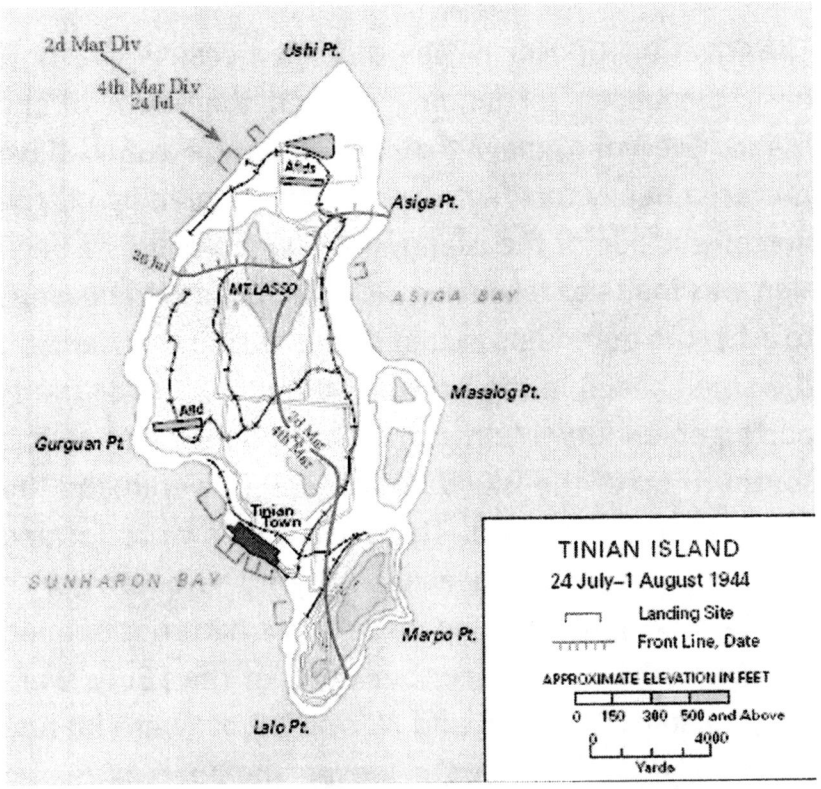

Tinian a mile southwest of Saipan. (Courtesy Wikipedia the free Encyclopedia-Public Domain)

The Battle of Tinian was fought in July 1944. In the course of the battle, the 9000-man Japanese garrison was eliminated. The island, along with Saipan and Guam, became the base for the Twentieth Air Force. It was from this island that the atomic bombs were loaded for the trips to Hiroshima and Nagasaki. Because of the flat terrain, this island was better suited for the B-29 airstrips than was Saipan. Fifteen thousand Seabees turned the island into the busiest airfield of the war.

The invasion of Tinian was difficult because the only desirable beach for landing was on the south of the island. Everyone knew that the Japanese would have this area heavy fortified. There was an opening on the northwest side of the island, but it was small. The decision was made to fake an invasion to the south beaches to draw the defenders in that direction and then land on the small beach in the north. The *Bell* and other transports got underway on July 24 and proceeded to the southern tip of the Island. Boats were lowered and the embarkation simulated. The boat waves were formed and sent toward the beaches. When the boats got to within 1500 yards, the Japanese shore batteries opened fire with a heavy barrage, but none of the LCVPs were hit. The ships *Colorado* and *Norman Scott* were hit and suffered heavy casualties, however. The boats retreated to a safe area and regrouped.

The boat waves were reformed and sent toward the beach a second time. This time, they turned off at 5000 yards and received no fire from the beach.

In the meantime, the *Bell*'s boat group commander, beach party, and boat crews played a major role in the amphibious strike on the northern beaches. We managed to put in place a floating dock that was long enough to reach just beyond the coral reef so we could bring vehicles and troops onto the shore. Several times a jeep failed to hit the ramp and was submerged in about ten feet of water. How I would like to have one of them back on the farm in Kentucky!

After hoisting the LCVPs back aboard, the *Bell* and other APAs proceeded to the north of the island where the actual landing was taking place. Assault troops were landed and casualties were brought back to our ship. It was during this landing that our boats came under heavy fire by Japanese field guns and mortars and William Kalnitsky in the *Bell*'s boat 22 was wounded.

On July 27, all the casualties were transferred to the field hospital on Saipan and 438 Japanese prisoners of war were brought aboard for transfer back to Pearl Harbor.

This happens to be one of my close calls to being a casualty, because we found a young Japanese soldier hiding in a bamboo thicket. He had spent all of his ammunition but attempted to use his bayonet; however, machetes and numbers of Allied troops won out. I was impressed with the fact that he was nearly six feet tall and very athletically built. He suffered machete wounds during the struggle to control him and was given a blood transfusion by a corpsman which did not go over well with a lot of our nearby troops.

It was on Tinian that I missed seeing my nephew Earl Hutchison. He had been a part of the Tarawa invasion and had been wounded in the head. By the time the Battle of Tinian occurred, he was fully recovered and was a part of the 2nd Marines landing on Tinian. He knew my ship number, APA16, so he contacted the crew of one of our LCVPs and wrote me a note on the inside wrapper of a pack of Camel cigarettes saying, "Sorry I missed seeing you, but see you back in Kentucky." And that he did.

The invasion of Tinian was the United States' most perfectly executed amphibious invasion yet has received relatively limited attention. According to reports, Admiral Raymond A. Spruance said that the seizure of Tinian was the most brilliantly conceived and executed amphibious operation in WWII.

Table 14 shows the troop casualties that occurred at Tinian.

Table 14. Tinian casualties

TROOPS	USA	JAPAN
Killed	326	5,542
Wounded	1,593	-
Captured		252*

*An additional 2,265 Japanese were missing.

The following men were awarded the Medal of Honor for their actions during the battle for Tinian. (Citations for each are noted in References.)

JOSEPH WILLIAM OZBOURN. Private U.S. Marine Corps born October 24, 1919, in Herrin, IL. As a BAR (Browning automatic rifleman) during the battle for enemy Japanese-held Tinian Island, Marianas Islands, July 30, 1944, and a member of a platoon assigned the mission of clearing the remaining Japanese troops from dugouts and pillboxes along a tree line, Private Ozbourn, flanked by two men on either side, was moving forward to throw an armed hand grenade into a dugout when a terrific blast from the entrance severely wounded the four other men and himself. Unable to throw the grenade into the dugout, and with no place to hurl it without endangering the other men, Private Ozbourn unhesitatingly grasped it close to his body and fell upon it, sacrificing his own life to absorb the full impact of the explosion but saving his comrades.

ROBERT L. WILSON. Private First Class U.S. Marine Corps born May 24, 1921, in Centralia, IL. During action against enemy Japanese forces at Tinian Island, Marianas Islands, on August 4, 1944, as one of a group of Marines advancing through heavy underbrush to neutralize isolated points of resistance, Private First Class Wilson daringly preceded his companions. Serving with the 2nd Marine Division (Reinforced), Wilson also received a second Presidential Unit Citation signed by Secretary of the Navy James Forrestal "for outstanding performance of duty in combat during the seizure and occupation of the Japanese-held Atoll of Tarawa, Gilbert Islands,

November 20, 24, 1943." In addition, Wilson received the Purple Heart with one gold star.

At the time of his death on Tinian, Wilson was serving with Company D, 2nd Pioneer Battalion, 18th Marines, and the 2nd Marine Division. The Medal of Honor was presented to his mother at a ceremony held on July 26, 1945, at the American Legion cottage in Centralia, Illinois. Private Wilson was initially buried in the military cemetery on Tinian but was reinterred in Hillcrest Cemetery, Centralia, in 1948.

THE BATTLES OF GUAM

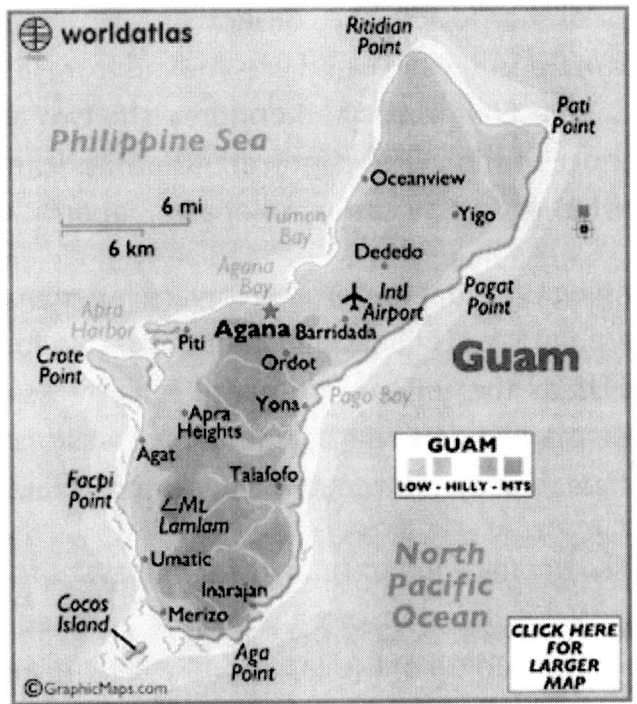

Guam the largest of the Marianas Islands (Courtesy WorldAtlas).

Guam, once belonging to Spain, had been taken over by the United States in 1898 during the Spanish-American War. The bombing of Guam by the Japanese started the same day as the attack on Pearl Harbor in preparation for the actual landing of Japanese troops on December 10, 1941, just three days after the Pearl Harbor attack. The Japanese also invaded and captured all of the Mariana Islands during December 1941.

Six US troops decided to fade into the jungle and evade capture but eventually 5 were captured and beheaded by the Japanese along with many of the local Chamorros (Indigenous people of the Mariana Islands) who were accused of harboring the Americans. However, one American, George Ray Tweed was moved from village to village by the Chamorros and endured the two and half years of occupation. The captured 406 Americans were transported to a POW camp at Kagawa, Japan.

Maintaining the ladder approach toward Japan made the islands of Saipan, Tinian, and Guam desirable locations for the US as the military prepared for attacks on the Japanese mainland as well as upcoming invasions of the Philippines (Leyte) and the Ryukyu Islands (Okinawa).

Originally, the invasion to retake Guam was set for three days after the invasion of Saipan, but because of the unexpected strength of the Japanese on Saipan and with the knowledge that a naval battle in the Philippine Sea (Only 180 miles west of Guam) was imminent, Admiral Spruance and his staff decided to delay the attack on Guam for a month and rescheduled the attack for July 21, 1944.

Guam, which is ringed with cliffs and reefs with heavy surf, was a challenge to any attacker. The Japanese were effective with their artillery, which sank twenty LVTs and inflicted heavy losses on the US troops, but by nightfall on the first day, the Americans had a beachhead nearly 7000 feet deep. Each counterattack by the Japanese during the night resulted in heavy losses for them.

The Japanese chose to withdraw to the mountainous region in the central and northern parts of the island in an effort to hold the island as long as possible. Rain and thick jungle made things difficult for the US troops. By August 10, 1944, however, organized Japanese resistance was essentially ended and it was estimated that about 7,500 were at large in the jungle. The commander for the Japanese on Guam committed ritual suicide at his headquarters. A few Japanese continued to hide out in the jungle, and nearly a year later, three Marines were ambushed and killed by the hiding Japanese. On January 24, 1972, Sergeant Shoichi Yokoi was found by hunters after he had had been living alone in a cave for twenty-seven years.

Table 15 shows the troop casualties for the first and second Battles of Guam. The first battle occurred just after Pearl Harbor on December 10, 1941 when the Japanese invaded the American Controlled Island. The second battle occurred July 21, 1944.

Table 15. Guam casualties

(First Battle 1941)			(Second Battle 1944)		
TROOPS	USA	JAPAN	TROOPS	USA	JAPAN
Killed	17	1	Killed	1,783	18,337
Wounded	35	6	Wounded	6,010	-
Captured	406	-	Captured	-	1,250

The following four troops were awarded the Medal of Honor for their actions during the Second Battle of Guam. (Citations for each are noted in References.)

LEONARD F. MASON, Private First Class U.S. Marine Corps born February 2, 1920, in Middleborough, KY. In action against the enemy on the island of Guam, Private First Class Mason was suddenly taken under fire by two enemy machine guns that were holding up the advance of his platoon through a narrow gulley. Private Mason, on his own initiative, climbed out of the gully and moved toward the enemy position. Although wounded, he, with complete disregard for his own safety, cleaned out an enemy position, killing five enemy soldiers and wounding another. He then rejoined his platoon and reported his action before succumbing to his critical wounds. His exceptionally heroic act in the face of almost certain death enabled his platoon to accomplish its mission.

LUTHER SKAGGS JR., Private First Class U. S. Marine Corps Reserve born March 3, 1923, in Henderson, KY. When the section leader became a casualty under heavy mortar barrage shortly after landing, Private First Class Skaggs promptly assumed command and led his section through intense fire for a distance of 200 yards to a position from which to deliver effective coverage of the assault on a strategic cliff. Private Skaggs was critically wounded when a grenade was tossed into his foxhole. He put a tourniquet on his leg and continued gallantly, returning the enemy fire with rifle and grenades for eight hours. Uncomplaining and calm throughout this critical period, Private Skaggs served as a heroic example of courage and fortitude to other wounded men.

LOUIS H. WILSON JR., Captain U.S. Marine Corps born February 11, 1920, in Brandon, MS. Ordered to take a portion of the hill in his zone of action, Captain Wilson initiated the attack in midafternoon, pushed up the rugged and open terrain against terrific machine-gun and rifle fire for 300 yards, and successfully captured the objective. He promptly took command of other units and organized his night defenses. Although wounded three times during a five-hour period, he made sure his troops were in position for an expected counterattack before he retired to the command post for medical attention. Shortly thereafter, when the enemy launched the first of a series of savage attacks lasting all night, he voluntarily rejoined his besieged unit, where he dashed fifty yards into the open to rescue a wounded Marine lying helplessly beyond the front lines. Fighting fiercely in hand-to-hand combat for ten hours, he succeeded in holding his position. Then, organizing a seventeen-man patrol, he, defying intense mortar, machine-gun, and rifle fire that struck down thirteen of his men, drove relentlessly forward with the remnants of his patrol to seize the vital ground. By his indomitable leadership, daring combat tactics, and valor in the face of overwhelming odds,

Captain. Wilson succeeded in capturing and holding the strategic high ground in his regimental sector.

FRANK P. WITEK, Private First Class U.S. Marine Corps Reserve born December 1921, in Derby, CN. When his rifle platoon was halted by heavy surprise fire from a well-camouflaged enemy position, Private First Class Witek daringly remained standing to fire a full magazine from his automatic at point-blank range into a depression housing Japanese troops, killing eight of the enemy and enabling the greater part of his platoon to take cover. During his platoon's withdrawal for consolidation of lines, he remained to safeguard a severely wounded comrade, courageously returning enemy fire until the arrival of stretcher bearers. Private Witek, on his own initiative, moved forward to within five to ten yards of the enemy position and destroyed an enemy machine-gun emplacement and killed an additional eight Japanese before he was struck down by an enemy rifleman.

THE BATTLE OF LEYTE

I shall return. — General Douglas Macarthur, Supreme Allied Commander of Southwest Pacific (speaking about the Philippines when he was forced to retreat to Australia in 1942)

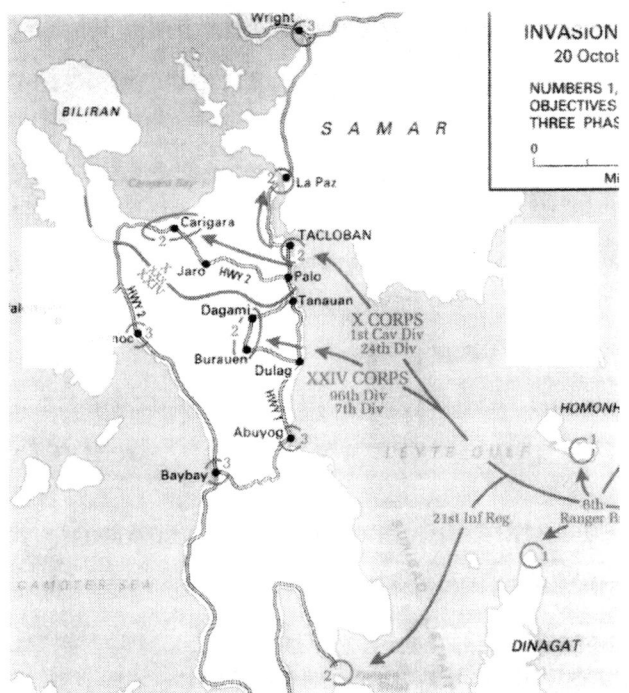

The Battle for Leyte in the Philippines (Courtesy Wikipedia the free Encyclopedia- Public Domain) Note: The arrows on the above map shows the direction of the US forces in the attack on Leyte.

After the Battle of Tinian, the USS *J. Franklin Bell* returned to Pearl Harbor, where we unloaded the prisoners of war and took on US troops and combat equipment. Amphibious practice landings were held at Maalaen Bay on the island of Maui for several days. After this, the troops were returned to their land base. During the next two weeks, final planning for the invasion of the island of Yap, in the Caroline Islands, was completed. Our first stop was at Eniwetok, in the Marshall Islands. The general in charge of the troops aboard left the ship for a meeting, and when he returned, he announced that our objective now was Leyte, in the Philippines. The *Bell* then headed for Manus, in the Admiralty Islands group. We held antiaircraft practice every day while in route to Manus.

Pityliu Island, one of the sections of the barrier reef north of the harbor, was set aside for rest and relaxation. I became very popular with the old salts on board because at my young age, I was not yet a beer drinker and we were restricted to just a couple beers for each shipmate. I quite frequently traded my beer for cokes.

The *Bell* assistant beach master, with some of the beach party members, was transferred to the LST 605 for the initial assault on Leyte beach. Other APAs made similar transfers to another five LSTs. The beach parties were accompanied by 926 assault troops. The goal for this group was to hit the beach to test the Japanese defense for the landing that was to follow.

The task group moved out of Seeadler Harbor; firing exercises were a daily routine. *Mindanao* was detected by radar late on October 19, 1944. During the night, the convoy sailed through Surigao Strait and entered Leyte Gulf. At dawn on October 20, Japanese planes flew just a few hundred feet over the convoy, dropping bombs that landed on each side of the *Bell* but did not inflict any damage. I can still to this day see a vision of the plane directly overhead through a gap in the smoke screen.

Directly behind the beach was a small ridge about 300–400 feet above sea level. The Japanese planes used the ridge to hide from our radar and would pop over the hill and be upon us without any warning. On one occasion, an American plane was chasing a Japanese plane that was flying in over the ridge. The Japanese plane was shot down, as was our plane. The American pilot was rescued from the gulf by one of our LCVPs and was brought aboard our ship. He was very angry and said all he would do if he could find out who shot him down. All of my shipmates said it was not us, but because I was captain of the aft 40 mm gun crew and was firing our guns with all the rest of the ships in the area, I could not rule us out being the guilty party, especially because the pilot said a round of ammunition that he suspected to be a 40 mm projectile had gone right between his legs.

Japanese Admiral Toyoda elected to divide his fleet into three groups, called the Northern, Center, and Southern Forces, to engage the US Third and Seventh Fleets. These US ships were stationed in the Leyte Gulf to provide coverage for the invasion of Leyte. Before the Center Force reached Leyte, however, it was attacked by US submarines and planes from the Third Fleet. The Southern Force was engaged that night in the Surigao

Strait by the Seventh Fleet and retreated from battle. Meanwhile, the Northern Force lured the Third Fleet away from Leyte Gulf but was outmaneuvered and outgunned by Admiral Bull Halsey, suffering heavy losses. At the same time, the Seventh Fleet, under Vice Admiral Kinkaid, engaged the retreating Japanese Center Force off the island of Samar, inflicting additional damage. This activity ended the naval battle for Leyte Gulf and was a crushing defeat for the once-powerful Japanese Navy.

General MacArthur kept his promise of returning by wading ashore on D-Day. He challenged the Philippine people by addressing them via radio: "People of the Philippines, I have returned," he proclaimed. "The hour of your redemption is here. ... Rally to me ... as the lines of battle roll forward to bring you within the zone of operation. Rise and strike."

The landing was accomplished with great precision by the American Forces, but the objective was barely visible through the cloak of bursting bombs and projectiles. *The Bell's* landing craft returned from the beach with twenty-eight wounded Army troops and two civilians for treatment by our ship's doctors and corpsman.

In midafternoon on D-Day (October 20, 1944), the cruiser *Honolulu,* which was anchored several thousand yards north of the *Bell,* was torpedoed by enemy planes. Several bombing attacks by Japanese planes during the day did no damage.

I still have the image in my mind of the LSM-34 as she came alongside our ship with the mangled bodies of her skipper and two members of the crew who had taken a mortar shell in their conning tower.

The *Bell* as well as other APAs in the invasion received a "well done" from Rear Admiral Connolly. We then took aboard the admiral of the British fleet, Lord Roger Keyes, for transport back to Manus in the Admiralty Islands.

Table 16 lists the troop casualties for the Battle of Leyte.

Table 16. Leyte casualties

TROOPS	USA	JAPAN
Killed	3,500	70,000
Wounded	11,991	
Captured	89*	

* USA Troops missing-probably drown

After a trip to New Guinea for troop transfers, the *Bell* arrived back in Manus on November 8. On the morning of November 10, for some unknown reason, Captain Ritchie moved our anchorage from next to an ammunition ship, the *Mount Hood*, to another location. I was working on top deck with the 20 mm guns later that day when the *Mount Hood* exploded. The resulting blast floored all of us who were topside. No one on the *Mount Hood* survived, except the ship's crew who had been sent for mail, and many ships adjacent were sunk or damaged. It was just another of those close calls that followed me throughout my navy career. Tim Churchill expressed our many close calls in his poem *Deathly Encounters*.

Deathly Encounters

Some close calls in my memory still,
When I think back in time,
Like Kamikaze reads I saw,
in ugly war and grime.

Another instance I recall
An ammo ship so near,
It blew itself to kingdom come
and filled my heart with fear.

And then a bad collision came,
two ships collide at sea,
A dreadful night for both the crews
But fortune smiled on me.

A bullet whizzed by left ear,
That left me dazed, in shock;
A thing you don't forget I guess,
It's something carved in rock.

Once while driving in the Alps,
I missed a crucial curve;
I left the roadway, yet remained,
with very shattered nerve.

At other times and events past,
With dangers on the line,
My close encounters seemed to say,
"Good fortune" has been mine.

After Leyte, the *Bell* spent considerable time shifting troops and casualties from island to island and finally ended up in San Francisco during the latter part of 1944 for three months of overhaul and repair to get ready for the invasion of Okinawa.

The following fourteen troops were awarded the Medal of Honor for their actions during the invasion of Leyte. (Citations for each are noted in References.)

GEORGE BENJAMIN JR., Private First Class U.S. Army born April 24, 1919, in Philadelphia, PA. Private First Class Benjamin was a radio operator advancing in the rear of his company as it engaged a well-defended Japanese strongpoint holding up the progress of the entire battalion. When a rifle platoon supporting a light tank hesitated in its advance, he voluntarily, and with utter disregard for personal safety, left his comparatively secure position and ran across a bullet-whipped terrain to the tank, waving and shouting to the men of the platoon to follow. Carrying his bulky radio and armed only with a pistol, he fearlessly penetrated intense machine-gun and rifle fire to the enemy position, where he killed one of the enemy in a foxhole and moved on to annihilate the crew of a light machine gun. Heedless of the terrific fire now concentrated on him, he continued to spearhead the assault, killing two more of the enemy and exhorting the other men to advance, until he fell mortally wounded. After being evacuated to an aid station, his first thought was still of the American advance. Overcoming great pain, he called for the battalion operations officer to report the location of enemy weapons and valuable tactical information he had secured in his heroic charge.

RICHARD I. BONG, Major U.S. Army Air Corps born September 24, 1920, in Poplar, WI. Though assigned to duty as gunnery instructor and neither required nor expected to perform combat duty, Major Bong voluntarily and at his own urgent request engaged in repeated combat missions, including unusually hazardous sorties over Balikpapan, over Borneo, and in the Leyte area of the Philippines. His aggressiveness and daring resulted in his shooting down eight enemy airplanes during this period.

LEONARD C. BROSTROM, Private First Class U.S. Army born November 23, 1919, in Preston, ID. Private First Class Brostrom was a rifleman with an assault platoon that ran into powerful resistance near Dagami, Leyte, Philippine Islands, on October 28, 1944. From pillboxes, trenches, and spider holes so well camouflaged that they could be detected at no more than twenty yards, the enemy poured machine-gun and rifle fire, causing severe casualties in the platoon. Realizing that a key pillbox in the center of the strongpoint would have to be knocked out if the company were to advance, Private Brostrom, without orders and completely ignoring his own safety, ran forward to attack the pillbox with grenades. He immediately became the prime target for all the riflemen in the area as he rushed to the rear of the pillbox and tossed grenades through the entrance. Six enemy soldiers left a trench in a bayonet charge against the heroic American, but Brostrom killed one and drove the others off with rifle fire. As he threw more grenades from his completely exposed position, he was wounded several times in the abdomen and was knocked to the ground. Although suffering intense pain and rapidly weakening from loss of blood, he slowly rose to his feet and once more hurled his deadly missiles at the pillbox. As he collapsed, the enemy began fleeing from the fortification and were killed by riflemen of Brostrom's platoon. Private Brostrom died while being carried from the battlefield.

ELMER E. FRYAR, Private U.S. Army born February 10, 1914, in Denver, CO. Private Fryar's battalion encountered the enemy strongly entrenched in a position supported by mortars and automatic weapons. The battalion attacked but, in spite of repeated efforts, was unable to take the position. Private Fryar's company was ordered to cover the battalion's withdrawal to a more suitable point from which to attack, but the enemy launched a strong counterattack that threatened to cut off the company. Seeing an enemy platoon moving to outflank his company, Fryar moved to higher ground and opened heavy and accurate fire. He was hit and wounded, but, continuing his attack, he drove the enemy back with a Japanese loss of twenty-seven killed. While withdrawing to overtake his squad, Private Fryar found a seriously wounded comrade, helped him to the rear, and soon overtook his platoon leader, who was assisting another wounded comrade. While these four were moving to rejoin their platoon, an enemy sniper appeared and aimed his weapon at the platoon leader. Private Fryar instantly sprang forward, received the full burst of automatic fire in his own body, and fell mortally wounded. With his remaining strength, he threw a hand grenade and killed the sniper.

LEROY JOHNSON, Sergeant U.S. Army born December 6, 1919, in Caney Creek, LA. Johnson was squad leader of a nine-man patrol sent to reconnoiter a ridge held by a well-entrenched enemy force. Seeing an enemy machine-gun position, he ordered his men to remain behind while he crawled to within six yards of the gun and reported the situation to his commanding officer. One of the enemy crew jumped up and prepared to man the weapon. Quickly withdrawing, Sergeant Johnson rejoined his patrol. Ordered to destroy the gun, which covered the approaches to several other enemy positions, he chose three other men, armed them with hand grenades, and led them to a point near the objective. After taking partial cover behind a log, the men had knocked out the gun and begun an assault when hostile troops on the flank hurled several grenades. As he started for cover, Sergeant Johnson saw two unexploded grenades that had fallen near his men. Knowing that his comrades would be wounded or killed by the explosion, he deliberately threw himself on the grenades and received their full charge in his body. Fatally wounded by the blast, he died soon afterward.

OVA A. KELLY, Private U.S. Army born March 27, 1914, in Norwood, MO. Before dawn, near the edge of the enemy-held Buri airstrip, the company was immobilized by heavy, accurate rifle and machine-gun fire from hostile troops entrenched in bomb craters and a ditch less than one hundred yards distant. The company commander ordered a mortar concentration, which destroyed one machine gun but failed to dislodge the main body of the enemy. At this critical moment, Private Kelly, on his own initiative, left his shallow foxhole with an armload of hand grenades and began a one-man assault on the foe. Throwing his missiles with great accuracy, he moved forward, killed or wounded five men, and forced the remainder to flee in a disorganized route. He picked up an M1 rifle and emptied its clip at the running Japanese, killing three. Discarding this weapon, Private Kelly took a carbine and killed three more of the enemy. Inspired by Private Kelly's example, his comrades followed him in a charge that destroyed the entire enemy force of thirty-four enlisted men and two officers and captured two heavy and one light machine gun. Private Kelly continued to press the attack on to an airstrip, where sniper fire wounded him so grievously that he died two days later.

WILLIAM A. MCWHORTER. Private First Class U.S. Army born December 7, 1918, in Liberty, SC. While engaged in operations against the enemy, Private First Class McWhorter, a machine gunner, was emplaced in a defensive position with one assistant when the enemy launched a heavy attack. Manning the gun and opening fire, Private McWhorter killed several members of an advancing demolition squad. When one of the enemy succeeded in throwing a fused demolition charge in the entrenchment, without hesitation and with complete disregard for his own safety, Private McWhorter picked up the improvised grenade and deliberately held it close to his body, bending over and turning away from his companion. The charge exploded, killing him instantly but leaving his assistant unharmed.

HAROLD H. MOON JR. Private U.S. Arm born March 15, 1921, in Albuquerque, NM. When powerful Japanese counterblows were being struck in a desperate effort to annihilate a newly won beachhead, Moon, in a forward position and manned with a submachine gun, met the brunt of a strong, well-supported night attack that quickly enveloped his platoon's flanks. Many men in nearby positions were killed or injured, and Private Moon was wounded as his foxhole became the immediate object of a concentration of mortar and machine-gun fire. Nevertheless, Moon maintained his stand, poured deadly fire into the enemy, and daringly exposed himself to hostile fire time after time to exhort and inspire what American troops were left in the immediate area. A Japanese officer, covered by machine-gun fire and hidden by an embankment, attempted to knock out his position with grenades, but Pvt. Moon, after protracted and skillful maneuvering, killed the officer. When the enemy advanced a light machine gun to within twenty yards of the shattered perimeter and fired with telling effects on the remnants of the platoon, Moon stood up to locate the gun and remained exposed while calling back range corrections to friendly mortars, which knocked out the weapon. A little later, he killed two Japanese as they charged an aid man.

By dawn, Private Moon's position, the focal point of the attack for more than four hours, was virtually surrounded. In a fanatical effort to reduce the position and kill its defender, an entire Japanese platoon charged with fixed bayonets. Firing from a sitting position, Private Moon calmly emptied his magazine into the advancing horde, killing eighteen and repulsing the attack. In a final display of bravery, he stood up to throw a grenade at a machine gun that had opened fire on the right flank. He was hit and instantly killed.

CHARLES E. MOWER, Sergeant U.S. Army born November 29, 1924, in Chippewa Falls, WI. Mower was an assistant squad leader in an attack against strongly defended enemy positions on both sides of a stream running through a wooded gulch. As the squad advanced through concentrated fire, the leader was killed and Sergeant Mower assumed command. To bring direct fire upon the enemy, he had started to lead his men across the stream, which by this time was churned by machine-gun and rifle fire, but he was severely wounded before reaching the opposite bank. After signaling his unit to halt, he realized that his own exposed position was the most advantageous point from which to direct the attack, and he stood fast. Half submerged, gravely wounded, but refusing to seek shelter or accept aid of any kind, he continued to shout and signal to his squad as he directed it in the destruction of two enemy machine guns and numerous riflemen. Discovering that the intrepid man in the stream was largely responsible for the successful action being taken against them, the remaining Japanese concentrated the full force of their firepower upon him and he was killed while still urging his men on.

ROBERT P. NETT, Captain U.S. Army born June 13, 1922, in New Haven, CT. Nett commanded Company E in an attack against a reinforced enemy battalion that had held up the American advance for two days from entrenched positions around a three-story concrete building. With another infantry company and armored vehicles, Company E advanced against heavy machine-gun and other automatic-weapons fire, with Lieutenant Nett spearheading the assault against the strongpoint. During the fierce hand-to-hand encounter that ensued, Lieutenant Nett killed seven deeply entrenched Japanese with his rifle and bayonet and, although seriously wounded, gallantly continued to lead his men forward, refusing to relinquish his command. Again he was severely wounded, but, still unwilling to retire, pressed ahead with his troops to ensure the capture of the objective. Wounded once more in the final assault, Nett calmly made all arrangements for the resumption of the advance, turned over his command to another officer, and then walked unaided to the rear for medical treatment. Lieutenant Nett received the Medal of Honor because of his remarkable courage in continuing forward through sheer determination despite successive wounds.

RICHARD H. O'KANE, Commander U.S. Navy born On February 2, 1911, in Dover, NH. Kane was commanding officer of the USS *Tang* as she operated against two enemy Japanese convoys on October 23 and 24, 1944, during her fifth and last war period. Boldly maneuvering on the surface into the midst of a heavily escorted convoy, Commander O'Kane stood in the fusillade of bullets and shells from all directions to launch smashing hits on three tankers, coolly swung his ship to fire at a freighter, and, in a split-second decision, shot out of the path of an onrushing transport, missing it by inches. Boxed in by blazing tankers, a freighter, a transport, and several destroyers, he blasted two of the targets with his remaining torpedoes and, with pyrotechnics bursting on all sides, cleared the area. Twenty-four hours later, he again made contact with a heavily escorted convoy steaming to support the Leyte campaign with reinforcements and supplies, with crated planks piled high on each unit. In defiance of the enemy's relentless fire, Commander O'Kane closed the concentration of ships and in quick succession sent two torpedoes each into the first and second transports and an adjacent tank, finding his mark with each torpedo in a series of violent explosions at fewer than 1,000 yards' range. With ships bearing down from all sides, he charged the enemy at high speed, exploding the tanker in a burst of flame, smashing the transport dead in the water, and blasting the destroyer with a mighty roar that rocked the *Tang* from stern to stern, expending his last two torpedoes into the remnants of a once-powerful convoy before his own ship went down.

JOHN F. THORSON, Private First Class U.S. Army born May 10, 1920, in Armstrong, IA. Thorson was an automatic rifleman on October 28, 1944, in the attack on Dagami, Leyte, Philippine Islands. A heavily fortified enemy position consisting of pillboxes and supporting trenches held up the advance of Thorson's company. His platoon was ordered to outflank and neutralize the strongpoint. Voluntarily moving well out in front of his group, Private Thorson came upon an enemy fire trench defended by several hostile riflemen and, disregarding the intense fire directed at him, attacked single-handedly. He was seriously wounded and fell about six yards from the trench. Just as the remaining twenty members of Thorson's platoon reached him, one of the enemy threw a grenade into their midst. Shouting a warning and making a final effort, Private Thorson rolled onto the grenade and smothered the explosion with his body. He was instantly killed.

DIRK J. VLUG, Private First Class U.S. Army born August 20, 1916, in Maple Lake, MN. When an American roadblock on the Ormoc Road was attacked by a group of enemy tanks. He left his covered position and, with a rocket launcher and six rounds of ammunition, advanced alone under intense machine-gun and 37 mm fire. Loading single-handedly, he destroyed the first tank, killing its occupants with a single round. As the crew of the second tank started to dismount and attack him, Vlug killed one of the foe with his pistol, forcing the survivors to return to their vehicle, which he then destroyed with a second round. Three more hostile tanks moved up the road, so he flanked the first and eliminated it and then, despite a hail of enemy fire, pressed forward again to destroy another. With his last round of ammunition, he struck the remaining vehicle, causing it to crash down a steep embankment. Through his sustained heroism in the face of superior forces, Private First Class Vlug alone destroyed five enemy tanks and greatly facilitated successful accomplishment of his battalion's mission.

CAPTAIN FRANCIS B. WAI, Captain U.S. Army born April 17, 1917, in Honolulu, HI. Captain Wai landed at Red Beach, Leyte, in the face of accurate, concentrated enemy fire from gun positions advantageously located in a palm grove bounded by submerged rice paddies. Finding the first four waves of American soldiers leaderless, disorganized, and pinned down on the open beach, he immediately assumed command. Issuing clear and concise orders, and disregarding heavy enemy machine-gun and rifle fire, he began to move inland through the rice paddies without cover. The men, inspired by his cool demeanor and heroic example, rose from their positions and followed him. During the advance, Captain Wai repeatedly determined the locations of enemy strongpoints by deliberately exposing himself to draw their fire. In leading an assault upon the last remaining Japanese pillbox in the area, he was killed by its occupants.

THE BATTLE OF LUZON

I just can't understand how such a damn fool could have gotten to be a general. — General Eisenhower, about General MacArthur in Ann Whitman's Diary, December 4, 1954

Eisenhower did admit that MacArthur was smart, decisive, and had a brilliant military mind. Additionally, when General Eisenhower spoke at London's Guild Hall in June 1945, he said, "Humility must always be the portion of any man who receives acclaim earned in the blood of his followers and the sacrifices of his friends."

Luzon in the Philippines (Courtesy WorldAtlas)

Because of the importance of the Philippines, prior to the Japanese attack, the United States had stationed 135,000 troops and 227 aircraft in the Philippines in late 1941. However, the Japanese captured Luzon, the largest island of the Philippines, in early 1942. The Japanese gained control of the Philippines in May 1942, and the defeat of the American forces led to General MacArthur's departure to Australia and to General Jonathan Wainwright's capture.

Almost immediately after arriving in Australia, MacArthur began promoting the need to recapture the Philippines. This was in direct conflict with Admiral Nimitz and Admiral King, whose argument was that the recapture of the Philippines had to wait until victory was certain. This resulted in MacArthur having to wait for two years to see himself wade ashore on both Leyte and Luzon. General MacArthur made sure that the cameras caught him wading ashore at Leyte on October 20, 1944, and again on January 9, 1945, at Luzon.

The invasion of Luzon needed a land-based air support to keep in step with the Navy's philosophy, so after Leyte, the island of Mindoro was invaded. Troops under General William C. Dunckel had captured Mindoro, and by December 16, 1944, two air bases on Mindoro were ready to assist the invasion of Luzon.

The United States went to great lengths to convince the Japanese that Luzon would be attacked from the south:

Dummies were parachuted into the southern area, mine sweepers cleared the bays in the south, and Filipino resistance fighters conducted sabotage operations in southern Luzon. Even with all this effort, however, Japanese General Yamashita was not fooled; he built significant defenses in the areas surrounding Lingayen Gulf in northern Luzon.

The assault on Luzon was launched on January 9, 1945, with heavy bombardment of Japanese shore positions starting at 7:00 AM, and the landings followed one hour later. The landing force faced heavy opposition from Japanese Kamikaze planes. The US escort carrier *Ommaney Bay* was destroyed by the attack, as were a destroyer and several other warships.

The Army landed about 175,000 troops along a twenty-mile beachhead within a few days. The plan was to drive south toward Clark Field and then on to Manila. Only after completing this phase was the Army to push north to control the roads leading into the northern part of Luzon.

The US forces did not meet much resistance until they reach Clark Air Base on January 23. The battle at Clark lasted until the end of January.

The United States had also launched a second amphibious landing on January 15, about forty-five miles southwest of Manila. Then on January 31, two regiments of the 11th Airborne Division made an airborne assault that allowed an approach from the south. On February 11, 1945, the 11th Airborne Division captured the last Japanese outer defenses, allowing the US and Filipino forces to encircle all of Manila.

Battles continued throughout the island of Luzon for several weeks. The Allies took control of the important locations of Luzon by March 1945, but pockets of Japanese soldiers held out in the mountains until the unconditional surrender of Japan on August 15, 1945. In one case, Soldier Hiroo Onada maintained warfare on an island in the Philippines until 1974. He ignored leaflets dropped saying the war was over, as he thought they were propaganda. He was found by a Japanese student who convinced him the war was over.

Although not the highest in US casualties, the Battle of Luzon had the highest *total* battle casualties during WWII. Nearly 205,000 Japanese combatants, 8,000 US combatants, and 120,000–140,000 Filipino civilians and combatants were killed.

Table 17 shows the troop casualties, including POWs, at Luzon.

Table 17. Luzon casualties

TROOPS	USA	JAPAN
Killed	8310	205,535
Wounded	29,560	-
Civilian Killed	93,400*	-
Captured	-	9050

*Non-Combat Philippine Losses

The following troops received the Medal of Honor for the Battle of Luzon. (Citations for each are noted in References.)

THOMAS E. ATKINS, Private First Class U.S. Army born February 5, 1921, in Campobello, SC. After his two companions were killed, Adkins remained in his precarious position to repel any subsequent assaults instead of returning to the American lines for medical treatment. An enemy machine gun set up within twenty yards of his foxhole vainly attempted to drive him off or silence his gun. The Japanese repeatedly made fierce attacks, but for four hours, Private First Class Atkins determinedly remained in his foxhole, bearing the brunt of each assault and maintaining steady and accurate fire until each charge was repulsed. At 7:00 AM, thirteen enemy dead lay in front of his position; he had fired 400 rounds, all he and his two dead companions possessed, and had used three rifles until each had jammed too badly for further operation. He withdrew during a lull to secure a rifle and more ammunition and was persuaded to remain for medical treatment. While waiting, he saw a Japanese within the perimeter and, seizing a nearby rifle, killed him. A few minutes later, while lying on a litter, he discovered an enemy group moving up behind the platoon's lines. Despite his severe wound, he sat up, delivered heavy rifle fire against the group, and forced them to withdraw. Private Atkins' superb bravery and his determination to hold his post against the main force of repeated enemy attacks, even though he was painfully wounded, were major factors in enabling his comrades to maintain their lines against a numerically superior enemy force.

ELMER CHARLES BIGELOW, Watertender First Class U.S. Navy Reserves born July 20, 1920, in Hebron, IL. Standing topside when an enemy shell struck the USS *Fletcher*, Bigelow, acting instantly as the deadly projectile exploded into fragments that penetrated the number-one gun magazine and set fire to several powder cases, picked up a pair of fire extinguishers and rushed below in a resolute attempt to quell the raging flames. Refusing to waste the precious time required to don a rescue-breathing apparatus, he plunged through the blinding smoke billowing out of the magazine hatch and dropped into the blazing compartment. Despite the acrid, burning powder smoke, which seared his lungs with every agonizing breath, he worked rapidly and with instinctive sureness and succeeded in quickly extinguishing the fires and cooling the cases and bulkheads, thereby preventing further damage to the stricken ship. Although he succumbed to his injuries on the following day, Bigelow, by his dauntless valor, unfaltering skill, and prompt action in the critical emergency, averted a magazine explosion that undoubtedly would have left his ship wallowing at the mercy of the furiously pounding Japanese guns on *Corregidor*, and his heroic spirit of self-sacrifice in the face of almost certain death enhanced and sustained the highest traditions of the US Naval Service. He gallantly gave his life in the service of his country.

JOSEPH J. CICCHETTI, Private First Class U.S. Army born June 8, 1923, in Waynesburg, OH. Private First Class Cicchetti was with troops assaulting the first important line of enemy defenses. The Japanese had converted the partially destroyed Manila Gas Works and adjacent buildings into a formidable system of mutually supporting strongpoints from which they were concentrating machine-gun, mortar, and heavy artillery fire on the American forces. Casualties rapidly mounted, and the medical aid men, finding it increasingly difficult to evacuate the wounded, called for volunteer litter bearers. Private Cicchetti immediately responded, organized a litter team, and skillfully led the team for more than four hours in rescuing fourteen wounded men, constantly passing back and forth over a 400-yard route that was the impact area for a tremendous volume of the most intense enemy fire. On one return trip, the path was blocked by machine-gun fire, but Private Cicchetti deliberately exposed himself to draw the automatic fire, which he neutralized with his own rifle while ordering the rest of the team to rush past to safety with the wounded. While gallantly continuing his work, he noticed a group of wounded and helpless soldiers some distance away and ran to their rescue although the enemy fire had increased to new fury. As he approached the casualties, he was struck in the head by a shell fragment, but with complete disregard for his gaping wound, he continued to his comrades, then lifted one and carried him on his shoulders fifty yards to safety. Private Cicchetti then collapsed and died. By his skilled leadership, indomitable will, and dauntless courage, Private Cicchetti saved the lives of many of his fellow soldiers at the cost of his own.

RAYMOND H. COOLEY, Staff Sergeant U.S. Army born May 7, 1914, in Dunlap, TN. Staff Sergeant Cooley was a platoon guide in an assault on a camouflaged entrenchment defended by machine guns, rifles, and mortars. When his men were pinned down by two enemy machine guns, he voluntarily advanced under heavy fire to within twenty yards of one of the guns and attacked it with a hand grenade. The enemy, however, threw the grenade back at him before it could explode. Arming a second grenade, Sergeant Cooley held it for several seconds of the safe period and then hurled it into the enemy position, where it exploded instantaneously, destroying the gun and crew. He then moved toward the remaining gun, throwing grenades into enemy foxholes as he advanced. Inspired by his actions, one squad of his platoon joined him. After he had armed another grenade and was preparing to throw it into the second machine-gun position, six enemy soldiers rushed at him. Knowing he could not dispose of the armed grenade without injuring his comrades because of the intermingling in close combat of the men of his platoon and the enemy in the melee which ensued, he deliberately covered the grenade with his body and was severely wounded as it exploded. By his heroic actions, Sergeant Cooley not only silenced a machine gun and so inspired his fellow soldiers that they pressed the attack and destroyed the remaining enemy emplacements, but also, in complete disregard of his own safety, accepted certain injury and possible loss of life to avoid wounding his comrades.

GEORGE FLEMING DAVIS, Commander U.S. Navy born March 23, 1911, in Manila, Philippines. Operating without gun support of other surface ships when four Japanese suicide planes were detected flying low overland to attack simultaneously, Commander Davis boldly took his position in the exposed wings of the bridge and directed control to pick up the leading plane and open fire. Alert and fearless as his ship the USS *Walke*'s deadly fire sent the first target crashing into the water and caught the second as it passed close over the bridge to plunge into the sea port side, he remained steadfast in the path of the third plane plunging swiftly to crash on the after end of the bridge structure. Seriously wounded when the craft struck, drenched with gasoline and immediately enveloped in flames, Davis conned the *Walke* in the midst of the wreckage; he rallied his command to heroic efforts; he exhorted his officers and men to save the ship and, still on his feet, saw the barrage from his guns destroy the fourth suicide bomber. With the fires under control and the safety of the ship assured, he consented to be carried below. Succumbing several hours later, Commander Davis by his example of valor and unhesitating self-sacrifice steeled the fighting spirit of his command into unyielding purpose in completing a vital mission. He gallantly gave his life in the service of his country.

JAMES H. DIAMOND, Private First Class U.S. Army born April 22, 1925, in New Orleans, LA. As a member of the machine-gun section, Diamond displayed extreme gallantry and intrepidity above and beyond the call of duty. When a Japanese sniper rose from his foxhole to throw a grenade into their midst, this valiant soldier charged and killed the enemy with a burst from his submachine gun; then, by delivering sustained fire from his personal arm and simultaneously directing the fire of 105 mm and 50-caliber weapons upon the enemy pillboxes immobilizing this and another machine-gun section, Diamond enabled them to put their guns into action. When two infantry companies established a bridgehead, he voluntarily assisted in evacuating the wounded under heavy fire and then, despite the fact that he was suffering from a painful wound, securing an abandoned vehicle, transported casualties to the rear through mortar and artillery fire so intense as to render the vehicle inoperative. The following day, he again volunteered, this time for the hazardous job of repairing a bridge under heavy enemy fire. On May 14, 1945, when leading a patrol to evacuate casualties from his battalion, which was cut off, he ran through a virtual hail of Japanese fire to secure an abandoned machine gun. Though mortally wounded as he reached the gun, he succeeded in drawing sufficient fire upon himself so that the remaining members of the patrol could reach safety. Private Diamond's indomitable spirit, constant disregard of danger, and eagerness to assist his comrades will ever remain a symbol of selflessness and heroic sacrifice to those for whom he gave his life.

DAVID M. GONZALES, Private First Class U.S. Army born June 9, 1923, in Pacoima, CA. Gonzales was pinned down with his company. As enemy fire swept the area, making any movement extremely hazardous, a 500-pound bomb smashed into the company's perimeter, burying five men with its explosion. Private First Class Gonzales, without hesitation, seized an entrenching tool and, under a hail of fire, crawled fifteen yards to his entombed comrades, where his commanding officer, who had also rushed forward, was beginning to dig the men out. Nearing his goal, Private Gonzales saw the officer struck and instantly killed by machine-gun fire. Undismayed, he set to work swiftly and surely with his hands and the entrenching tool while enemy sniper and machine-gun bullets struck all about him. He succeeded in digging one of the men out of the pile of rock and sand. To dig faster, he stood up, regardless of the greater danger from so exposing himself. He extricated a second man, and then another. As he completed the liberation of the third, he was hit and mortally wounded, but the comrades for whom he so gallantly gave his life were safely evacuated. Private Gonzales's valiant and intrepid conduct exemplifies the highest tradition of the military service.

WILLIAM J. GRABIARZ, Private First Class U.S. Army born March 25, 1925, in Buffalo, NY. Grabiarz was a scout when his unit advanced with tanks along a street in Manila, Luzon, Philippine Islands. Without warning, enemy machine-gun and rifle fire from concealed positions in the customs building swept the street, striking down the troop commander and driving his men to cover. As the officer lay in the open road, unable to move and completely exposed to the point-blank enemy fire, Private First Class Grabiarz voluntarily ran from behind a tank to carry the officer to safety but was himself wounded in the shoulder. Ignoring both the pain in his injured, useless arm and his comrades' shouts to seek the cover that was only a few yards distant, the valiant rescuer continued his efforts to drag his commander out of range. Finding this impossible, he rejected the opportunity to save himself and deliberately covered the officer with his own body to form a human shield, calling as he did so for a tank to maneuver into position between him and the hostile emplacement. The enemy riddled Private Grabiarz with concentrated fire before the tank could interpose itself. The American troops found that he had been successful in preventing bullets from striking his leader, who survived. Through his magnificent sacrifice in gallantly giving his life to save that of his commander, Private Grabiarz provided an outstanding and lasting inspiration to his fellow soldiers.

HARRY R. HARR, Corporal U.S. Army born February 22, 1921, in Pine Croft, PA. In a fierce counterattack, the Japanese closed in on Harr's machine-gun emplacement, hurling hand grenades, one of which exploded under the gun, putting it out of action and wounding two of the crew. While the remaining gunners were desperately attempting to repair their weapon, another grenade landed squarely in the emplacement. Quickly realizing he could not safely throw the unexploded missile from the crowded position, Captain Harr unhesitatingly covered it with his body to smother the blast. His supremely courageous act, which cost him his life, saved four of his comrades and enabled them to continue their mission.

DEXTER J. KERSTETTER, Private First Class U.S. Army born December 21, 1907, in Centralia, WA. Kerstetter was with his unit in a dawn attack against hill positions approachable only along a narrow ridge paralleled on each side by steep cliffs that were heavily defended by enemy mortars, machine guns, and rifles in well-camouflaged spider holes and tunnels leading to caves. When the leading element was halted by intense fire that inflicted five casualties, Private First Class Kerstetter passed through the American line with his squad. Placing himself well in advance of his men, he grimly worked his way up the narrow steep hogback, meeting the brunt of enemy action. With well-aimed shots and rifle-grenade fire, Private Kerstetter forced the Japanese to take cover. He left the trail and, moving down a cliff that offered only precarious footholds, dropped among four Japanese at the entrance to a cave, fired his rifle from his hip, and killed them all. Climbing back to the trail, he advanced against heavy enemy machine-gun, rifle, and mortar fire to silence a heavy machine gun by killing its crew of four with rifle fire and grenades. He expended his remaining ammunition and grenades on a group of approximately twenty Japanese, scattering them, and returned to his squad for more ammunition and first aid for his left hand, which had been blistered by the heat from his rifle. Resupplied, he guided a fresh platoon into a position from which a concerted attack could be launched, killing three hostile soldiers on the way. In all, he dispatched sixteen Japanese that day. The hill was taken and held against the enemy's counterattacks, which continued for three days. Private Kerstetter's dauntless and gallant heroism was largely responsible for the capture of this key enemy position, and his fearless attack in the face of great odds was an inspiration to his comrades in their dangerous task.

ANTHONY L. KROTIAK, Private First Class U.S. Army born August 15, 1915, in Chicago, IL. Private First Class Krotiak was an acting squad leader directing his men in consolidating a newly won position on Hill B when the enemy concentrated small-arms fire and grenades upon him and four others, driving them to cover in an abandoned Japanese trench. A grenade thrown from above landed in the center of the group. Instantly pushing his comrades aside and jamming the grenade into the earth with his rifle butt, Private Krotiak threw himself over it, making a shield of his body to protect the other men. The grenade exploded under him, and he died a few minutes later. By his extraordinary heroism in deliberately giving his life to save those of his comrades, Private Krotiak set an inspiring example of utter devotion and self-sacrifice that reflected the highest traditions of the military service.

ROBERT E, LAWS, Staff Sergeant U.S. Army born January 18, 1921, in Altoona, PA. Laws led the assault squad when his Company G attacked enemy hill positions. The enemy force, estimated to be a reinforced infantry company, was well supplied with machine guns, ammunition, grenades, and blocks of TNT and could be attacked only across a narrow ridge seventy yards long. At the end of this ridge, an enemy pillbox and rifle positions were set in rising ground. Covered by his squad, Staff Sergeant Laws traversed the hogback through vicious enemy fire until close to the pillbox, where he hurled grenades at the fortification. Enemy grenades wounded him, but he persisted in his assault until one of his missiles found its mark and knocked out the pillbox. With more grenades, passed to him by members of his squad who had joined him, Laws led the attack on the entrenched riflemen. In the advance up the hill, he suffered additional wounds in both arms and legs, about the body, and in the head as grenades and TNT charges exploded near him. Three Japanese rushed him with fixed bayonets, and he emptied the magazine of his machine pistol at them, killing two. He closed in hand-to-hand combat with the third, seizing the Japanese's rifle as he met the onslaught. The two fell to the ground and rolled some fifty or sixty feet down a bank. When the dust cleared, the Japanese lay dead and the valiant American was climbing up the hill with a large gash across the head. He was given first aid and was evacuated from the area while his squad completed the destruction of the enemy position. Sergeant Laws's heroic actions provided great inspiration to his comrades, and his courageous determination in the face of formidable odds and while suffering from multiple wounds enabled them to secure an important objective with minimum casualties.

MELVIN MAYFIELD, Corporal U.S. Army born March 24, 1919, in Salem, WV. Mayfield displayed conspicuous gallantry and intrepidity above and beyond the call of duty while fighting in the Cordillera Central Mountains of Luzon, Philippine Islands. When two Filipino companies were pinned down under a torrent of enemy fire that converged on them from a circular ridge commanding their position, Corporal Mayfield, in a gallant single-handed effort to aid them, rushed from shell hole to shell hole until he reached four enemy caves atop the barren, fire-swept hill. With grenades and his carbine, he assaulted each of the caves while enemy fire pounded about him. Before Corporal Mayfield annihilated the last hostile redoubt, however, a machine-gun bullet destroyed his weapon and slashed his left hand. Disregarding his wound, he secured more grenades and dauntlessly charged again into the face of point-blank fire to help destroy a hostile observation post. By his gallant determination and heroic leadership, Corporal Mayfield inspired the men to eliminate all remaining pockets of resistance in the area and to press the advance against the enemy.

LLOYD G. MCCARTER, Private U.S. Army born April 11, 1917, in St. Maries, ID. Private McCarter was a scout with the regiment that seized the fortress of Corregidor,

Philippine Islands. Shortly after the initial parachute assault on February 16, 1945, he crossed thirty yards of open ground under intense enemy fire and, at point-blank range, silenced a machine gun with hand grenades. On the afternoon of February 18, he killed six snipers. That evening, when a large force attempted to bypass his company, he voluntarily moved to an exposed area and opened fire. The enemy attacked his position repeatedly throughout the night and was each time repulsed. By 2:00 AM, all the men about him had been wounded, but, shouting encouragement to his comrades and defiance at the enemy, Private McCarter continued to bear the brunt of the attack, fearlessly exposing himself to locate enemy soldiers and then pouring heavy fire on them. He repeatedly crawled back to the American line to secure more ammunition. When his submachine gun would no longer operate, he seized an automatic rifle and continued to inflict heavy casualties. This weapon, in turn, became too hot to use and, discarding it, he continued with an M1 rifle. At dawn, the enemy attacked with renewed intensity. Completely exposing himself to hostile fire, Private McCarter stood erect to locate the most dangerous enemy positions. He was seriously wounded, but though he had already killed more than thirty of the enemy, he refused to evacuate until he had pointed out immediate objectives for attack. Through his sustained and outstanding heroism in the face of grave and obvious danger, Private McCarter made outstanding contributions to the success of his company and to the recapture of Corregidor.

CHARLES L. MCGAHA, Master Sergeant U.S. Army born February 26, 1914, in Crosby, TN. McGaha displayed conspicuous gallantry and intrepidity. His platoon and one other were pinned down in a roadside ditch by heavy fire from five Japanese tanks supported by ten machine guns and a platoon of riflemen. When one of his men fell wounded forty yards away, McGaha unhesitatingly crossed the road under a hail of bullets and moved the man seventy-five yards to safety. Although he had suffered a deep arm wound, McGaha returned to his post. Finding the platoon leader seriously wounded, he assumed command and rallied the men. Once more, he braved enemy fire, to go to the aid of a litter party removing another wounded soldier. A shell exploded in their midst, wounding McGaha in the shoulder and killing two of the party. McGaha picked up the remaining man, carried him to cover, and then moved out in front deliberately to draw the enemy fire while the American forces, thus protected, withdrew to safety. When the last man had gained the new position, McGaha rejoined his command and there collapsed from loss of blood and exhaustion. Master Sergeant McGaha set an example of courage and leadership in keeping with the highest traditions of the service.

THOMAS B. MCGUIRE, JR., Major U.S. Army Air Corps born August 2, 1920, in Ridgewood, NJ. Major McGuire fought with conspicuous gallantry and intrepidity over Luzon, Philippine Islands. Voluntarily, he led a squadron of fifteen P-38s as top cover for heavy bombers striking Mabalacat Airdrome, where his formation was attacked by twenty aggressive Japanese fighters. In the ensuing action he repeatedly flew to the aid of embattled comrades, driving off enemy assaults while himself under attack and at times outnumbered three to one, and, even after his guns jammed, continued the fight by forcing a hostile plane into his wingman's line of fire. Before he started back to his base, he had shot down three Zeros. The next day, he again volunteered to lead escort fighters on a mission to strongly defend Clark Field. During the resultant engagement, he again exposed himself to attacks so he might rescue a crippled bomber. In rapid succession, he shot down one aircraft; parried the attack of four enemy fighters, one of which he shot down; single-handedly engaged three more Japanese, destroying one; and then shot down still another, his thirty-eighth victory in aerial combat.

On January 7, 1945, while leading a voluntary fighter sweep over Los Negros Island, he risked an extremely hazardous maneuver at low altitude in an attempt to save a fellow flyer from attack. In the attempt, he crashed and was reported missing in action. With gallant initiative, deep and unselfish concern for the safety of others, and heroic determination to destroy the enemy at all costs, Major McGuire set an inspiring example in keeping with the highest traditions of the military service.

JOHN R. MCKINNEY, Sergeant U.S. Army born on February 26, 1921, in Woodcliff, GA. Private McKinney fought with extreme gallantry to defend the outpost that had been established near Dingalan Bay. Just before daybreak, approximately one hundred Japanese stealthily attacked the perimeter defense, concentrating on a light-machine-gun position manned by three Americans. Having completed a long tour of duty at this gun, Private McKinney was resting a few paces away when an enemy soldier dealt him a glancing blow on the head with a saber. Although dazed by the stroke, McKinney seized his rifle, bludgeoned his attacker, and then shot another assailant who was charging him. Meanwhile, one of his comrades at the machine gun had been wounded and his other companion withdrew, carrying the injured man to safety. Alone, Private McKinney was confronted by ten infantrymen who had captured the machine gun with the evident intent of reversing it to fire into the perimeter. Leaping into the emplacement, he shot seven of them at point-blank range and killed three more with his rifle butt. In the melee, the machine gun was rendered inoperative, leaving McKinney only his rifle with which to meet the advancing Japanese, who hurled grenades and directed knee-mortar shells into the perimeter. He warily changed position, secured more ammunition, and, reloading repeatedly, cut down waves of the fanatical enemy with devastating fire or clubbed them to death in hand-to-hand combat. When assistance arrived, he had thwarted the assault and was in complete control of the area. Thirty-eight dead Japanese around the machine gun and two more at the side of a mortar forty-five yards distant was the amazing toll he had exacted single-handedly. By his indomitable spirit, extraordinary fighting ability, and unwavering courage in the face of tremendous odds, Private McKinney saved his company from possible annihilation and set an example of unsurpassed intrepidity.

LAVERNE PARRISH, Technician 4th Grade born July 16, 1918, in Knox City, MO. Parrish was medical aid man during the fighting in Binalonan, Luzon, Philippine Islands. On January 18, 1945 he observed two wounded men under enemy fire and immediately went to their rescue. After moving one to cover, he crossed twenty-five yards of open ground to administer aid to the second.

In the early hours of January 24, 1945, his company, crossing an open field near San Manuel, encountered intense enemy fire and was ordered to withdraw to the cover of a ditch. While treating the casualties, Technician Parrish observed two wounded still in the field. Without hesitation, he left the ditch, crawled forward under enemy fire, and in two successive trips brought both men to safety. He next administered aid to twelve casualties in the same field, crossing and recrossing the open area raked by hostile fire. Making successive trips, he then brought three wounded in to cover. After treating nearly all of the thirty-seven casualties suffered by his company, he was mortally wounded by mortar fire and shortly after was killed. The indomitable spirit, intrepidity, and gallantry of Technician Parrish saved many lives at the cost of his own.

MANUEL PEREZ JR., Private First Class U.S. Army born March 3, 1923, in Oklahoma City, OK. Perez was lead scout for his company, which had destroyed eleven of twelve pillboxes in a strongly fortified sector defending the approach to enemy-held Fort William McKinley on Luzon, Philippine Islands. In the reduction of these pillboxes, Perez killed five Japanese in the open and blasted others in pillboxes with grenades. Realizing the urgent need for taking the last emplacement, which contained two twin-mount 50-caliber dual-purpose machine guns, he took a circuitous route to within twenty yards of the position, killing four of the enemy in his advance. He threw a grenade into the pillbox and, as the crew started withdrawing through a tunnel just to the rear of the emplacement, shot and killed four before exhausting his clip. Perez had reloaded and killed four more when an escaping Japanese threw his rifle with fixed bayonet at him. As Perez warded off this thrust, his own rifle was knocked to the ground. Seizing the Japanese rifle, Perez continued firing, killing two more of the enemy.

He rushed the remaining Japanese, killed three of them with the butt of the rifle, and entered the pillbox, where he bayoneted the one surviving hostile soldier. Single-handedly, he had killed eighteen of the enemy in neutralizing the position that had held up the advance of his entire company. Through his courageous determination and heroic disregard of grave danger, Private First Class Perez made possible the successful advance of his unit toward a valuable objective and provided a lasting inspiration for his comrades.

JOHN N. REESE JR., Private First Class U.S. Army born June 13, 1923, in Muskogee, OK. Reese was engaged in the attack on the Paco railroad station, which was strongly defended by 300 determined enemy soldiers with machine guns and rifles, supported by several pillboxes, three 20 mm guns, one 37 mm gun, and heavy mortars. While making a frontal assault across an open field, Reese's platoon was halted one hundred yards from the station by intense enemy fire. On his own initiative, he left the platoon accompanied by a comrade and continued forward to a house sixty yards from the objective. Although under constant enemy observation, the two men remained in this position for an hour, firing at targets of opportunity, killing more than thirty-five Japanese and wounding many more. Moving closer to the station and discovering a group of Japanese replacements attempting to reach pillboxes, Reese and his comrade opened heavy fire, killed more than forty enemy soldiers, and stopped all subsequent attempts to man the emplacements. Enemy fire became more intense as Reese and his companion advanced to within twenty yards of the station. From that point, Private First Class Reese provided effective covering fire and courageously drew enemy fire to himself while his companion killed seven Japanese and destroyed a 20 mm gun and a heavy machine gun with hand grenades.

With their ammunition running low, the two men started to return to the American lines, alternately providing covering fire for each other as they withdrew. During this movement, Private Reese was killed by enemy fire as he reloaded his rifle. The intrepid team, in two and a half hours of fierce fighting, killed more than eighty-two Japanese.

CLETO RODRIGUEZ, Technical Sergeant U.S. Army born April 26, 1923, in San Marcos, TX. Rodriguez was an automatic rifleman when his unit attacked the strongly defended Paco railroad station during the battle for Manila, Philippine Islands. While making a frontal assault across an open field, his platoon was halted one hundred yards from the station by intense enemy fire. On his own initiative, he left the platoon, accompanied by a comrade, and continued forward to a house sixty yards from the objective. Although under constant enemy observation, the two men remained in this position for an hour, firing at targets of opportunity, killing more than thirty-five hostile soldiers and wounding many more. Moving closer to the station and discovering a group of Japanese replacements attempting to reach pillboxes, they opened heavy fire, killed more than forty, and stopped all subsequent attempts to man the emplacements. Enemy fire became more intense as Rodriguez and his companion advanced to within twenty yards of the station. Then, covered by his companion, Private Rodriguez boldly moved up to the building and threw five grenades through a doorway, killing seven Japanese, destroying a 20 mm gun and wrecking a heavy machine gun.

With their ammunition running low, Rodriguez and his companion started to return to the American lines, alternately providing covering fire for each other's withdrawal. During this movement, Private Rodriguez's companion was killed. In two and a half hours of fierce fighting, the intrepid team killed more than eighty-two Japanese, completely disorganized their defense, and paved the way for the subsequent overwhelming defeat of the enemy at this strongpoint.

Two days later, Private Rodriguez again enabled his comrades to advance when he single-handedly killed six Japanese and destroyed a well-placed 20 mm gun by his outstanding skill with his weapons.

DONALD E. RUDOLPH, Second Lieutenant U.S. Army born February 21, 1921, in South Haven, MN. Second

Lieutenant (at the time Technical Sergeant) Rudolph was acting as platoon leader at Munoz, Luzon, Philippine Islands. While administering first aid on the battlefield, he observed enemy fire issuing from a nearby culvert. Crawling to the culvert with rifle and grenades, he killed three of the enemy concealed there. He then worked his way across open terrain toward a line of enemy pillboxes that had immobilized his company. Nearing the first pillbox, he hurled a grenade through its embrasure and charged the position. With his bare hands he tore away the wood and tin covering, then dropped a grenade through the opening, killing the enemy gunners and destroying their machine gun. Ordering several riflemen to cover his further advance, Rudolph seized a pick mattock and made his way to the second pillbox. Piercing its top with the mattock, he dropped a grenade through the hole, fired several rounds from his rifle into it, and smothered any surviving enemy by sealing the hole and the embrasure with earth. In quick succession, he attacked and neutralized six more pillboxes. Later, when his platoon was attacked by an enemy tank, he advanced under covering fire, climbed to the top of the tank, and dropped a white phosphorus grenade through the turret, destroying the crew. Through his outstanding heroism, superb courage and leadership, and complete disregard for his own safety, Rudolph cleared a path for an advance that culminated in one of the most decisive victories of the Philippines Campaign.

WILLIAM R. SHOCKLEY, Private First Class U.S. Army born December 4, 1918, in Bokoshe, OK. Shockley was in position with his unit on a hill when the enemy, after a concentration of artillery fire, launched a counterattack. He maintained his position under intense enemy fire and urged his comrades to withdraw, saying that he would "remain to the end" to provide cover. Although he had to clear two stoppages that impeded the reloading of his weapon, he halted one enemy charge. Hostile troops then began moving in on his left flank, and he quickly shifted his gun to fire on them. Knowing that the only route of escape was being cut off by the enemy, he ordered the remainder of his squad to withdraw to safety and deliberately remained at his post. He continued to fire until he was killed during the ensuing enemy charge. Later, four Japanese were found dead in front of his position. Private First Class Shockley, facing certain death, sacrificed himself to save his fellow soldiers, but the heroism and gallantry he displayed enabled his squad to reorganize and continue its attack.

WILLIAM A. SHOMO, Major U.S. Army Air Corps born May 30, 1918, in Jeannette, PA. Major Shomo was lead pilot of a flight of two fighter planes charged with an armed photographic and strafing mission against the Aparri and Laoag airdromes. While en route to the objective, he observed an enemy twin-engine bomber, protected by twelve fighters, flying about 2,500 feet above him and in the opposite direction. Although the odds were thirteen to two, Major Shomo immediately ordered an attack. Accompanied by his wingman, he closed on the enemy formation in a climbing turn and scored hits on the leading plane of the third element, which exploded in midair. Major Shomo then attacked the second element from the left side of the formation and shot another fighter down in flames. When the enemy formed for counterattack, Major Shomo moved to the other side of the formation and hit a third fighter, which exploded and fell. Diving below the bomber, he put a burst into its underside and the bomber crashed and burned.

Pulling up from this pass, he encountered a fifth plane, firing head on and destroying it. He next dived upon the first element and shot down the lead plane. Then, diving to 300 feet in pursuit of another fighter, Major Shomo caught it with his initial burst and it crashed in flames. During this action, Major Shomo's wingman shot down three planes, and the three remaining enemy fighters fled into a cloudbank and escaped.

JOHN C. SJOGREN, Staff Sergeant U.S. Army born August 16, 1916, in Rockford, MI. Sjogren led an attack against a high precipitous ridge defended by a company of enemy riflemen who were entrenched in spider holes and supported by well-sealed pillboxes housing automatic weapons with interlocking bands of fire. The terrain was such that only one squad could advance at one time, and from a knoll atop a ridge, a pillbox covered the only approach with automatic fire. Against this enemy stronghold, Staff Sergeant Sjogren led the first squad to open the assault. Deploying his men, he moved forward and was hurling grenades when he saw that his next in command, at the opposite flank, was gravely wounded. Without hesitation, Sjogren crossed twenty yards of exposed terrain in the face of enemy fire and exploding dynamite charges, moved the man to cover, and administered first aid. He then worked his way forward and, advancing directly into the enemy fire, killed eight Japanese in spider holes guarding the approach to the pillbox. Crawling to within a few feet of the pillbox while his men concentrated their bullets on the fire port, Sjogren began dropping grenades through the narrow firing slit. The enemy immediately threw two or three of these unexploded grenades out, and fragments from one wounded Sergeant Sjogren in the hand and back. By hurling grenades through the embrasure faster than the enemy could return them, however, Sjogren succeeded in destroying the occupants.

Despite his wounds, Staff Sergeant Sjogren directed his squad to follow him in a systematic attack on the remaining positions, which he eliminated in like manner, taking tremendous risks, overcoming bitter resistance, and never hesitating in his relentless advance. To silence one of the pillboxes, he wrenched a light machine gun out through the embrasure as it was firing before blowing up the occupants with hand grenades. During this action, Staff Sergeant Sjogren, by his heroic bravery, aggressiveness, and skill as a soldier, single-handedly killed forty-three enemy soldiers and destroyed nine pillboxes, thereby paving the way for his company's successful advance.

WILLIAM H. THOMAS, Private First Class U.S Army born January 13, 1923, in Wynne, AR. Thomas was a member of the leading squad of his company, which was attacking along a narrow wooded ridge. The enemy, strongly entrenched in camouflaged emplacements on the hill beyond, directed heavy fire and hurled explosive charges on the attacking riflemen. Private First Class Thomas, an automatic rifleman, was struck by one of these charges, which blew off both his legs below the knees. He refused medical aid and evacuation and continued to fire at the enemy until his weapon was put out of action by an enemy bullet. Still refusing aid, he threw his last two grenades. He destroyed three of the enemy after suffering the wounds from which he would die later that day. The effective fire of Private Thomas prevented the repulse of his platoon and ensured the capture of the hostile position.

YSMAEL R. VILLEGAS, Staff Sergeant U.S. Army born March 21, 1924, in Casa Blanca, CA. Villegas was a squad leader when his unit, in a forward position, clashed with an enemy strongly entrenched in connected caves and foxholes on commanding ground. He moved boldly from man to man in the face of bursting grenades and demolition charges, through heavy machine-gun and rifle fire, to bolster the spirit of his comrades. Inspired by his gallantry, Villegas's men pressed forward to the crest of the hill. Numerous enemy riflemen, refusing to flee, continued firing from their foxholes. Staff Sergeant Villegas, with complete disregard for his own safety and of the bullets that kicked up the dirt at his feet, charged an enemy position and, firing at point-blank range, killed the Japanese in a foxhole. He rushed a second foxhole, bullets missing him by inches, and killed one more of the enemy. In rapid succession, Sergeant Villegas charged a third, fourth, and fifth foxhole, each time destroying the enemy within. The fire against him increased in intensity, but he pressed onward to attack a sixth position. As he neared his goal, he was hit and killed by enemy fire.

ROBERT M. VIALE, Second Lieutenant U.S. Army born April 21, 1916, in Bayside, CA. Forced by the enemy's detonation of prepared demolitions to shift the course of his advance through the city, Viale led his platoon toward a small bridge, where heavy fire from three enemy pillboxes halted the unit. With two men, Viale crossed the bridge behind screening grenade smoke to attack the pillboxes. The first, he knocked out himself while covered by his men's protecting fire; the other two pillboxes were silenced by one of his companions and a bazooka team that he had called up. Viale suffered a painful wound in the right arm during the action. After his entire platoon had joined him, he pushed ahead through mortar fire and encircling flames.

Blocked from the only escape route by an enemy machine gun placed at a street comer, he entered a nearby building with his men to explore possible means of reducing the emplacement. In one room, he found civilians huddled together, in another, a small window placed high in the wall and reached by a ladder. Because of the relative positions of the window, ladder, and enemy emplacement, he decided that he, being left-handed, could better hurl a grenade than one of his men, who had made an unsuccessful attempt. Grasping an armed grenade, Viale started up the ladder. His wounded right arm weakened, and as he tried to steady himself, the grenade fell to the floor. In the five seconds before the grenade would explode, he dropped down, recovered the grenade, and looked for a place to dispose of it safely. Finding no way to get rid of the grenade without exposing his own men or the civilians to injury or death, Viale turned to the wall, held the grenade close to his body, and bent over the grenade as it exploded. Second Lieutenant Viale died in a few minutes, but his heroic act saved the lives of others.

HOWARD E. WOODFORD, Staff Sergeant U.S. Army born June 21, 1921, in Barberton, OH. Woodford volunteered to investigate the delay in a scheduled attack by an attached guerrilla battalion. Reaching the line of departure, he found that the lead company, in combat for the first time, was immobilized by intense enemy mortar, machine-gun, and rifle fire, which had caused casualties to key personnel. Knowing that further failure to advance would endanger the flanks of adjacent units, as well as delay capture of the objective, Woodford immediately took command of the company, evacuated the wounded, reorganized the unit under fire, and prepared to attack. He repeatedly exposed himself to draw revealing fire from the Japanese strongpoints and then moved forward with a five-man covering force to determine exact enemy positions. Although intense enemy machine-gun fire killed two and wounded his other three men, Staff Sergeant Woodford resolutely continued his patrol before returning to the company. Then, against bitter resistance, he guided the guerrillas up a barren hill and captured the objective, personally accounting for two hostile machine gunners and courageously reconnoitering strong defensive positions before directing neutralizing fire. After organizing a perimeter defense for the night, he was given permission by radio to return to his battalion, but, feeling that he was needed to maintain proper control, he chose to remain with the guerrillas.

Before dawn the next morning, the enemy launched a fierce suicide attack with mortars, grenades, and small-arms fire and infiltrated the perimeter. Though wounded by a grenade, Sergeant Woodford remained at his post, calling for mortar support until bullets knocked out his radio. Then, seizing a rifle, he began working his way around the perimeter, encouraging the men until he reached a weak spot where two guerrillas had been killed. Filling this gap himself, he fought off the enemy. At daybreak, he was found dead in his foxhole, but thirty-seven enemy dead were lying in and around his position.

THE BATTLE OF PELELIU

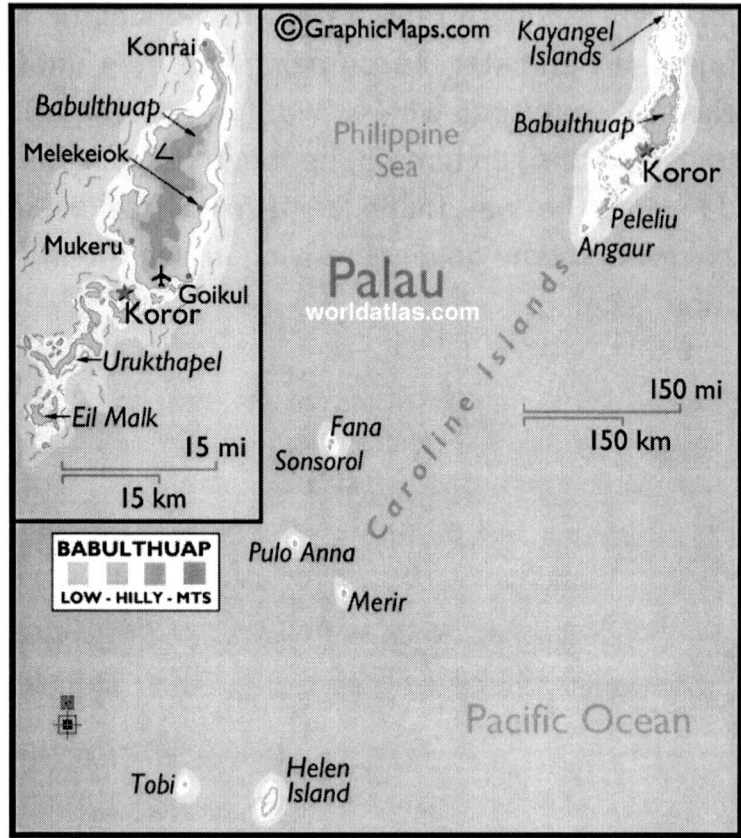

The Battle for Peleliu -upper right (Courtesy WorldAtlas)

The Battle of Peleliu was fought in the months of September and November 1944. The war in the Pacific brought two different opinions for winning. The strategy proposed by General MacArthur was to work our way through the Philippines, then take Okinawa, then attack the Japanese mainland. Admiral Nimitz favored a more direct route, bypassing the Philippines and seizing Okinawa and Taiwan as staging areas for the assault on

Japan. President Roosevelt traveled to Pearl Harbor to meet with both men to settle the strategy. MacArthur's plan was adopted.

After their repeated losses throughout the Pacific, the Japanese adopted a new strategy whereby they would allow US troops to reach the beach with little resistance, but then, through carefully placed bunkers and artillery with tunnels connecting these positions, they would inflict heavy losses to American troops. This, the Japanese thought, would force the United States into a war of attrition requiring more and more resources.

The Japanese defenses were based on Peleliu's highest point, Umurbrogol Mountain, a collection of hills and steep ridges located at the center of the island. This mountain contained more than 500 caves, all connected by tunnels. Many of the tunnels were mine shafts that the Japanese had turned into defense positions.

The battle with the Japanese troops around Umurbrogol Mountain is considered to be the most difficult military battle the United States encountered during WWII. After this battle, the 1st Marine Division was so depleted by casualties that it did not see action again until the Battle for Okinawa which started in early April, 1944. In hindsight, the Battle of Peleliu became controversial because of the island's strategic value, as the airfield became unnecessary and the island was never used as a staging area for future battles. No one had thought the battle would be as tough as it was. In fact, a marine officer had predicted that the battle would be over in three days, with little resistance from the Japanese.

Table 18 shows the troop casualties that occurred during the Battle for Peleliu.

Table 18. Peleliu casualties

TROOPS	USA	JAPAN
Killed	1,794	10,695-10,999
Wounded	8,010	-
Captured	-	202

The Battle for Peleliu resulted in eight people receiving the Medal of Honor. (Citations for each are noted in References.)

LEWIS K. BAUSELL, Corporal U.S. Marine Corps born April 17, 1924, in Pulaski, VI. Valiantly placing himself at the head of his squad, Corporal Bausell led the charge forward against a hostile pillbox that was covering a vital sector of the beach and, as the first to reach the emplacement, immediately started firing his automatic weapon into the aperture while the remainder of his men closed in on the enemy. Swift to act as a Japanese grenade was hurled into his men, Corporal Bausell unhesitatingly threw himself on the grenade, heroically sacrificing his own life so that the others might live and fulfill their mission.

ARTHUR J. JACKSON, Private First Class U.S. Marine Corps born October 18, 1924, in Cleveland, OH. Private First Class Jackson unhesitatingly proceeded forward of American lines and, courageously defying heavy barrages, charged a large pillbox housing approximately thirty-five enemy soldiers. Pouring his automatic fire into the opening of the fixed installation to trap the occupying troops, Private Jackson hurled white phosphorus grenades and explosive charges brought up by a fellow Marine, demolishing the pillbox and killing all the enemy. Determined to crush the entire pocket of resistance, he stormed one-gun position after another and succeeded in wiping out a total of twelve pillboxes and fifty enemy soldiers and, by his cool decision and relentless fighting spirit during a critical situation, contributed essentially to the complete annihilation of the enemy.

RICHARD E. KRAUS, Private First Class U.S. Marine Corps Reserve born November 24, 1925, in Chicago, IL. Unhesitatingly volunteering for the extremely hazardous mission of evacuating a wounded comrade from the front lines, Private First Class Kraus and three companions courageously made their way forward and successfully penetrated the lines for some distance before the enemy opened with an intense, devastating barrage of hand grenades that forced the stretcher party to take cover and subsequently abandon the mission. While returning to the rear, they observed two men approaching who appeared to be Marines, and they immediately demanded the password. When, instead of answering, one of the two men threw a hand grenade into the midst of the group, Private Kraus heroically flung himself upon the grenade and, covering it with his body, absorbed the full impact of the explosion and was instantly killed. By his prompt action and great personal valor in the face of almost certain death, he saved the lives of his three companions.

JOHN D. NEW, Private First Class U.S. Marine Corps Reserve born August 12, 1925, in Mobile, AL. New was a member of the 2nd Battalion, 7th Marines, 1st Marine Division, in action against enemy Japanese forces on Peleliu Island, Palau Group, September 25, 1944. When a Japanese soldier emerged from a cave in a cliff directly below an observation post and suddenly hurled a grenade into the position from which two Americans were directing mortar fire against enemy emplacements, Private First Class New instantly perceived the dire peril to the other Marines and, with utter disregard for his own safety, unhesitatingly flung himself upon the grenade and absorbed the full impact of the explosion, thus saving the lives of the two observers.

WESLEY PHELPS, Private U.S. Marine Corps Reserve born June 12, 1923, in Neafus, KY. Stationed with another Marine in an advanced position when a Japanese hand grenade landed in his foxhole, Private First Class Phelps instantly shouted a warning to his comrade and rolled over on the deadly bomb, absorbing with his own body the full, shattering impact of the exploding charge. Courageous and indomitable, Private Phelps fearlessly gave his life that another might be spared serious injury.

EVERETT P. POPE, Captain U.S. Marine Corps born July 16, 1919, in Milton, MA. Subjected to point-blank cannon fire that caused heavy casualties and badly disorganized his company while assaulting a steep coral hill, Captain Pope rallied his men and gallantly led them to the summit in the face of machine-gun, mortar, and sniper fire. Forced by widespread hostile attack to deploy the remnants of his company thinly in order to hold the ground won, with his machine guns out of order and with insufficient water and ammunition, he remained on the exposed hill with twelve men and one wounded officer, determined to hold through the night. Attacked continuously with grenades, machine guns, and rifles from three sides, he and his valiant men fiercely beat back or destroyed the enemy, resorting to hand-to-hand combat as the supply of ammunition dwindled, and still maintained their lines with his eight remaining riflemen. When daylight brought more deadly fire, he was ordered to withdraw.

CHARLES H. ROAN, Private First Class U.S. Marine Corps Reserve born August 16, 1923, in Claude, TX. Shortly after his leader ordered a withdrawal upon discovering that the squad was partly cut off from their company as a result of the rapid advance along an exposed ridge during an aggressive attack on the strongly entrenched enemy, Private First Class Roan and his companions were suddenly engaged in a furious exchange of hand grenades by Japanese forces emplaced in a cave on higher ground to the rear of the squad. Seeking protection with four other Marines in a depression in the rocky, broken terrain, Private Roan was wounded by an enemy grenade that fell close to their position and, immediately realizing the eminent peril to his comrades when another grenade landed in the midst of the group, unhesitatingly flung himself upon it, covering it with his body and absorbing the full impact of the explosion. By his prompt action and selfless conduct in the face of almost certain death, he saved the lives of four men.

CARLTON R. ROUH, First Lieutenant U.S. Marine Corps Reserve born May 11, 1919, in Lindenwood, NJ. Before permitting his men to use an enemy dugout as a position for an 81 mm mortar observation post, First Lieutenant Rouh made a personal reconnaissance of the pillbox and, upon entering, was severely wounded by Japanese rifle fire from within. Emerging from the dugout, he was immediately assisted by two Marines to a less exposed area but while receiving first aid was further endangered by an enemy grenade thrown into their midst. Quick to act in spite of his weakened condition, Lieutenant Rouh lurched to a crouching position and thrust both men aside, placing his own body between them and the grenade and taking the full blast of the explosion himself.

THE BATTLE OF IWO JIMA

Among the men who fought on Iwo Jima, uncommon valor was a common virtue. — Admiral Chester Nimitz

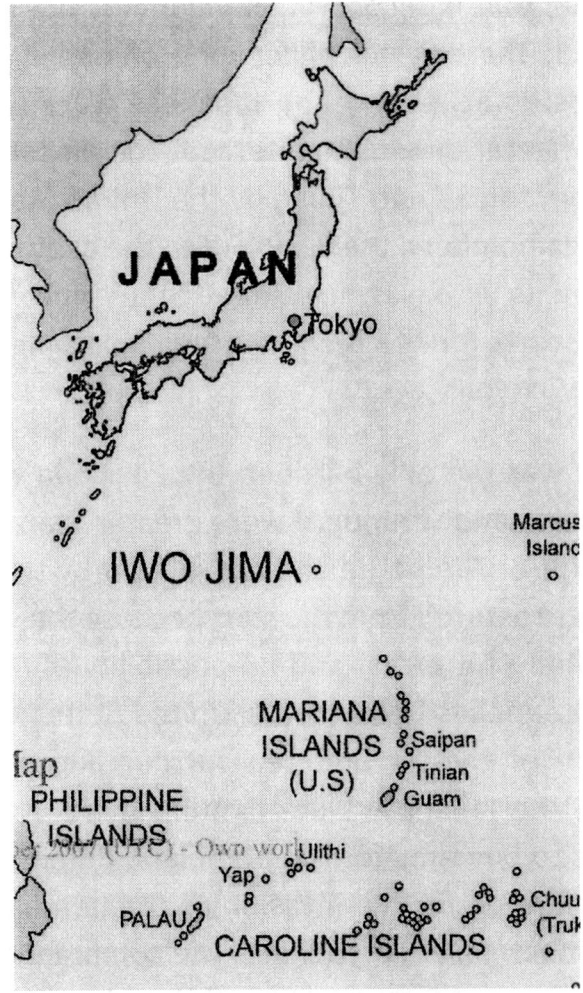

The Battle of Iwo Jima (Courtesy Wikipedia the free Encyclopedia- Public Domain)

The Battle for Iwo Jima was fought in February and March of 1945. Iwo Jima was another step closer to the

Japanese mainland and had three airfields that would be of great value for land-based aircraft for the invasion of Okinawa. Critics question the need for the airfields, especially after the heavy losses to US troops at Peleliu, but to me, that is second-guessing and is not in agreement with the original philosophy of moving up the ladder a step at a time. The Japanese were using this base for fighter aircraft to intercept the air raids being flown from Saipan and Tinian by the United States' new long-range bombers, the B-29s. With the capture of this Island and its air bases, the United States could provide fighter escorts for the B-29s on their bombing raids to and from Tokyo.

Iwo Jima was the only battle in the Pacific in which US losses (killed and wounded) were greater than those of the Japanese. The battle and the victory by the United States were assured from the start because the Japanese had nowhere to retreat and no possibility of reinforcements or supplies because the United States was now in control of the air and sea surrounding Iwo Jima. Basically, the Japanese were fighting there as a delaying tactic to buy time for the homeland defenses to get well established for the invasion of the homeland that was obviously fast approaching. The commander of the Japanese forces on Iwo Jima used the same philosophy as was used on Peleliu: Do not try to stop the landing at the beach, but build a strong defense with heavy weapons of machine guns and artillery at strategic locations.

As a result, hundreds of bunkers, pillboxes, and tunnels connecting the network were placed all over the island. These included hidden artillery and mortars positioned along with land mines.

The Japanese allowed the first wave of Marines to reach a certain point and then opened fire from the concealed bunkers and firing positions. The first wave took devastating losses from the machine guns. The Japanese also attacked with heavy artillery from their position on Mount Suribachi.

The Marines soon realized that firearms were relatively ineffective against the Japanese defenders and relied mostly on flamethrowers and hand grenades. The tunnel system was also difficult to overcome because once the Marines had cleared a bunker with a flamethrower or grenade and moved on, the Japanese would reoccupy through the tunnel connections and come at the Marines from the rear as they advanced. An additional problem with using the flamethrower was the very short range, requiring the person using it to be very close and often exposed to enemy fire.

Mount Suribachi is the dominant geographical feature on the island of Iwo Jima and became world famous because of the photograph taken by Joe Rosenthal on February 23, 1945, of five Marines and a Navy corpsman raising the US flag atop Mount Suribachi. The fact that the photograph is of a second flag being raised caused some to say it was staged. The first flag was a much smaller flag, however. It so happened that Secretary of the Navy James Forrestal had decided to go ashore and witness the fight for Mount Suribachi. After seeing the flag flying above the mountain, he decided he wanted it for a souvenir. The commander of the Marines who had put the flag there said, "Hell no, that flag belongs to the battalion," and sent a Marine to get another flag and, at the last minute, told the Marine to make it a bigger flag. It was the second flag, which Rosenthal snapped, that caught the eye of the world. He said he had set his camera down and out of the corner of his eye saw the flag going up so grabbed the camera, turned, and snapped. It became the only photograph in history to win the Pulitzer Prize for Photography in the same year it was taken.

Two of my favorite entertainers in show business were Johnny Carson and Lee Marvin, but I have to say I was offended by the fabricated story they told on the *Tonight Show* about the action of Marvin and of Captain Kangaroo (Bob Keeshan) during the Battle of Iwo Jima. The truth according to Snopes.com is that neither was ever on Iwo Jima and neither was awarded the Navy Cross. Lee did get the Purple Heart for being wounded on Saipan, and Bob Keeshan joined the Marines, but too late to see any action in the Pacific during the war. When I think of the 464 Medals of Honor awarded during WWII, particularly the 197 in the Pacific Theater, 266 of the 464 awarded posthumously, I believe bravery and claims for medals not awarded are not things to be joked about. People such as John Basilone, Richard Kraus, Richard Fleming, and the 464 others who gave their lives for their country make joking about medals awarded off limits, in my opinion.

Table 19 shows the troop and aircraft carrier casualties for the Battle of Iwo Jima.

Table 19. Iwo Jima casualties

TROOPS	USA	JAPAN	SHIPS/AIR CRAFT	USA	JAPAN
Killed	6,821	18,844	Escort Carrier	1	-
Wounded	20,000				
Captured		216*			

*An additional 3000 Japanese troops missing (hiding in the jungle).

The following troops were awarded the Medal of Honor for their actions during the Battle of Iwo Jima. (Citations for each are noted in References.)

CHARLES JOSEPH BERRY, Corporal U.S. Marine Corps born July 10, 1923, in Lorain, OH. Berry was a member of a machine-gun crew serving with the 1st Battalion, 26th Marines, 5th Marine Division, in action against enemy Japanese forces during the seizure of Iwo Jima in the Volcano Islands on March 3, 1945. When infiltrating Japanese soldiers launched a surprise attack shortly after midnight in an attempt to overrun his position, Berry engaged in a pitched hand-grenade duel, returning the dangerous weapons with prompt and deadly accuracy until an enemy grenade landed in his foxhole. Determined to save his comrades, Berry unhesitatingly chose to sacrifice himself and immediately dived on the deadly missile, absorbing the shattering violence of the exploding charge in his own body and protecting the others from serious injury.

WILLIAM R. CADDY, Private First Class U.S. Marine Corps Reserve born August 8, 1925, in Quincy, MA. Caddy served as a rifleman with Company 1, 3rd Battalion, 26th Marines, 5th Marine Division, in action against enemy Japanese forces during the seizure of Iwo Jima in the Volcanic Islands. Consistently aggressive, Private First Class Caddy boldly defied shattering Japanese machine-gun and small-arms fire to move forward with his platoon leader and another Marine during the determined advance of his company through an isolated sector and, gaining the comparative safety of a shell hole, took temporary cover with his comrades. Immediately pinned down by deadly sniper fire from a well-concealed position, Private Caddy made several unsuccessful attempts to again move forward and then, joined by his platoon leader, engaged the enemy in a fierce exchange of hand grenades until a Japanese grenade fell beyond reach in the shell hole. Fearlessly disregarding all personal danger, Private Caddy instantly dived on the deadly missile, absorbing the exploding charge with his own body and protecting the others from serious injury.

JUSTICE M. CHAMBERS, Colonel U.S. Marine Corps Reserve born February 2, 1908, in Huntington, WV. Under a furious barrage of enemy machine-gun and small-arms fire from the commanding cliffs on the right, Colonel (then Lieutenant Colonel) Chambers landed immediately after the initial assault waves of his battalion on D-Day to find the momentum of the assault threatened by heavy casualties from withering Japanese artillery, mortar-rocket, machine-gun, and rifle fire. Exposed to relentless hostile fire, Chambers coolly reorganized his battle-weary men, inspiring them to heroic efforts by his own valor and leading them in an attack on the critical impregnable high ground from which the enemy was pouring an increasing volume of fire directly onto troops ashore as well as onto amphibious craft in succeeding waves. Constantly in the front lines, encouraging his men to push forward against the enemy's savage resistance, Chambers led the eight-hour battle to carry the flanking ridge top and reduce the enemy's fields of aimed fire, thus protecting the vital foothold gained.

DARRELL SAMUEL COLE, Sergeant U.S. Marine Corps Reserve born July 20, 1920, in Flat River, MO. Assailed by a tremendous volume of small-arms, mortar, and artillery fire as he advanced with one squad of his section in the initial assault wave, Sergeant Cole boldly led his men up the sloping beach toward Airfield No. 1 despite the blanketing curtain of flying shrapnel and, personally destroying with hand grenades two hostile emplacements that menaced the progress of his unit, continued to move forward until a merciless barrage of fire emanating from three Japanese pillboxes halted the advance. Instantly placing his one remaining machine gun in action, Cole delivered a shattering fusillade and succeeded in silencing the nearest and most threatening emplacement before his weapon jammed and the enemy, reopening fire with knee mortars and grenades, pinned down his unit for the second time. Shrewdly gauging the tactical situation and evolving a daring plan of counterattack, Sergeant Cole, armed solely with a pistol and one grenade, coolly advanced alone to the hostile pillboxes. Hurling his one grenade at the enemy in sudden, swift attack, he quickly withdrew, returned to his own lines for additional grenades, and again advanced, attacked, and withdrew. With enemy guns still active, he ran the gauntlet of slashing fire a third time to complete the total destruction of the Japanese strongpoint and the annihilation of the defending garrison in this final assault. Although instantly killed by an enemy grenade as he returned to his squad, Sergeant. Cole had eliminated a formidable Japanese position.

ROBERT H. DUNLAP, Captain U.S. Marine Corps Reserve born October 19, 1920, in Abingdon, IL. Captain Dunlap led his troops in a determined advance from low ground uphill toward the steep cliffs from which the enemy poured a devastating rain of shrapnel and bullets. They steadily inched forward until the tremendous volume of enemy fire from the caves located high to the front temporarily halted their progress. Determined not to yield, Captain Dunlap crawled alone approximately 200 yards forward of his front lines, took observation at the base of the cliff fifty yards from Japanese lines, located the enemy gun positions, and returned to his own lines, where he relayed the vital information to supporting artillery and naval gunfire units. Persistently disregarding his own personal safety, he then placed himself in an exposed vantage point to more accurately direct the supporting fire and, working without respite for two days and two nights under constant enemy fire, skillfully directed a smashing bombardment against the almost impregnable Japanese positions despite numerous obstacles and heavy Marine casualties.

ROSS F. GRAY, Sergeant U.S. Marine Corps Reserve born August, 1920, in Marble Valley, AL. Shrewdly gauging the tactical situation when his platoon was held up by a sudden barrage of hostile grenades while advancing toward the high ground northeast of Airfield No. 1, Sergeant Gray promptly organized the withdrawal of his men from enemy grenade range, quickly moved forward alone to reconnoiter, and discovered a heavily mined area extending along the front of a strong network of emplacements joined by covered trenches. Although assailed by furious gunfire, he cleared a path leading through the minefield to one of the fortifications, then returned to the platoon position and, informing his leader of the serious situation, volunteered to initiate an attack under cover of three fellow Marines. Alone and unarmed but carrying a huge satchel charge, he crept up on the Japanese emplacement, boldly hurled the short-fused explosive, and sealed the entrance. Instantly taken under machine-gun fire from a second entrance to the same position, he unhesitatingly braved the increasingly vicious fusillades to crawl back for another charge, returned to his objective, and blasted the second opening, thereby demolishing the position. Repeatedly covering the ground between the savagely defended enemy fortifications and his platoon area, Gray systematically approached, attacked, and withdrew under blanketing fire to destroy a total of six Japanese positions, more than twenty-five Japanese troops, and a quantity of vital ordnance gear and ammunition.

WILLIAM G. HARRELL Sergeant United States Marine Corps born June 16, 1922, in Rio Grande City, TX. Standing watch alternately with another Marine in a terrain studded with caves and ravines, Sgt. Harrell was holding a position in a perimeter defense around the company command post when Japanese troops infiltrated our lines in the early hours of dawn. Awakened by a sudden attack, he quickly opened fire with his carbine and killed two of the enemy as they emerged from a ravine in the light of a star shellburst. Unmindful of his danger as hostile grenades fell closer, he waged a fierce lone battle until an exploding missile tore off his left hand

and fractured his thigh. He was vainly attempting to reload the carbine when his companion returned from the command post with another weapon. Wounded again by a Japanese who rushed the foxhole wielding a saber in the darkness, Sgt. Harrell succeeded in drawing his pistol and killing his opponent and then ordered his wounded companion to a place of safety. Exhausted by profuse bleeding but still unbeaten, he fearlessly met the challenge of two more enemy troops who charged his position and placed a grenade near his head. Killing one man with his pistol, he grasped the sputtering grenade with his good right hand, and, pushing it painfully toward the crouching soldier, saw his remaining assailant destroyed but his own hand severed in the explosion. At dawn Sgt. Harrell was evacuated from a position hedged by the bodies of 12 dead Japanese, at least five of whom he had personally destroyed in his self-sacrificing defense of the command post. His grim fortitude, exceptional valor, and indomitable fighting spirit against almost insurmountable odds reflect the highest credit upon himself and enhance the finest traditions of the U.S. Naval Service.

RUFUS G. HERRING, Lieutenant U.S. Marine Corps Reserve born June 11, 1921, in Roseboro, NC. Boldly closing the strongly fortified shores and under the devastating fire of Japanese coastal defense guns, Lieutenant Herring directed shattering barrages of 40 mm and 20 mm gunfire against hostile beaches until struck down by the enemy's savage counter-fire, which blasted the LCIs (Landing Craft Infantry) heavy guns and whipped her decks into sheets of flame. Regaining consciousness despite profuse bleeding, he was critically wounded a second time when a Japanese mortar crashed the conning station, instantly killing most of the officers and leaving the ship wallowing without navigational control. Upon recovering the second time, Herring climbed down to the pilot house and, fighting against waning strength, took over control and established communication with the engine room. When no longer able to stand, he propped himself against an empty shell case and rallied his men to aid the wounded; he maintained a position in the firing line with his 20 mm guns in the face of sustained fire.

DOUGLAS T. JACOBSON, Private First Class U.S. Marine Corps Reserve born November 25, 1925, in Rochester, NY. Promptly destroying a stubborn 20 mm antiaircraft gun and its crew after assuming the duties of a bazooka man who had been killed, Private First Class Jacobson waged a relentless battle as his unit fought desperately toward the summit of Hill 382 in an effort to penetrate the heart of Japanese cross-island defense. Employing his weapon with ready accuracy when his platoon was halted by overwhelming enemy fire on February 26, he first destroyed two hostile machine-gun positions, then attacked a large blockhouse, completely neutralizing the fortification before dispatching the five-man crew of a second pillbox and exploding the installation with a terrific demolitions blast. Moving steadily forward, he wiped out an earth-covered rifle emplacement and, confronted by a cluster of similar emplacements that constituted the perimeter of enemy defenses in his assigned sector, fearlessly advanced, quickly reduced all six positions to a shambles, killed ten of the enemy, and enabled American forces to occupy the strongpoint. Determined to widen the breach thus forced, he volunteered his services to an adjacent assault company, neutralized a pillbox holding up the company's advance, opened fire on a Japanese tank pouring a steady stream of bullets on one of the supporting American tanks, and smashed the enemy tank's gun turret in a brief but furious action culminating in a single-handed assault against still another blockhouse and the subsequent neutralization of its firepower. By his dauntless skill and valor, Private Jacobson destroyed a total of sixteen enemy positions and annihilated approximately seventy-five Japanese.

JOSEPH RODOLPH JULIAN, Platoon Sergeant U.S. Marine Corps Reserve born April 3, 1918, in Sturbridge, MA. Julian was in action against enemy Japanese forces during the seizure of Iwo Jima in the Volcano Islands, March 9, 1945. Determined to force a breakthrough when Japanese troops occupying trenches and fortified positions on the left front laid down a terrific machine-gun and mortar barrage in a desperate effort to halt his company's advance, Platoon Sergeant Julian quickly established his platoon's guns in strategic supporting positions and then, acting on his own initiative, fearlessly moved forward to execute a one-man assault on the nearest pillbox. He hurled deadly demolition and white phosphorus grenades into the emplacement, killing two of the enemy and driving the remaining five out into the adjoining trench system. Seizing a discarded rifle, Sergeant Julian jumped into the trench and dispatched the five before they could make an escape. Intent on wiping out all resistance, he obtained more explosives and, accompanied by another Marine, charged the hostile fortifications and knocked out two more cave positions. Immediately thereafter, he launched a bazooka attack unassisted, firing four rounds into the one remaining pillbox and completely destroying it before he fell, mortally wounded by a vicious burst of enemy fire.

JAMES D. LA BELLE, Private First Class U.S. Marine Corps Reserve born November 22, 1925, in Columbia Heights, MN. Private First Class La Belle was filling a gap in the front lines during a critical phase of the battle. He had dug into a foxhole with two other Marines and, grimly aware of the enemy's persistent attempts to blast a way through American lines with hand grenades, applied himself with steady concentration to maintaining a sharply vigilant watch during the hazardous night hours. Suddenly, a hostile grenade landed beyond reach in his foxhole. Quickly estimating the situation, he determined to save the others if possible, shouted a warning, and instantly dived on the deadly missile, absorbing the exploding charge in his own body and thereby protecting his comrades from serious injury.

JOHN H. LEIMS, Second Lieutenant U.S. Marine Corps Reserve born June 8, 1921, in Chicago, IL. Launching a surprise attack against the rock-imbedded fortification of a dominating Japanese hill position, Second Lieutenant Leims spurred his company forward with indomitable determination and, skillfully directing his assault platoons against the cave-emplaced enemy troops and heavily fortified pillboxes, succeeded in capturing the objective in later afternoon. When it became apparent that his assault platoons were cut off in this newly won position approximately 400 yards forward of adjacent units and lacking all communication with the command post, he personally advanced and laid telephone lines across the isolating expanse of open fire-swept terrain. Ordered to withdraw his command after he had joined his forward platoons, he immediately complied, adroitly affecting the withdrawal of his troops without incident. Upon arriving at the rear, he was informed that several casualties had been left at the abandoned ridge position beyond the front lines. Although suffering acutely from the strain and exhaustion of battle, he instantly went forward despite darkness and the slashing fury of hostile machine-gun fire, located and carried to safety one seriously wounded Marine, and then, running the gauntlet of enemy fire for the third time that night, again made his tortuous way into the bullet-riddled deathtrap and rescued another of his wounded men.

JACKLYN H. LUCAS, Private First Class U.S. Marine Corps Reserve born February 14, 1928, in Plymouth, NC. While creeping through a treacherous, twisting ravine that ran in close proximity to a fluid and uncertain front line on D-Day-plus-one, Private First Class Lucas and three other men were suddenly ambushed by a hostile patrol that savagely attacked with rifle fire and grenades. Quick to act when the lives of the small group were endangered by two grenades that landed directly in front of them, Private Lucas unhesitatingly hurled himself over his comrades upon one grenade and pulled the other under him, absorbing the whole blasting forces of the explosions in his own body in order to shield his companions from the concussion and murderous flying fragments. By his inspiring action and valiant spirit of self-sacrifice, he not only protected his comrades from certain injury or possible death but also enabled them to rout the Japanese patrol and continue the advance.

JACK LUMMUS, First Lieutenant U.S. Marine Corps Reserve born October 22, 1915, in Ennie, TX. Resuming his assault tactics with bold decision after fighting without respite for two days and nights, First Lieutenant Lummus slowly advanced his platoon against an enemy deeply entrenched in a network of mutually supporting positions. Suddenly halted by a terrific concentration of hostile fire, he unhesitatingly moved forward of his front lines in an effort to neutralize the Japanese position. Although knocked to the ground when an enemy grenade exploded close by, he immediately recovered himself and, again moving forward despite the intensified barrage, quickly located, attacked, and destroyed the occupied emplacement. Instantly taken under fire by the garrison of a supporting pillbox and further assailed by the slashing fury of hostile rifle fire, he fell under the impact of a second enemy grenade but, courageously disregarding painful shoulder wounds, staunchly continued his heroic one-man assault and charged the second pillbox, annihilating all the occupants. Subsequently returning to his platoon position, he fearlessly traversed his lines under fire, encouraging his men to advance and directing the fire of supporting tanks against other stubbornly holding Japanese emplacements. Held up again by a devastating barrage, he again moved into the open, rushed a third heavily fortified installation, and killed the defending troops. Determined to crush all resistance, he led his men indomitably, personally attacking foxholes and spider traps with his carbine and systematically reducing the fanatic opposition until, stepping on a land mine, he sustained fatal wounds.

HARRY L. MARTIN, First Lieutenant US Marine Corps Reserve born January 4, 1911, in Bucyrus, OH: With his sector of the 5th Pioneer Battalion bivouac area penetrated by a concentrated enemy attack launched a few minutes before dawn, Lieutenant Martin instantly organized a firing line with the Marines nearest his foxhole and succeeded in checking momentarily the headlong rush of the Japanese. Determined to rescue several of his men trapped in positions overrun by the enemy, he defied intense hostile fire to work his way through the Japanese to the surrounded Marines. Although sustaining two severe wounds, he blasted the Japanese who attempted to intercept him, located his beleaguered men, and directed them to their own lines. When four of the infiltrating enemy took possession of an abandoned machine-gun pit and subjected his sector to a barrage of hand grenades, First Lieutenant Martin, alone and armed with only a pistol, boldly charged the hostile position and killed all of its occupants. Realizing that his few remaining comrades could not repulse another organized attack, he called to his men to follow and then charged into the midst of the strong enemy force, firing his weapon and scattering them until he fell, mortally wounded by a grenade.

JOSEPH J. MCCARTHY, Captain U.S. Marine Corps Reserve born August 11, 1911, in Chicago, IL. Determined to break through the enemy's cross-island defenses, Captain McCarthy acted on his own initiative when his company advance was held up by uninterrupted Japanese rifle, machine-gun, and high-velocity 47 mm fire during the approach to Motoyama Airfield No. 2. Quickly organizing a demolitions and flamethrower team to accompany his picked rifle squad, he fearlessly led the way across seventy-five yards of fire-swept ground, charged a heavily fortified pillbox on the ridge of the front, and, personally hurled hand grenades into the emplacement as he directed the combined operations of his small assault group and completely destroyed the hostile installation.

GEORGE PHILLIPS, Private U.S. Marine Corps Reserve born July 14, 1926, in Rick Hill, MO. Standing the foxhole watch while other members of his squad rested after a night of bitter hand-grenade fighting against infiltrating Japanese troops, Private Phillips was the only member of his unit alerted when an enemy hand grenade was tossed into their midst. Instantly shouting a warning, he unhesitatingly threw himself on the deadly missile, absorbing the shattering violence of the exploding charge in his own body and protecting his comrades from serious injury. Stouthearted and indomitable, Private Phillips willingly yielded his own life that his fellow Marines might carry on the relentless battle against a fanatic enemy.

FRANCIS J. PIERCE, Pharmacist's Mate First Class U.S. Navy born December 7, 1924, in Earlville, IA. Almost continuously under fire while carrying out the most dangerous volunteer assignments, Pierce gained valuable knowledge of the terrain and disposition of troops. Caught in heavy enemy rifle and machine-gun fire that wounded a corpsman and two of the eight stretcher bearers who were carrying two wounded Marines to a forward aid station on March 15, Pierce quickly took charge of the party, carried the newly wounded men to a sheltered position, and rendered first aid. After directing the evacuation of three of the casualties, he stood in the open to draw the enemy's fire and, with his weapon blasting, enabled the litter bearers to reach cover. Turning his attention to the other two casualties, he was attempting to stop the profuse bleeding of one man when a Japanese fired from a cave fewer than twenty yards away and wounded his patient again. Risking his own life to save his patient, Pierce deliberately exposed himself to draw the attacker from the cave and destroyed him with the last of his ammunition. Then, lifting the wounded man to his back, Pierce advanced, unmanned, through deadly rifle fire across 200 feet of open terrain. Despite exhaustion, and in the face of warnings against such a suicidal mission, he again traversed the same fire-swept path to rescue the remaining Marine. On the following morning, he led a combat patrol to the sniper nest and, while aiding a stricken Marine, was seriously wounded. Refusing aid for himself, he directed treatment for the casualty, at the same time maintaining protective fire for his comrades. Completely fearless, completely devoted to the care of his patients, Pierce inspired the entire battalion.

DONALD J. RUHL, Private First Class U.S. Marine Corps Reserve born July 2, 1923, in Columbus, MT. Quick to press the advantage after eight Japanese had been driven from a blockhouse on D-Day, Private First Class Ruhl singlehandedly attacked the group, killing one of the enemy with his bayonet and another by rifle fire in his determined attempt to annihilate the escaping troops. Cool and undaunted as the fury of hostile resistance steadily increased throughout the night, he voluntarily left the shelter of his tank trap early in the morning of D-Day-plus-one and moved out under a tremendous volume of mortar and machine-gun fire to rescue a wounded Marine lying in an exposed position approximately forty yards forward of the line. Half pulling and half carrying the wounded man, Ruhl removed him to a defiladed position, called for an assistant and a stretcher, and, again running the gauntlet of hostile fire, carried the casualty to an aid station some 300 yards distant on the beach. Returning to his platoon, Private Ruhl continued his valiant efforts, volunteering to investigate an apparently abandoned Japanese gun emplacement seventy-five yards forward of the right flank during consolidation of the front lines, and subsequently occupying the position through the night to prevent the enemy from repossessing the valuable weapon. Pushing forward in the assault against the vast network of fortifications surrounding Mount Suribachi the following morning, he crawled with his platoon guide to the top of a Japanese bunker to bring fire to bear on enemy troops located on the far side of the bunker. Suddenly, a hostile grenade landed between the two Marines. Instantly,

Private called a warning to his fellow Marine and dived on the deadly missile, absorbing the full impact of the shattering explosion in his own body and protecting all within range from the danger of flying fragments.

FRANKLIN E. SIGLER, Private U.S. Marine Corps Reserve born November 6, 1924, in Glen Ridge NJ. Voluntarily taking command of his rifle squad when the leader became a casualty, Private Sigler fearlessly led a bold charge against an enemy gun installation that had held up the advance of his company for several days and, reaching the position in advance of the others, assailed the emplacement with hand grenades, personally annihilating the entire crew. As additional Japanese troops opened fire from concealed tunnels and caves above, he quickly scaled the rocks leading to the attacking guns, surprised the enemy with a furious one-man assault, and, although severely wounded in the encounter, deliberately crawled back to his squad position, where he steadfastly refused evacuation, persistently directing heavy machine-gun and rocket barrages on the Japanese cave entrances. Undaunted by the merciless rain of hostile fire during the intensified action, he gallantly disregarded his own painful wounds to aid casualties, carrying three wounded squad members to safety behind the lines and returning to continue the battle with renewed determination until ordered to retire for medical treatment.

TONY STEIN, Corporal U.S. Marine Corps Reserve born September 30, 1921, in Dayton, OH. First man of his unit to be on station after hitting the beach in the initial assault, Corporal Stein, armed with a personally improvised aircraft-type weapon, provided rapid covering fire as the remainder of his platoon attempted to move into position. When his comrades were stalled by a concentrated machine-gun and mortar barrage, he gallantly stood upright and exposed himself to the enemy's view, thereby drawing the hostile fire to his own person and enabling him to observe the location of the furiously blazing hostile guns. Determined to neutralize the strategically placed weapons, he boldly charged the enemy pillboxes one by one and succeeded in killing twenty of the enemy during the furious single-handed assault. Cool and courageous under the merciless hail of exploding shells and bullets that fell on all sides, he continued to deliver the fire of his skillfully improvised weapon at a tremendous rate of speed, which rapidly exhausted his ammunition. Undaunted, he removed his helmet and shoes to expedite his movements and ran back to the beach for additional ammunition, making a total of eight trips under intense fire and carrying or assisting a wounded man back each time. Despite the unrelenting savagery and confusion of battle, he rendered prompt assistance to his platoon whenever the unit was in position, directing the fire of a halftrack against a stubborn pillbox until he had effected the ultimate destruction of the Japanese fortification. Later in the day, although his weapon was twice shot from his hands, he personally covered the withdrawal of his platoon to the company position.

GEORGE E. WAHLEN, Pharmacist's Mate Second Class U.S. Navy born August 8, 1924, in Ogden, UT. Painfully wounded in the bitter action on February 26, Wahlen remained on the battlefield, advancing well forward of the front lines to aid a wounded Marine and carrying him back to safety despite a terrific concentration of fire. Tireless in his ministrations, he consistently disregarded all danger to attend his fighting comrades as they fell under the devastating rain of shrapnel and bullets, and he rendered prompt assistance to various elements of his combat group as required. When an adjacent platoon suffered heavy casualties, he defied the continuous pounding of heavy mortars and deadly fire of enemy rifles to care for the wounded, working rapidly in an area swept by constant fire, and treating fourteen casualties before returning to his own platoon. Wounded again on March 2, he gallantly refused evacuation, moving out with his company the following day in a furious assault across 600 yards of open terrain and repeatedly rendering medical aid while exposed to the blasting fury of powerful Japanese guns. Stouthearted and indomitable, he persevered in his determined efforts as his unit waged fierce battle and, unable to walk after sustaining a third agonizing wound, resolutely crawled fifty yards to administer first aid to still another fallen fighter.

WILLIAM GARY WALSH, Gunnery Sergeant U.S. Marine Corps Reserve born April 7, 1922, in Roxbury, MA. With the advance of his company toward Hill 362 disrupted by vicious machine-gun fire from a forward position that guarded the approaches to this key enemy stronghold, Gunnery Sergeant Walsh fearlessly charged at the head of his platoon against the Japanese entrenched on the ridge above him, utterly oblivious to the unrelenting fury of hostile automatic-weapons fire and hand grenades employed with fanatic desperation to smash his daring assault. Thrown back by the enemy's savage resistance, he once again led his men in a seemingly impossible attack up the steep, rocky slope, boldly defiant of the annihilating streams of bullets that saturated the area. Despite his own casualty losses and the overwhelming advantage held by the Japanese in superior numbers and dominant position, he gained the ridge's top only to be subjected to an intense barrage of hand grenades thrown by the remaining Japanese staging a suicidal last stand on the reverse slope. When one of the grenades fell in the midst of his surviving men huddled together in a small trench, Gunnery Sergeant Walsh, in a final valiant act of complete self-sacrifice, instantly threw himself upon the deadly bomb, absorbing with his own body the full and terrific force of the explosion.

WILSON D. WATSON, Private U.S. Marine Corps Reserve born February 18, 1921, in Tuscumbia, AL. With his squad abruptly halted by intense fire from enemy fortifications in the high rocky ridges and crags commanding the line of advance, Private Watson boldly rushed one pillbox and fired into the embrasure with his weapon, keeping the enemy pinned down single-handedly until he was in a position to hurl in a grenade, and then ran to the rear of the emplacement to destroy the retreating Japanese and enable his platoon to take its objective. Again pinned down at the foot of a small hill, he dauntlessly scaled the jagged incline under fierce mortar and machine-gun barrages and, with his assistant BAR man, charged the crest of the hill, firing from his hip. Fighting furiously against Japanese troops attacking with grenades and knee mortars from the reverse slope, he stood fearlessly erect in his exposed position to cover the hostile entrenchments and held the hill under savage fire for fifteen minutes, killing sixty Japanese before his ammunition was exhausted and his platoon was able to join him. His courageous initiative and valiant fighting spirit against devastating odds were directly responsible for the continued advance of his platoon.

HERSHEL W. WILLIAMS, Corporal U.S. Marine Corps Reserve born October 2, 1923, in Quiet Dell, WV. Quick to volunteer his services when American tanks were maneuvering vainly to open a lane for the infantry through the network of reinforced concrete pillboxes, buried mines, and black volcanic sands, Corporal Williams daringly went forward alone to attempt the reduction of devastating machine-gun fire from the unyielding positions. Covered only by four riflemen, he fought desperately for four hours under terrific enemy small-arms fire and repeatedly returned to his own lines to prepare demolition charges and obtain serviced flamethrowers, struggling back, frequently to the rear of hostile emplacements, to wipe out one position after another. On one occasion, he daringly mounted a pillbox to insert the nozzle of his flamethrower through the air vent, killing the occupants and silencing the gun; on another, he grimly charged enemy riflemen who attempted to stop him with bayonets and destroyed them with a burst of flame from his weapon.

JACK WILLIAMS, Pharmacist's Mate Third Class U.S. Marines Corps Reserve born October 18, 1924, in Harrison, AR. Gallantly going forward on the front lines under intense enemy small arms fire to assist a Marine wounded in a fierce grenade battle, Williams dragged the man to a shallow depression and was kneeling, using his own body as a screen from the sustained fire as he administered first aid, when struck in the abdomen and groin three times by hostile rifle fire. Momentarily stunned, he quickly recovered and completed his ministrations before applying battle dressings to his own multiple wounds. Unmindful of his own urgent need for medical attention, he remained in the perilous fire-swept area to care for another Marine casualty. Heroically completing his task despite pain and profuse bleeding, he then endeavored to make his way to the rear in search of adequate aid for himself when struck down by a Japanese sniper bullet, which caused his collapse. Succumbing later as a result of his self-sacrificing service to others, Williams. by his courageous determination, unwavering fortitude, and valiant performance of duty, served as an inspiring example of heroism.

JOHN H. WILLIS, Pharmacist's Mate First Class U.S. Navy born June 10, 1921, in Columbia, TN. Constantly imperiled by artillery and mortar fire from strong and mutually supporting pillboxes and caves studding Hill 362 in the enemy's cross-island defenses, Willis resolutely administered first aid to the many Marines wounded during the furious close-in fighting until he himself was struck by shrapnel and was ordered back to the battle-aid station. Without waiting for official medical release, he quickly returned to his company and, during a savage hand-to-hand enemy counterattack, daringly advanced to the extreme front lines under mortar and sniper fire to aid a Marine lying wounded in a shell hole. Completely unmindful of his own danger as the Japanese intensified their attack, Willis calmly continued to administer blood plasma to his patient, promptly returning the first hostile grenade that landed in the shell hole while he was working, and hurling back seven more in quick succession, before the ninth one exploded in his hand and instantly killed him.

THE BATTLE OF OKINAWA

Let us pray that peace be now restored to the world and that God will preserve it always. — General Douglas Macarthur, Supreme Allied Commander of the Southwest Pacific (1945)

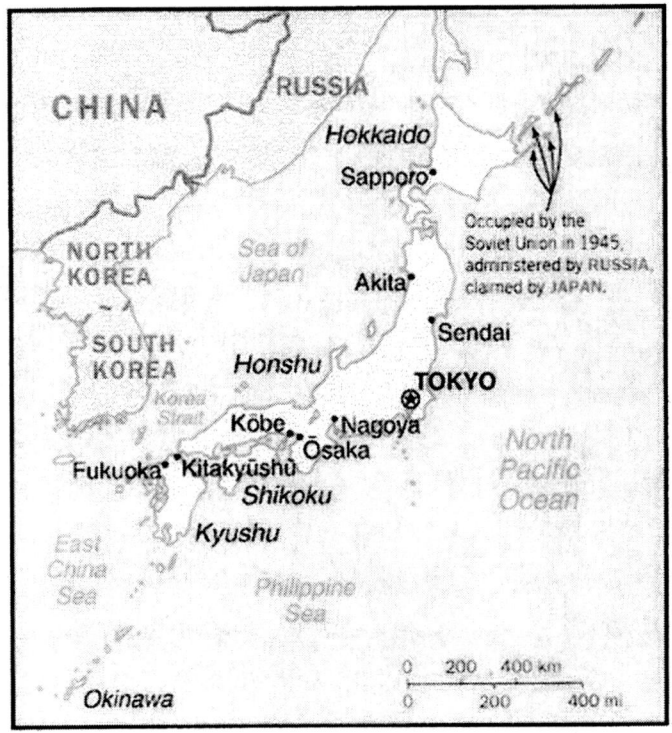

The Battle of Okinawa (Courtesy WorldAtlas)

The Battle of Okinawa lasted eighty-two days, from April until mid-June 1945. With this island in hand serving as one of the bases for the invasion of Japan, the United States would be only about 340 miles from the Japanese mainland. The battle would come to represent the highest casualties of all the battles in the Pacific Theater. Okinawa government sources report that a total of

77,166 Japanese soldiers were killed or committed suicide. The United States and its allies suffered total casualties of 65,000, with 14,009 killed. It is estimated that 42,000–50,000 local civilians either were killed or committed suicide.

The USS *J. Franklin Bell* left San Francisco on February 28, 1945, for this battle, which would be the final battle of WWII. I remember the journey well because after we loaded officers and troops in Pearl Harbor, eighteen Army nurses came aboard. All the enlisted men were restricted to the lower decks. (We assumed that the officers did not want any competition.) After a short stop at Eniwetok, we went on to Saipan, where all the passengers were unloaded. The *Bell* then headed for Noumea, New Caledonia. Another reason I remember this trip is that our top speed was about ten knots as result of the loss of power in one of the turbines. At that speed, we were sitting ducks for Japanese submarines, but the trip was uneventful. After repairs were made at Noumea, we spent time transferring troops between Guadalcanal, Ulithi Atoll, and Eniwetok.

In the Battle of Okinawa, the Japanese established the kamikaze tactics as a defensive measure for the first time (though you will remember that kamikazes were first used in the Battle of Leyte). Between April and May 1945, the Japanese made seven major kamikaze attacks, involving more than 1500 planes. We were also aware of the possibility of suicide boats, and that awareness created an experience that I will never forget. I was in one of our LCVPs, creating smoke along with another gunner's mate, a coxswain, and a naval officer. We were one of several boats to lay smoke screens to hide the ships from Japanese planes. If we were challenged, we had a special light to give as a response. It so happened that in the thick of smoke, we came upon a US gunboat, and when attempting to answer the challenge, the officer dropped the light, whereupon the gunboat opened fire with small-caliber guns. We all went to the bilges, and fortunately, the officer found the light and signaled for the shooting to stop. The gunboat turned out to be on its first action of the war, and its crew were very apologetic about having fired on us. They welcomed us aboard and treated us like royalty.

At Okinawa, The *Bell* anchored in the Hagushi anchorage and unloaded our troops, which were the US Naval Construction Battalion. The *Bell* remained at Okinawa for several days and was subject to numerous air raids. The Japanese planes dropped four bombs on the first day that were near misses. The only casualty was William Wrenn, who received non-life-threatening facial wounds while serving in one of our smoke boats.

Table 20 shows the troop, ship, carrier, and artillery casualties during the Battle of Okinawa.

Table 20. Okinawa casualties

TROOPS	USA	JAPAN	SHIPS/AIR CRAFT/ETC.	USA	JAPAN
Killed	12,513	77,166-110,000	Ships	38	16
Wounded	31,000-40,000	Unknown	Aircraft	763	7800
Captured		7,000	Tanks	225	27
	See Note:		Artillery Pieces	-	743

Note: An additional 30,000 USA non-combat losses

The Battle of Okinawa resulted in twenty-two Medals of Honor being awarded, (Citations for each are noted in References.)

BEAUFORD T. ANDERSON, Technical Sergeant U.S. Army born July 6, 1922, in Eagle, WI. When a powerfully conducted predawn Japanese counterattack struck his unit's flank, Anderson ordered his men to take cover in an old tomb, and then, armed with only a carbine, faced the onslaught alone. After emptying one magazine at point-blank range into the screaming attackers, he seized an enemy mortar dud and threw it back among the charging Japanese, killing several when it burst. Securing a box of mortar shells, he extracted the safety pins, banged the bases upon a rock to arm them, and alternately hurled shells and fired his piece among the fanatical foe, finally forcing them to withdraw. Despite the protests of his comrades, and bleeding profusely from a severe shrapnel wound, he made his way to his company commander to report the action. Technical Sergeant Anderson's intrepid conduct in the face of overwhelming odds accounted for twenty-five enemy troops killed and several machine guns and knee mortars destroyed; thus, he single-handedly removed a serious threat to the company's flank.

RICHARD E. BUSH, Corporal U.S. Marine Corps Reserve born December 23, 1923, in Glasgow, KY. Rallying his men forward with indomitable determination, Corporal Bush boldly defied the slashing fury of concentrated Japanese artillery fire pouring down from the gun-studded mountain fortress to lead his squad up the face of the rocky precipice, sweep over the ridge, and drive the defending troops from their deeply entrenched position. With his unit, the first to break through to the inner defense of Mount Yae-Take, he fought relentlessly in the forefront of the action until seriously wounded and evacuated with others under protecting rocks. Although prostrate under medical treatment when a Japanese hand grenade landed in the midst of the group, Corporal Bush, alert and courageous in extremity as in battle, unhesitatingly pulled the deadly missile to himself and absorbed the shattering violence of the exploding charge in his body, thereby saving his fellow Marines from severe injury or death despite the certain peril to his own life. By his valiant leadership and aggressive tactics in the face of savage opposition, Corporal Bush contributed materially to the success of the sustained drive toward the conquest of this fiercely defended outpost of the Japanese Empire.

ROBERT EUGENE BUSH, Hospital Apprentice First Class U.S. Navy Reserves born October 4, 1926, in Tacoma, WA. Fearlessly braving the fury of artillery, mortar, and machine-gun fire from strongly entrenched hostile positions, Bush constantly and unhesitatingly moved from one casualty to another to attend the wounded falling under the enemy's murderous barrages. As the attack passed over a ridgetop, Bush was advancing to administer blood plasma to a Marine officer lying wounded on the skyline when the Japanese launched a savage counterattack. In this perilously exposed position, Bush resolutely maintained the flow of life-giving plasma. Holding the bottle high in one hand, Bush drew his pistol with the other and fired into the enemy's ranks until his ammunition was expended. Quickly seizing a discarded carbine, he trained his point-blank fire on the Japanese charging over the hill, accounting for six of the enemy despite his own serious wounds and the loss of one eye during his desperate battle in defense of the helpless man. With the hostile force finally routed, Bush calmly disregarded his own critical condition to complete his mission, valiantly refusing medical treatment for himself until his officer patient had been evacuated, and collapsed only after attempting to walk to the battle aid station.

HENRY A. COURTNEY JR., Major U.S. Marine Corps Reserve born January 6, 1916, in Duluth, MN. Ordered to hold for the night in static defense behind Sugar Loaf Hill after leading the forward elements of his command in a prolonged firefight, Major Courtney weighed the effect of a hostile night counterattack against the tactical value of an immediate Marine assault, resolved to initiate the assault, and promptly obtained permission to advance and seize the forward slope of the hill. Quickly explaining the situation to his small remaining force, he declared his personal intention of moving forward and then proceeded on his way, boldly blasting nearby cave positions and neutralizing enemy guns as he went. Inspired by his courage, every man followed without hesitation, and together, the intrepid Marines braved a terrific concentration of Japanese gunfire to skirt the hill on the right and reach the reverse slope. Temporarily halting, Major Courtney sent guides to the rear for more ammunition and possible replacements. Subsequently reinforced by twenty-six men and an LVT-load of grenades, he determined to storm the crest of the hill and crush any planned counterattack before it could gain sufficient momentum to effect a breakthrough. Leading his men by example rather than by command, he pushed ahead with unrelenting aggressiveness, hurling grenades into cave openings on the slope with devastating effect. Upon reaching the crest and observing large numbers of Japanese forming for action less than 100 yards away, he instantly attacked, waged a furious battle, and succeeded in killing many of the enemy and in forcing the remainder to take cover in the caves. Determined to hold, he ordered his men to dig in and, coolly disregarding the continuous hail of flying enemy shrapnel to rally his weary troops, tirelessly aided casualties and assigned his men to more advantageous positions. He was instantly killed by a hostile mortar burst while moving among his men.

CLARENCE B. CRAFT, Private First Class U.S. Army born September 23, 1921, in San Bernardino, CA. Craft was a rifleman when his platoon spearheaded an attack on Hen Hill, the tactical position on which the entire Naha-Shuri-Yonabaru line of Japanese defense on Okinawa, Ryukyu Islands, was hinged. For twelve days, American forces had been stalled, and repeated heavy assaults by one battalion, and then another had been thrown back by the enemy with serious casualties. With five comrades, Private First Class Craft was dispatched in advance of Company G to feel out the enemy resistance. The group had proceeded only a short distance up the slope when rifle and machine-gun fire, coupled with a terrific barrage of grenades, wounded three and pinned down the others. Against odds that appeared suicidal, Private Craft launched a remarkable one-man attack. He stood up in full view of the enemy and began shooting with deadly marksmanship wherever he saw hostile movement. He steadily advanced up the hill, killing Japanese soldiers with rapid fire, driving others to cover He unhesitatingly faced alone the strength that had previously beaten back attacks of battalion strength. He reached the crest of the hill, where he stood silhouetted against the sky while quickly throwing grenades at extremely short range into the enemy positions. His extraordinary assault lifted the pressure from his company for the moment, allowing members of his platoon to comply with his motions to advance and pass him more grenades. With a chain of his comrades supplying him while he stood atop the hill, he furiously hurled a total of two cases of grenades into a main trench and other positions on the reverse slope of Hen Hill, meanwhile directing the aims of his fellow soldiers, who threw grenades from the slope below him. He left his position, where grenades from both sides were passing over his head and bursting on either slope, to attack the main enemy. Pursuing the enemy, he came upon a heavy machine gun that was still creating havoc in the American ranks. With rifle fire and a grenade, he wiped out this position. By this time, the Japanese were in complete rout and American forces were swarming over the hill. Private Craft continued down the central trench to the mouth of a cave where many of the enemy had taken cover. A satchel charge was brought to him, and he tossed it into the cave. It failed to explode. With great daring, the intrepid fighter retrieved the charge from the cave, relighted the fuse, and threw the charge back, sealing the Japanese in a tomb. In the local action, against tremendously superior forces heavily armed with rifles, machine guns, mortars, and grenades, Private Craft killed at least twenty-five, but his contribution to the campaign on Okinawa was of much more far-reaching consequence, for Hen Hill was the key to the entire defense line, which rapidly crumbled after his utterly fearless and heroic attack strongly disposed trenches.

JAMES DAY, Major General U.S. Marine Corps born October 5, 1925, in East St. Louis, IL. On the first day of the invasion of Okinawa, Corporal (at that time) Day rallied his squad and the remnants of another unit and led them to a critical position forward of the front lines of Sugar Loaf Hill. Soon thereafter, they came under an intense mortar and artillery barrage that was quickly followed by a ferocious ground attack by some forty Japanese soldiers. Despite the loss of half of his men, Corporal Day remained at the forefront, shouting encouragement, hurling hand grenades, and directing deadly fire, thereby repelling the determined enemy. Reinforced by six men, he led his squad in repelling three fierce night attacks but suffered five additional Marines killed and one wounded, whom he assisted to safety. Upon hearing nearby calls for corpsman assistance, Corporal Day braved heavy enemy fire to escort four seriously wounded Marines, one at a time, to safety. Corporal Day then manned a light machine gun, assisted by a wounded Marine, and halted another night attack. In the ferocious action, his machine gun was destroyed and he suffered multiple white-phosphorous and fragmentation wounds. He reorganized his defensive position in time to halt a fifth enemy attack with devastating small-arms fire. On three separated occasions, Japanese soldiers closed to within a few feet of his foxhole but were killed by Corporal Day. During the second day, the enemy conducted numerous unsuccessful swarming attacks against his exposed position. When the attacks momentarily subsided, more than seventy enemy dead were counted around his position. On the third day, a wounded and exhausted Corporal Day repulsed the enemy's final attack, killing a dozen enemy soldiers at close range. Having yielded no ground and with more than one hundred enemies dead around his position, Corporal Day preserved the lives of his fellow Marines and made a significant contribution to the success of the Okinawa campaign. He later rose to the rank of Major General and served in Korean and Vietnam campaigns.

DESMOND T. DOSS, Corporal U.S. Army born February 7, 1919, in Lynchburg, VA. Doss was a company aid man when the 1st Battalion assaulted a jagged escarpment 400 feet high. As American troops gained the summit, a heavy concentration of artillery, mortar, and machine-gun fire crashed into them, inflicting approximately seventy-five casualties and driving the others back. Private First Class Doss refused to seek cover and remained in the fire-swept area with the many stricken, carrying them one by one to the edge of the escarpment and there lowering them on a rope-supported litter down the face of a cliff to friendly hands. On May 2, he exposed himself to heavy rifle and mortar fire in rescuing a wounded man 200 yards forward of the lines on the same escarpment. Two days later, he treated four men who had been cut down while assaulting a strongly defended cave; he advanced through a shower of grenades to within eight yards of enemy forces in a cave's mouth and dressed his comrades' wounds before making four separate trips under fire to evacuate them to safety. On May 5, he unhesitatingly braved enemy shelling and small-arms fire to assist an artillery officer. He applied bandages, moved his patient to a spot that offered protection from small-arms fire, and, while artillery and mortar shells fell close by, painstakingly administered plasma. Later that day, when an American was severely wounded by fire from a cave, Private Doss crawled to him where he had fallen twenty-five feet from the enemy position, rendered aid, and carried the man one hundred yards to safety while continually exposed to enemy fire. On May 21, in a night attack on high ground near Shuri, Private Doss remained in exposed territory while the rest of his company took cover, fearlessly risking the chance that he would be mistaken for an infiltrating Japanese and giving aid to the injured until he was himself seriously wounded in the legs by the explosion of a grenade. Rather than call another aid man from cover, Private Doss cared for his own injuries and waited five hours before litter bearers reached him and started carrying him to cover. The trio was caught in an enemy tank attack, and Private Doss, seeing a more critically wounded man nearby, crawled off the litter and directed the bearers to give their first attention to the other man. Awaiting the litter bearers' return, Doss was again struck, this time suffering a compound fracture of his arm. With magnificent fortitude, he bound a rifle stock to his shattered arm as a splint and then crawled 300 yards over rough terrain to the aid station.

JOHN P. FARDY, Corporal U.S. Marine Corps born August 8, 1922, in Chicago, IL. When his squad was suddenly assailed by extremely heavy small-arms fire from the front during a determined advance against strongly fortified, fiercely defended Japanese positions, Corporal Fardy temporarily deployed his men along a nearby drainage ditch. Shortly thereafter, an enemy grenade fell among the Marines in the ditch. Instantly throwing himself upon the deadly missile, Corporal Fardy absorbed the exploding blast in his own body, thereby protecting his comrades from certain and perhaps fatal injuries. Concerned solely for the welfare of his men, he willingly relinquished his own hope of survival that his fellow Marines might live to carry on the fight against a fanatic enemy. A stouthearted leader and indomitable fighter, Corporal Fardy, by his prompt decision and resolute spirit of self-sacrifice in the face of certain death, rendered valiant service.

WILLIAM A. FOSTER, Private First Class U.S. Marine Corps Reserve born February 17, 1915, in Cleveland, OH. Dug in with another Marine on the point of the perimeter defense after waging a furious assault against a strongly fortified Japanese position, Private First Class Foster and his comrade engaged in a fierce hand-grenade duel with infiltrating enemy soldiers. Suddenly, an enemy grenade landed beyond reach in the foxhole. Instantly diving on the deadly missile, Private Foster absorbed the exploding charge in his own body, thereby protecting the other Marine from serious injury. Although mortally wounded as a result of his heroic action, he quickly rallied, handed his own remaining two grenades to his comrade, and said, "Make them count." Stouthearted and indomitable, he had unhesitatingly relinquished his own chance of survival that his fellow Marine might carry on a relentless fight against a fanatic enemy.

HAROLD GONSALVES, Private First Class U.S. Marine Corps Reserve born January 28, 1926, in Alameda, CA. Undaunted by the powerfully organized opposition encountered on Motobu Peninsula during the fierce assault waged by his battalion against the Japanese stronghold at Mount Yae-Take, Private First Class Gonsalves repeatedly braved the terrific enemy bombardment to aid his forward observation team in directing well-placed artillery fire. When his commanding officer determined to move into the front lines to register a more effective bombardment in the enemy's defensive position, Gonsalves unhesitatingly advanced uphill with the officer and another Marine despite a slashing barrage of enemy mortar and rifle fire. As they reached the front, a Japanese grenade fell close within the group. Instantly, Private Gonsalves dived on the deadly missile, absorbing the exploding charge in his own body and thereby protecting the others from serious and perhaps fatal wounds. Stouthearted and indomitable, Private Gonsalves readily yielded his own chances of survival that his fellow Marines might carry on a relentless battle against a fanatic enemy.

DALE MERLIN HANSEN, Private U.S. Marine Corps born December 13, 1922, in Wisner, NE. Cool and courageous in combat, Private Hansen unhesitatingly took the initiative during a critical stage of the action and, armed with a rocket launcher, crawled to an exposed position where he attacked and destroyed a strategically located hostile pillbox. With his weapon subsequently destroyed by enemy fire, he seized a rifle and continued his one-man assault. Reaching the crest of a ridge, he leaped across, and opened fire on six Japanese, killing four before his rifle jammed. Attacked by the remaining two Japanese, Private Hansen beat them off with the butt of his rifle and then climbed back to cover. Promptly returning with another weapon and a supply of grenades, he fearlessly advanced, destroyed a strong mortar position, and annihilated eight more of the enemy.

LOUIS JAMES HAUGE JR., Corporal U.S. Marine Corps Reserve born December 12, 1924, in Ada, MN. Alert and aggressive during a determined assault against a strongly fortified Japanese hill position, Corporal Hauge boldly took the initiative when his company's left flank was pinned down under a heavy machine-gun and mortar barrage with resultant severe casualties and, quickly locating the two machine guns that were delivering the uninterrupted stream of enfilade fire, ordered his squad to maintain a covering barrage as he rushed across an exposed area toward the furiously blazing enemy weapons. Although painfully wounded as he charged the first machine gun, he launched a vigorous single-handed grenade attack, destroyed the entire hostile gun position, and moved relentlessly forward toward the other emplacement despite the increasingly heavy Japanese fire. Undaunted by the savage opposition, he again hurled his deadly grenades with unerring aim and succeeded in demolishing the second enemy gun before he fell under the slashing fury of Japanese sniper fire. By his ready grasp of the critical situation and his heroic one-man assault tactics, Corporal Hauge eliminated two strategically placed enemy weapons, thereby releasing the besieged troops from an overwhelming volume of hostile fire and enabling his company to advance.

ELBERT LUTHER KINSER, Sergeant U.S. Marine Corps Reserve born October 21, 1922, in Greenville, TN. Taken under sudden, close attack by hostile troops entrenched on the reverse slope while moving up a strategic ridge along which his platoon was holding newly won positions, Sergeant Kinser engaged the enemy in a fierce hand-grenade battle. Quick to act when a Japanese grenade landed in the immediate vicinity, Sergeant Kinser unhesitatingly threw himself on the deadly missile, absorbing the full charge of the shattering explosion in his own body, thereby protecting his men from serious injury and possible death. Stouthearted and indomitable, he yielded his own chance of survival that his comrades might live to carry on a relentless battle against a fanatic enemy.

FRED FAULKNER LESTER, Hospital Apprentice First Class U.S. Navy born April 29, 1926, in Downers Grove, IL. Quick to spot a wounded Marine lying in an open field beyond the front lines following the relentless assault against a strategic Japanese hill position, Lester unhesitatingly crawled toward the casualty under a concentrated barrage from hostile machine guns, rifles, and grenades. Torn by enemy rifle bullets as he inched forward, he stoically disregarded the mounting fury of Japanese fire and his own pain to pull the wounded man toward a covered position. Struck by enemy fire a second time before he reached cover, Lester exerted tremendous effort and succeeded in pulling his comrade to safety where, too seriously wounded himself to administer aid, he instructed two of his squad in proper medical treatment of the rescued Marine. Realizing that his own wounds were fatal, Lester staunchly refused medical attention for himself and, gathering his fast waning strength with calm determination, coolly and expertly directed his men in the treatment of two other wounded Marines, succumbing shortly thereafter himself. Completely selfless in his concern for the welfare of his fighting comrades, Lester, by his indomitable spirit, outstanding valor, and competent direction of others, saved the life of one who otherwise must have perished and contributed to the safety of countless others.

MARTIN O. MAY, Private First Class U.S. Army born April 18, 1922, in Phillipsburg, NJ. May gallantly maintained a three-day stand in the face of terrible odds when American troops fought for possession of the rugged slopes of Legusuku-Yama on Ie Shima, Ryukyu Islands. After placing his heavy machine gun in an advantageous yet vulnerable position on a ridge to support riflemen, he became the target of fierce mortar and small-arms fire from counterattacking Japanese. He repulsed this assault by sweeping the enemy with accurate bursts while explosions and ricocheting bullets threw blinding dust and dirt about him. He broke up a second counterattack by hurling grenades into the midst of the enemy forces and then refused to withdraw, volunteering to maintain his post and cover the movement of American riflemen as they reorganized to meet any further hostile action. The major effort of the enemy did not develop until the morning of April 21, which found Private First Class May still supporting the rifle company in the face of devastating rifle, machine-gun, and mortar fire.

RICHARD MILES MCCOOL, Lieutenant U.S. Navy born January 4, 1922, in Tishomingo, OK. Sharply vigilant during hostile air raids against Allied ships on radar picket duty off Okinawa on June 10, Lieutenant McCool aided materially in evacuating all survivors from a sinking destroyer that had sustained mortal damage under the devastating attacks. When his own craft was attacked simultaneously by two of the enemy's suicide squadron early in the evening of June 11, he instantly hurled the full power of his gun batteries against the plunging aircraft, shooting down the first and damaging the second before it crashed his station in the conning tower and engulfed the immediate area in a mass of flames. Although suffering from shrapnel wounds and painful bums, McCool rallied his concussion-shocked crew and initiated vigorous firefighting measures, then proceeded to the rescue of several trapped in a blazing compartment, subsequently carrying one man to safety despite the excruciating pain of additional severe burns. Unmindful of all personal danger, he continued his efforts without respite until aid arrived from other ships and he was evacuated. By his staunch leadership, capable direction, and indomitable determination throughout the crisis, Lieutenant McCool saved the lives of many who otherwise might have perished and contributed materially to the saving of his ship for further combat service.

ROBERT MILLER MCTUREOUS JR., Private U.S. Marine Corps born March 26, 1924, in Altoona, FL. Alert and ready for any hostile counteraction following his company's seizure of an important hill objective, Private McTureous was quick to observe the plight of company stretcher bearers who were suddenly assailed by slashing machine-gun fire as they attempted to evacuate wounded troops at the rear of the newly won position. Determined to prevent further casualties, he quickly filled his jacket with hand grenades and charged the enemy-occupied caves from which the concentrated barrage was emanating. Coolly disregarding all personal danger as he waged his furious one-man assault, he smashed grenades into the cave entrances, thereby diverting the heaviest fire from the stretcher bearers to his own person and, resolutely returning to his own lines under a blanketing hail of rifle and machine-gun fire to replenish his supply of grenades, dauntlessly continued his systematic reduction of Japanese strength until he himself sustained serious wounds after silencing a large number of the hostile guns. Aware of his own critical condition and unwilling to further endanger the lives of his comrades, he stoically crawled a distance of 200 yards to a sheltered position within friendly lines before calling for aid. By his fearless initiative and bold tactics, Private McTureous succeeded in neutralizing enemy fire, killing six Japanese troops and effectively disorganizing the remainder of the savagely defending garrison.

JOHN MEAGHER, Technical Sergeant U.S. Army born December 5, 1917, in Jersey City, NJ. Meagher mounted an assault tank, and, with bullets splattering about him, designated targets to the gunner. Seeing an enemy soldier carrying an explosive charge dash for the tank treads, Meagher shouted fire orders to the gunner, leaped from the tank, and bayoneted the charging soldier. After he was knocked unconscious and his rifle destroyed, Meagher regained consciousness, secured a machine gun from the tank, and began a furious one-man assault on the enemy. Firing from his hip, moving through vicious crossfire that ripped through his clothing, he charged the nearest pillbox, killing six Japanese. Going on amid the hail of bullets and grenades, he dashed for a second enemy gun, running out of ammunition just as he reached the position. He grasped his empty gun by the barrel and, in a violent onslaught, killed the crew. By his fearless assaults, Technical Sergeant Meagher single-handedly broke the enemy resistance, enabling his platoon to take its objective and continue the advance.

EDWARD J. MOSKALA, Private First Class U.S. Army born November 6, 1921, in Chicago, IL. Moskala was the leading element when grenade explosions and concentrated machine-gun and mortar fire halted the unit's attack on Kakazu Ridge, Okinawa, Ryukyu Islands. With utter disregard for his personal safety, he charged forty yards through withering grazing fire and wiped out two machine-gun nests with well-aimed grenades and deadly accurate fire from his automatic rifle. When strong counterattacks and fierce enemy resistance from other positions forced his company to withdraw, he voluntarily remained behind with eight others to cover the maneuver. Fighting from a critically dangerous position for three hours, he killed more than twenty-five Japanese before following his surviving companions through screening smoke down the face of the ridge to a gorge where it was discovered that one of the group had been left behind wounded. Unhesitatingly, Private Moskala climbed the bullet-swept slope to assist in the rescue and then, returning to lower ground, volunteered to protect other wounded while the bulk of the troops quickly took up more favorable positions. He had saved another casualty and had killed four enemy infiltrators when he was struck and mortally wounded while aiding still another disabled soldier. With gallant initiative, unfaltering courage, and heroic determination to destroy the enemy, Private Moskala gave his life in his complete devotion to his company's mission and his comrades' well-being. His intrepid conduct provided a lasting inspiration for those with whom he served.

JOSEPH E. MULLER, Sergeant U.S. Army born June 23, 1908, in Holyoke, MA. Muller directed men to points where they could cover his attack. Then, through vicious machine-gun and automatic fire, crawling forward alone, he suddenly jumped up, hurled his grenades, charged the enemy, and drove them into the open, where his squad shot them down. Seeing enemy survivors about to man a machine gun, he fired his rifle at pointblank range, hurled himself upon them, and killed them. Before dawn the next day, the enemy counterattacked fiercely to retake the position. Sergeant Muller crawled forward through the flying bullets and explosives, then, leaping to his feet, hurling grenades, and firing his rifle, charged the Japanese and routed them. As Sergeant Muller moved into his foxhole shared with two other men, a lone enemy who had been feigning death threw a grenade. Quickly seeing the danger to his companions, Sergeant Muller threw himself over the grenade and smothered the blast with his body, heroically sacrificing his life to save his comrades.

LEJANDRO R. RENTERIA RUIZ, Private First Class U.S. Army born June 23, 1923, in Loving, NM. When his unit was stopped by a skillfully camouflaged enemy pillbox, Ruiz displayed conspicuous gallantry and intrepidity above and beyond the call of duty. His squad, suddenly brought under a hail of machine-gun fire and a vicious grenade attack, was pinned down. Jumping to his feet, Private First Class Ruiz seized an automatic rifle and lunged through the flying grenades and rifle and automatic fire for the top of the emplacement. When an enemy soldier charged him, Ruiz's rifle jammed. Undaunted, Private Ruiz whirled on his assailant and clubbed him down. Then he ran back through bullets and grenades, seized more ammunition and another automatic rifle, and again made for the pillbox. Enemy fire now was concentrated on him, but he charged on, miraculously reaching the position, and in plain view, he climbed to the top. Leaping from one opening to another, he sent burst after burst into the pillbox, killing twelve of the enemy and completely destroying the position.

ALBERT EARNEST SCHWAB, Private First Class U.S. Marine Corps Reserve born July 17, 1920, in Washington, DC. Quick to take action when his company was pinned down in a valley and suffered resultant heavy casualties under blanketing machine-gun fire emanating from a high ridge to the front, Private First Class Schwab, unable to flank the enemy emplacement because of steep cliffs on either side, advanced up the face of the ridge in bold defiance of the intense barrage and, skillfully directing the fire of his flamethrower, quickly demolished the hostile gun position, thereby enabling his company to occupy the ridge. Suddenly, a second enemy machine gun opened fire, killing and wounding several Marines with its initial bursts. Estimating in a split second the tactical difficulties confronting his comrades, Private Schwab elected to continue his one-man assault despite a diminished supply of fuel for his flamethrower. Cool and indomitable, he moved forward in the face of a direct concentration of hostile fire, relentlessly closed on the enemy position, and attacked. Although severely wounded by a vicious blast from the enemy weapon, Private Schwab had succeeded in destroying two highly strategic Japanese gun positions during a critical stage of the operation and, by his dauntless, single-handed efforts, had materially furthered the advance of his company.

SEYMOUR W. TERRY, Captain U.S. Army born December 11, 1918, in Little Rock, AR. Terry was leading an attack against heavily defended Zebra Hill when devastating fire from five pillboxes halted the advance. He braved the hail of bullets to secure satchel charges and white phosphorus grenades, then ran thirty yards directly at the first enemy stronghold with an ignited charge, demolished the stronghold, and moved on to the other pillboxes, bombarding them with his grenades and calmly cutting down their defenders with rifle fire as they attempted to escape. When he had finished this job by sealing four pillboxes with explosives, he had killed twenty Japanese and destroyed three machine guns.

The advance was again held up by an intense grenade barrage, which inflicted several casualties. Locating the source of enemy fire in trenches on the reverse slope of the hill, First Lieutenant Terry, burdened by six satchel charges, launched a one-man assault. He wrecked the enemy's defenses by throwing explosives into their positions and himself accounted for ten of the twenty hostile troops killed when his men overran the area.

Pressing forward again toward a nearby ridge, Terry's two assault platoons were stopped by slashing machine-gun and mortar fire. Terry fearlessly ran across one hundred yards of fire-swept terrain to join the support platoon and urge it on in a flanking maneuver. This thrust, too, was halted by stubborn resistance. Lieutenant Terry began another one-man drive, hurling grenades upon the strongly entrenched defenders until they fled in confusion, leaving five dead behind them. Inspired by this bold action, the support platoon charged the retreating enemy and annihilated them. Soon afterward, while organizing his company to repulse a possible counterattack, the gallant company commander Terry was mortally wounded by the burst of an enemy mortar shell.

PART IV: THE USS *J. FRANKLIN BELL*, AND HER HISTORY AND DEMISE

I know not with what World War III will be fought, but World War IV will be fought with sticks and stones — **Albert Einstein**

The *J. Franklin Bell* was a Harris-class attack transport ship. She was built in 1921 and served in the merchant service for twenty years. The ship was acquired by the Army in 1940 and transferred to the Navy shortly after Pearl Harbor. The Army renamed the ship *J. Franklin Bell* in honor of the man who was Army chief of staff from 1906 to 1910. General Bell was also a Medal of Honor winner for bravery during the Luzon campaign in the Philippines. (He grew up on a farm just outside Shelbyville, Kentucky, so I was proud to have served on the *J. Franklin Bell* for more than one reason.)

The poem "The Spirit of the *J. Franklin Bell*" by Timothy Churchill expresses the thoughts of all of us who served aboard the *Bell:*

The *Bell* camouflaged to avoid detection by the enemy (Courtesy U.S. Navy)

The Spirit of the *J. Franklin Bell*

I am the spirit of a ship, the USS *J. Franklin Bell,*
I live in the hearts and minds of men;
Men who served on my decks and fired my guns,
And who guided me through troubled waters.

I was born in the time of peace, and calm before the storm;
My decks carried travelers, revelers, and students of the east;
The flag at my mast was red white and blue,
The country I served was a beacon of light for the world.

My mission changed drastically with my nation attacked,
I was filled with combatants and ordered to war;
I was fitted with hardware, munitions and men of steel,
My decks were then trodden by heroes, waiting to die.

There was no glory in war, but my crewmates stood tall,
Defending our nation with courage, determined to win;
They sailed me through storms, battles, torpedoes and bombs,
They gave me more men, with the mission to fight, and for some, to die.

I was brought to the gates of hell, with
troops assaulting the shore,
I scoured the beaches with cannon, and brave men who died;
I met the enemy, with smoke on the water, and fire in the sky.
And I lived to see victory, preserving freedom for my country.

My crewmates have gone now, my guns
are silent; and my engines are still,
And the world is now different, with new
dangers, and different foes;
My decks no longer exist, to support a new crop of heroes,
The memories of what we did will soon be gone ... Forever.

These battles were relived over and over by my shipmates for twenty-one years after Shipmate Chet Maki made the first reunion happen in 1987. I am proud to have hosted three such reunions in Kentucky, and for one, I wish they had not stopped, but age and travel caught up with most shipmates.

Shipmates at tenth reunion in Canton, Ohio

Attendance at last reunion in 2009 in Tyler, Texas

During the reunions, we fought the battles repeatedly, and I detected that the intensity of our many battles increased from year to year—or maybe, like our Kentucky bourbon, they just got better with age. The fact is we were all very young that day in December when the Japanese attacked Pearl Harbor.

People often ask what it was like to serve on board a ship during wartime. Because I was an enlisted man, I cannot describe life for an officer, but it was obvious that officers had more privacy, better meals, and more free time. If we seamen were not on watch (duty station ready for combat), which usually was four hours each day, we had to be ready for General Quarters (manning our battle stations), which always occurred an hour before dusk and again an hour before dawn, when the enemy was most likely to attack. Midnight to 4:00 AM was the most hated period for having to stand watch because after you had just gotten to sleep, it was time for General Quarters. During the day, we worked at whatever duty we had been assigned. For example, I had been assigned to be a gunner's mate, so I worked on cleaning and lubricating guns, chipping paint, and painting the gun emplacements. Salt water enhances corrosion, so chipping and painting were constant chores, as was swabbing decks.

In our free time, we played cards, read books, wrote letters, watched movies when available, which was not too often, or just visited with friends. We were always looking for some reason to have a special event. The one I remember best was crossing the equator. If we had never crossed, we were known as Pollywogs. After crossing, we became Shellbacks, but to become Shellbacks, we had to be initiated into that society. The *J. Franklin Bell* had long canvas funnels that were used to send air belowdecks when we had troops aboard. The Shellbacks saved the garbage for days and filled a funnel laid out on the deck with the garbage, requiring each Pollywog to crawl through the mess. If a Pollywog tried to raise himself up to avoid crawling through the garbage in the funnel, he was hit in the butt with a club by the Shellbacks stationed along the length of the funnel. When the Pollywog finally reached the end of the funnel, he encountered King Neptune—the Shellback with the biggest belly on the ship—sitting on his throne. The Pollywog was required to kiss King Neptune's navel, which was covered with hair recovered from the barber shop and soaked in wintergreen. Our lips burned for days. Also, leading up to the initiation day sailors had to respond to any command given by a shellback.

The officers did not escape this ritual, and in some cases, this was a chance for the enlisted men to get even. Being assign different duties was also part of the initiation. For example, we had an officer who never saw a fog nozzle (the brass control at the end of a water hose) that did not need cleaning, regardless of how many times it had been cleaned or how much it shined, so he was put on a four-hour watch in the crow's nest with two fog nozzles, to scan the horizon, instead of binoculars.

The Shellback ritual was fun and a diversion from the daily routine of life in the middle of the Pacific. Also, sailors just prayed that there would be at least one more crossing of the equator, because now they were Shellbacks.

There was only one galley for the whole ship, and when we were carrying combat troops, the chow lines were endless. I am thankful that the ship's crew had special access and did not have to wait, but I always felt sorry for the Army and Marine troops that we often carried into combat because of the long endless chow lines.

The food was pretty good, but the coffee was terrible, and as a result, most of the divisions, like us in the Ordnance Division, had a hot plate stashed away in a locker and brewed our own coffee.

I had a hard time getting used to navy beans for breakfast but have to admit that after two years, I started looking forward to Wednesday because that was navy bean day.

Our greatest fears were not necessarily the Japanese but the surprise spur-of-the-moment ship inspections. In these inspections, we had to open our lockers, lower our bunks, and wait for the inspection team to pass through our crew quarters. Only those on duty at the time were exempt from the inspection. All kinds of things occurred during the inspections. We had to hide our coffee makers and supplies. Alcohol was not allowed on board for us enlisted men, but one group was occasionally in the process of making home brew in the engine room, where the warm temperatures enhanced the brew time. The group had a scheme whereby they managed to fall in behind the inspection team while carrying their brew and, with a lot of lookouts along the way, made their way back to the engine room undetected.

The crew's quarters were two bunks high, and each had a full-length locker. A shower was centrally located to serve several groups. We almost always had fresh-water showers, but occasionally, we had to put up with saltwater showers. At one of those times, if we had a thunderstorm with rain, the announcement would come over the PA system: "All men desiring a freshwater shower come topside with soap and towel." The troop quarters were different, as they had to sleep in bunks four deep, which provided little space between bunks.

While life on the shipboard presented numerous experiences, some delightful and then on occasion frightening, I once had a terrifying experience that I will never forget. Huelen Watts, a gunner's mate from Cullman, Alabama, was my best friend on board ship. The ammunitions storage room needed painting, and Huelen and I volunteered. Access to the room was by ladder and an elevator that was about four feet square. The purpose of the elevator was to send ammunition for the guns, which were located directly above. We almost always used the elevator rather than the several flights by ladder. On one occasion when I was in the ammunition room by myself, I decided to go topside, so I got in the elevator and reached around the opening to push the button to send the elevator upward. I discovered that someone had bolted down the hatch at the top of the elevator. My first thought was of being crushed against the steel hatch that was bolted down because the normal run stopped about a foot from the top, but then I remembered that a switch on one side of the elevator shaft stopped the upward motion. I could not remember which side, however. To this day, I do not know how I covered all four sides of the elevator with two arms, but I did, and I am surer than ever that it was the result of my Mother's prayers. About forty-five minutes later, a sailor walking by the hatch heard my tapping and opened the hatch. I never again started the elevator without looking up to see daylight.

After Okinawa, the *Bell* headed for Guadalcanal, but en route, the destination was changed to Espiritu Santo.

Then after a stop in Noumea, New Caledonia, the *Bell* was on its way home, only to hit one of the worst storms it had ever experienced. Waves came over the bridge, which was about seventy-five feet from normal waterline. When the bow of the ship would go down into a trough created by the waves, the screws would come out of the water and it was like hitting a brick wall. Someone eating in the galley had to hold his tray with one hand and eat with the other. Two army soldiers who didn't obey the command to avoid topside were washed overboard. Because the storm was so bad they could never be found.

After arriving in San Francisco and unloading passengers, the *Bell* went to Pier 62 for about seven weeks of repair. During this period, word was received, on August 15, 1945, that the Japanese had surrendered. With repairs made, the ship then went to Seattle, where I served on Shore Patrol for a few weeks. In November 1945, I was sent home on home leave and told to report to Louisville, Kentucky to be discharged on December 15; however, when I went to Louisville, they did not have my records, so I was sent home again and told to report back on January 6, 1946. That time, I was discharged from the Navy.

It felt strange to be back to free life, without being ordered to stand watch or have General Quarters every night at dusk and morning at sunrise, free to do my own thing. The most difficult part was the realization that I did not have a home to call my own. With the passing of my mother during the war, my older brother Vernon and his family had moved in to care for my father. I was left without a home, and my oldest brother, Preston, his wife, Florence, and his family of Alice, Preston Jr., and Coleman were about my age and they invited me to move in with them.

It also took time to adjust to all the world changes in 1945, such as the death of President Roosevelt and the swearing in of President Harry S. Truman. The Dow Jones high and low for the year was 195/155, unemployment was at a low of 1.9 percent, and a postage stamp cost only $0.03. One could buy a woman's fur coat for $70.00 and a man's dress shirt for $2.50 The USS *Indianapolis*, which had just delivered parts needed for the atomic bomb to the island of Tinian, was sunk with 883 seamen. Fifty nations signed the United Nations Tablet to create the United Nations. Percy Spencer accidentally discovered that microwaves can heat food, and only about 5000 homes had television.

In the fall of 1945, the USS *J. Franklin Bell* had some changes to adjust to, as well. She was called into service to help move people along the West coast because the surface transportation facilities were inadequate to handle the large increase in movement of people and troops up and down the coast. The proud history of the USS *J. Franklin Bell* included nine battle stars for the Aleutians (with landings at Adak, Attu, and Kiska), Tarawa, Kwajalein, Saipan, Tinian, Leyte, and Okinawa. During the war, the *Bell* had had to dodge torpedoes, outmaneuver bombs, battle strafing planes, and survive friendly fire such as the accidental explosion of the *Mount Hood*. All of this heroic action came to an embarrassing end as the *Bell* on its final journey overshot the pier in San Francisco where a band and a large number of guests were on dock to meet the troops that she was carrying. In every case, when a ship comes into a harbor, a pilot who knows the channel is brought aboard to guide the ship into dock. We, the *Bell's* proud shipmates, take some comfort in that fact and also the local newspaper reported the cause of her overshooting as engine failure.

The USS J. Franklin Bell overshooting the pier in San Francisco

Timothy Churchill describes our feelings about the *J. Franklin Bell* quite well in the following poem.

Farewell Salute to the _Bell_

A Valiant ship we all once knew
"J. Franklin Bell" by name
With battle scars from World War Two
Awash in victory fame.

A ship that served her country well
Composed of steel and men
A ship that sailed right into hell
And lived to fight again.

At last, triumphant, homeward bound
Her brave crew through with war
She suffered one last fateful round
At San Francisco's shore.

Her mission ended suddenly,
With holes ripped in her fore
Her brave crew knew, unhappily
The Bell would sail no more.

Alas, the decades took their toll;
Brave men who sailed _The Bell_
Whose names adorn the Honor Roll
Remember here as well,

But to survivors, we now toast,
J. Franklin Bell be praised,
The memories we all can share,
Once more, with glasses raised.

After this accident, the USS _J. Franklin Bell_ was sent to Suisun Bay, California, and on March 20, 1946, was decommissioned. She was sold for scrap on April 3, 1948, to Boston Metals of Baltimore, Maryland.

Listed below are the commanding officers of the USS *J. Franklin Bell* during the war in the Pacific.

- Captain Herbert J. Grassie, USN, April 2, 1942 to November 2, 1942
- Captain John B. McGovern, USN, November 2, 1942 to October 22, 1943
- Captain Oliver H. Ritchie, USNR, October 22, 1943 to end of war

On August 13, 1943, the commander of amphibious forces, US Pacific Fleet, came aboard the *Bell* to award the Silver Star Medal (the third highest military decoration awarded for gallantry in action against an enemy of the United States) to the following people for their action during the invasion of Attu Island:

- Captain John B. McGovern
- Lieutenant William K. Rummel
- Ensign Charles J. Boyle
- Chief Boatswain's Mate William B. Stanchfield
- Boatswain's Mate First Class Edward A. Salatka
- Boatswain's Mate Second Class Robert E. Hart
- Coxswain Robert H. Sturl
- Seaman First Class Marion L. Williams

On August 19, 1944, the commanding officer, on behalf of the commander in chief of the US Pacific Fleet, presented the Commendation Ribbon for Special Services, for services rendered on Kwajalein Island by scouting the beach under machine-gun fire to determine the conditions of the beach and the Japanese defenses for the invasion, to the following people:

- Ensign Commodore M. Combs
- Seaman First Class Charles W. Mize
- Seaman First Class Leslie W. Schmudlach
- Seaman First Class Kendal P. Cahill
- Seaman First Class Carl B. Carlson
- Radioman First Class Thaddeus K. Kubala
- Motor Machinist's Mate Second Class James E. Belfrage
- Quartermaster Second Class Warren H. DeWitt

By letter from the commander in chief of the US Pacific Fleet, the Commendation Ribbon was awarded to the following for services during the invasion of Saipan and Tinian:

- Lieutenant Jehue R. Connelly
- Chief Boatswain's Mate Edward A. Salatka
- Pharmacist's Mate William C. Hartmann

By letter from the commander of the Third Amphibious Forces for action against the enemy at Leyte Island, a letter of commendation was given to:

- Lieutenant Carl F. Rohleder.

One final story about the *J. Franklin Bell* and a shipmate comes from Susan Walker, the daughter of Shipmate Clark Wierhake. Susan's mother found out that the *Bell* was going to be in San Francisco during the war, so she left Detroit, Michigan, where she had met and fallen in love with Clark, and headed west. When she arrived in San Francisco, she went to the dockside and told the officer of deck to call the captain. When the captain appeared, she told him to call Clark Wierhake because they were getting married. Susan says it was a surprise for her father but that he felt it was the only honorable thing he could do, even though it was a little earlier than he had planned, and especially after all the trouble his bride-to-be had gone to, making it happen.

PART V: THE OTHER FORGOTTEN WARRIORS

They have given their sons to the military services. They have stoked the furnaces and hurried the factory wheels. They have made the planes and welded the tanks. Riveted the ships and rolled the shells. — President Franklin D. Roosevelt (addressing the women's contribution to the war)

It took more than just the soldiers and sailors of the Navy, Army, and Marines to win WWII. This section deals with other warriors who were involved: US women, Coast Guards, Submariners, and Seabees.

US WOMEN OF WORLD WAR II

Before the war, it was generally expected that a working man was the provider for his family. It was thought that any women who took a job was taking it from a man who needed the job to support his family. With so many men away in the services during WWII, however, this approach could not continue. Women were recruited for jobs that had previously been thought to be too physical for women, such as welding, machine repair, and the operation of tractors and other large machines. Women also made uniforms, weapons and ammunition, tanks, planes, and trucks.

During the early part of WWII, all the branches of service established women's auxiliary corps. This included a group known as the Women Airforce Service Pilots

(WASP), which was created in 1943 to ferry planes to stateside locations where male pilots were in short supply. During WWII, 350,000 women served in the military. Sixteen of those were killed in combat. Sixty-seven were captured by the Japanese in 1942 and were held as POWs for two and a half years.

Recruitment of African American women was limited to 10 percent to match the percentage of them in the US population at that time, and a total of 6,520 served during the war. Enlisted basic training was segregated for training, living, and dining.

Asian Pacific American women first entered military service during WWII. The Army lowered the height and weight requirement for this group, and the unit was referred to as the Madame Chiang Kai-Shek Air WAC unit. These women served in a variety of jobs such as aerial photo interpretation, air traffic control, and weather forecasting.

More than 14,000 Navy nurses served stateside, overseas on hospital ships, and as flight nurses during the war. Nursing could be a dangerous job during the war. As the Japanese closed in on Singapore in early 1942, sixty-five nurses were evacuated by ship. The Japanese sank the ship they were on, and twelve nurses were drowned. A group of twenty-two nurses was captured by the Japanese on the Indonesian island of Banka.

They were marched to the waterfront and executed by machine-gun fire.

In 1942, the director of the Women's Bureau, Mary Anderson, reported that about 2,800,000 women were engaged in war work and the number was expected to double by the end of that year. When including all the services, such as the Office of Strategic Services, the American Red Cross, and the United Service Organizations plus the "Rosie the Riveters" in factories, transportation, agriculture, and office work, nearly nineteen million women supported the war effort.

It was interesting to read Denise Kiernan's *The Girls of Atomic City*. The book is about the building of a city in Tennessee for the continued development and building the atomic bomb. I find it almost unimaginable that these young girls in their late teens and early twenties could be trusted to not talk about what they were doing. They did not talk to outsiders or to each other about their work duties. This commitment of silence just had to come from a deep and sincere devotion to their country and the willingness to support the overall war effort to the maximum extent.

Numerous women deserve to be listed as forgotten warriors, but one stands out in my mind from my research of the American Women of WWII for my book. This lady was Ruby Bradley, a career nurse who was serving as a hospital administrator on the island of Luzon in the

Philippines when the Japanese arrived in early 1942. She and another nurse along with a doctor chose to hide out in the hills after the takeover by the Japanese. They were turned over by the locals and sent back to their camp, which had become a prisoner camp. They once again went to attending the sick and injured with little supply of medicines or equipment. Ruby spent more than three years in this camp, trying to comfort the sick and dying. When finally freed, she was down to 84 pounds from 110.

After the war, she earned her bachelor's degree. Then, in 1950, she went to Korea as the 8th Army Chief Nurse. Working at the front lines, she was the last to leave by plane, her ambulance destroyed by enemy shelling as she departed. During her career, Ruby was awarded thirty-four medals and citations, including two Legions of Merit, two Bronze Stars, and a promotion to Army colonel. She was also awarded the Florence Nightingale Medal, the International Red Cross's highest award, by that organization.

Needless to say, WWII changed the lives of most women, and the process is continuing today, with a constant fight for equal pay, promotions, and opportunities. I would guess that it is fair to say the genie is out of the bottle.

THE UNITED STATES SUBMARINE SERVICE

In the year 2000, the United States celebrated its first century with the submarine, which was important to the winning of WWII. Through a design competition, the Navy had given John Holland the contract to build the first submarine—the *Plunger*. In 1900, John Holland again won the competition to build the sixty-four-ton vessel named the USS *Holland,* or SS-1, at a cost of $160,000. It was commissioned on October 12, 1900. Initially, the engines were run on gasoline, but because of the volatility of gas, the engines were soon switched to diesel.

During WWII, the submarine service had the highest casualty percentage of all the armed services. Fifty-two submarines were lost during this period. Some 16,000 personnel served on submarines during the war, of which 375 officers and 3131 enlisted men were killed.

WWII submarines were basically surface ships that could travel for a limited time under water. The air-breathing diesel engines gave them high surface speed and long range, but their speed and range under water were greatly reduced because they had to use electric motors powered by batteries. Recharging the batteries meant surfacing to run the diesels, which was required about 90 percent of the time even on combat patrols.

The USS *Balao*, which was commissioned in February 1943, carried a crew of ten officers and seventy enlisted men, was 312 feet long, carried twenty-four torpedoes, and was equipped with deck guns. The *Balao* had a surface speed of more than twenty miles per hour, and this speed was cut in half when submerged. If her underwater speed was reduced to two knots per hour, she could stay submerged for forty-eight hours.

The submarine service played a significant role in the defeat of the Japanese not only in sinking ships but also in penetrating hostile areas (for picking up aviators who had been shot down by the enemy), extracting Coastwatchers or moving them to different areas, doing reconnaissance for potential invasion sites, and performing many other activities associated with fighting a war that needs covert action.

It was either a stroke of luck or divine intervention that the Japanese commanders who brought destruction to Pearl Harbor ignored the submarine base. They elected to bypass the submarine base, which allowed the United States to keep its most effective warship, the submarine, active in the early stages of WWII. It was the submarine force that carried the load in those early years of the war so the industrial might of the United States could spring into action.

MacArthur saw the value of the submarine in the delivery of personnel and supplies at Corregidor. He used the submarine for special missions more than any other commander did. This did not sit well with some of the submarine commanders, as they felt their mission was to seek and destroy Japanese shipping; however, the experience that submarine crews gained while performing special missions paid huge dividends in the guerrilla and resistance operations throughout the South Pacific.

I have great admiration for the sailors who served in our submarine fleet. The thought of having to talk in whispers and to walk in stockinged feet when in enemy waters to avoid creating a noise that could be detected by the enemy is hard to imagine, and enduring the bone-chilling explosions of depth charges going off nearby while the ship was submerged in enemy waters requires courage and bravery of a special breed. An example of this special breed is illustrated by an event that took place in enemy waters just off the coast of Japan for Sergeant Richard Heuver. He was a tail gunner in a B-29 bomber that had lost all but one engine during a bombing raid over Japan. Below is his story about how the submarine service saved his life and that of his crew mates when they had to ditch their plane:

> A "buddy" Superfort crew guided the troubled crew over a pickup area and the troubled crew bailed out and landed in about a mile-wide area. The last crew member jumped at an elevation on only 800 feet above the water. Within 45 minutes all crew members of the plane were in the submarine.

Another real-life illustration of how engaged the submarine service was during WWII is that the fewer than 2 percent of sailors who served in the Navy sank a total of 214 Japanese ships. This included 4 large aircraft carriers, 4 small aircraft carriers, 1 battleship, 3 heavy cruisers, 8 light cruisers, 43 destroyers, 23 large submarines, and 1,178 merchant ships. These combined represented more than 55 percent of all Japanese ships. The submarine service also strangled the Japanese economy by sinking almost five million tons of imports of material the Japanese needed badly for the war effort. This means that the US submarine service did more than all the others, including Navy surface forces, Navy Air Forces, and US Army Air Corps, combined.

After the war was over, Fleet Admiral Chester W. Nimitz said, "We who survived World War II and were privileged to rejoin our loved ones at home salute those gallant officers and men of our submarines who lost their lives in that long struggle. We shall never forget that it was our submarines that held the lines against the enemy while our fleets replaced losses and repaired wounds." Our wholehearted thanks should go to all submariners, who, along with the pilots who fought at Midway and the troops who conquered the Solomon Island jungles, should all get our praise and thanks. They, above all, should never be put into the category of the forgotten warrior.

THE US COAST GUARD

Coast Guard and Marines on Island of Guam- (Courtesy U.S. Navy Photograph- Public Domain)

Another group that should not be forgotten is our Coast Guard. All too often, this group is thought to be a military agency that protects US borders from outsiders. Nothing could be further from the truth. The Coast Guard played a major role in the march across the Pacific. At the same time, it did patrol the coast of the United States. For example, Seaman Second Class John Cullen received the Legion of Merit for catching the German sabotage team that tried to enter the United States at Amagansett, New York, on June 13, 1942.

The history of the United States Coast Guard goes back to the United States Revenue Service, which was created on August 4, 1790, as part of the Department of Treasury. The US Revenue Cutter Service and the US Life-Saving Service were merged to become the Coast Guard on January 28, 1915, to be a military service and a branch of the armed forces at all times. In 2006, a law was passed stating, "In case of war, and upon the direction of Congress, or [if] the President directs, the Coast Guard shall operate as a service under the Department of the Navy."

Coast Guardsmen watching depth chargers explode (Courtesy U.S. Navy Photograph-Public Domain)

The Coast Guard had numerous ships under its command during WWII, including, twenty-two troopships, twenty amphibious cargo ships, nine APAs, and thirty Edsall-class destroyer escorts. The Edsall-class destroyer escort was used primarily for convoy escorts duty in the Atlantic.

I personally became acquainted with the Coast Guard during the invasion of Tinian in the Mariana Islands. I, along with all the others of the *Bell*'s beach party for this invasion, were transferred to the Coast Guard ship the USS *Cavalier* (APA-37) because the *Bell* was going to be part of the fake landing on the south of Tinian. We of the *J. Franklin Bell* beach party had to go with the landing on the North side of Tinian.

The *Cavalier* was also in our convoy for the invasion of Leyte and it was in the Philippines a little later that she was torpedoed, which resulted in injury to fifty shipmates and damage to the extent that she had to be towed for repairs, but she went on to serve in the Korean and Vietnam Wars.

Several Hollywood movie stars became sailors in the Coast Guard, including Gig Young, Cesar Romero, and Richard Cromwell, who all served in different capacities in the Pacific for several years. During WWII, 214,239 persons, including 12,846 women, served in the Coast Guard. The Coast Guard lost a total of 1,917 sailors, with 574 losing their life in action.

The Coast Guard was involved in many activities during WWII. For example, the Coast Guard sent a team of beach control experts—twenty-one enlisted men and three officers—to China in 1944 to help train the Nationalist Chinese Army in the use of dogs and horses for patrol and counterinsurgency duty. They trained more than 500 Chinese troops.

**Group of Chinese and their Coast Guard Trainers
(Courtesy U.S. Navy Photograph- Public Domain)**

On January 29, 1945, the USS *Serpens* (AK-97), a Coast Guard-manned Liberty ship, exploded off Guadalcanal in the Solomon Islands while loading depth charges. This was the biggest single loss of the war for the Coast Guard and included 193 Coast Guardsmen, 56 Army stevedores, and one US Public Health Service officer.

THE US SEABEES NAVAL CONSTRUCTION BATALLIONS

In the late 1930s, it became evident that the United States was not far from being involved in the war in Europe. With this concern, Congress authorized the expansion of the Naval shore activities. The result was construction projects initiated in the Caribbean and the Central Pacific. At that time, it was Navy policy to award the construction to civilian contractors who employed locals as well as American civilians. Under international law, civilians were encouraged not to resist enemy military attacks. Resistance meant the employees could be executed as guerrillas; therefore, the need for a militarized Naval construction force was obvious.

Rear Admiral Ben Morrell became chief of the Bureau of Yards and Docks in 1937. This office is in charge of the Civil Engineer Corps. On December 28, 1941, he requested specific authority to develop the force. He received authority to do so on January 5, 1942, and the Naval Construction Force was officially named on March

5, 1942. The average age of the men being enlisted was thirty-seven years.

A problem developed immediately over who should command the construction battalions. The Bureau of Naval Personnel objected to the command being given to the Civil Engineer Corps, but Admiral Morrell personally presented this question to the Secretary of the Navy. On March 19, 1942, the Secretary of the Navy gave authority to the Civil Engineer Corps. It has been said that Admiral Morrell's success in achieving this contributed greatly to the success and fame of the Seabees.

The term "Seabees" was created by Frank J. Infrate, who was working as a file clerk at the Naval Air Station, Quonset, Rhode Island. He was known for drawing caricatures of the men in his area, and a Navy lieutenant asked him to draw a Disney-type insignia that would identify and represent this new battalion. After considerable thought, Infrate concluded that the bee would be appropriate because "busy as a bee" was a well-known phrase and bees would not hurt people unless they were bothered first. Infrate gave the bee in the insignia a tommy gun to illustrate its fierce nature. He added the C.E.C. insignia for the Civil Engineer Corps and encircled the logo with a Q for Quonset. The next day, the logo was sent off to Admiral Morrell. The only change made was to switch the Q with a rope, which Admiral Morrell felt tied it to the Navy.

During WWII, the Seabees worked in both the Atlantic and Pacific Theaters. At a cost of $11 billion and many casualties, they constructed more than 400 advanced bases. In the Pacific, this was along three figurative roads: the North Pacific Road through the Aleutians; the Central Pacific Road through the Hawaiian, Marshall, Gilbert, Mariana, and Ryukyu Islands; and the South Pacific Road through the South Sea Islands to Samoa, the Solomons, New Guinea, and the Philippines. All the roads converged on Japan.

Along these three roads, the Seabees constructed 111 major airstrips, 441 piers, 2,558 ammunition magazines, 700 square blocks of warehouses, hospitals to serve 70,000 patients, tanks for the storage of 100,000,000 gallons of gasoline, and housing to serve 1,500,000 men.

All of these accomplishments were not easy, as the Seabees suffered more than 200 combat deaths and earned more than 2,000 Purple Hearts while they were active on four continents and served on more than 300 islands.

The Seabees' first major activity was setting up bases in the Aleutian Islands, with a base at Adak to serve the troops for the battles of Attu and Kiska. Although the United States never pushed toward Japan from this direction, these bases kept the Japanese looking over their shoulders for fear of an attack from that direction.

The road through the South Pacific had to go through steaming jungles toward the Philippines. The first stop was the Society Islands. The Seabees landed on an island in this group called Bora Bora. The code name given to this island for military purpose was BOBCAT, so the Seabees called themselves the Bobcats. They were the advanced party of more than 325,000 men who served in the Naval Construction Force during WWII.

D Ralph Young on Bora Bora (Courtesy D. Ralph Young)

I recently had the opportunity to see some of the gun emplacements on Bora Bora (Society Islands.) and said to myself, "It is not possible to get the guns up here and build the concrete foundations that they sat on at these peaks," but there they were, defying all logic, thanks to the Bobcats.

The purpose of building the facilities on the Society Islands was to have a station that would fuel the ships and planes necessary to keep the shipping lanes open to Australia. After landing on what seemed like a tropical paradise, the Bobcats discovered that they had to deal with continual rainfall, fifty varieties of dysentery, skin disease and the dreaded elephantiasis.

The need to destroy the Japanese airfield nearing completion on Guadalcanal was imperative, but for US troops to destroy that airfield, US planes would need an airfield on Espiritu Santo, the closest island in the New Hebrides to the Japanese-held Guadalcanal. Within an incredible twenty days, the Seabees carved out a 6,000-foot airstrip in a virgin jungle. As a result of this effort, the United States was able to destroy the Japanese air base.

When the Marines landed on Guadalcanal, the Seabees followed them ashore and became the first Seabees to build under combat conditions. The Seabees then began repairing the airfield that their effort had just permitted the United States to destroy. This airfield became known as Henderson Field, after the Marine pilot lost at Midway, and the Japanese tried many times to retake it but were repulsed on every attempt. The Seabees had to work continuously at repairing this airstrip because the Japanese kept bombing it, but, the Seabees managed to keep it open, which was critical to the success of the Guadalcanal invasion.

The Seabees continued their march across the Pacific, often landing with the invasion force and setting up construction projects within hours after the initial invasion, as at Tarawa in the Gilbert Islands; Kwajalein, Eniwetok, and Majuro in the Marshall Islands, and Saipan, Tinian, and Guam in the Mariana Islands.

It was at Henderson Field that the first decorated hero of the Seabees was named: Seaman Second Class Lawrence C. "Bucky" Meyer, USNR. He salvaged an abandoned machine gun and used it to shoot down a Japanese Zero that was strafing his area. He was awarded the Silver Star posthumously because he was killed thirteen days later when Japanese naval gunfire hit a gasoline barge on which he was working.

Another act of heroism occurred on the landing on Treasury Island in the Solomons. Fireman First Class Aurelio Tassone, USNR, was driving his bulldozer ashore when he was told by a Lieutenant Turnbull that a Japanese pillbox was holding up their advance. Tassone drove his dozer toward the pillbox with blade up as a shield while the lieutenant provided cover fire with his carbine. The result was that all twelve occupants of the pillbox were killed. For this, Tassone received the Silver Star.

Although the Seabees were expected to fight only to defend what they had built, throughout WWII, they were awarded thirty-three Silver Stars and five Navy Crosses. They lost 272 enlisted men and 18 officers killed in action during the war. An additional 500 Seabees died in construction accidents.

When you stop for a moment to think about all the troops, ships, and aircraft in the Pacific and Atlantic Theaters having to be maintained and supplied with provisions to keep them in fighting shape, you realize just how important the Seabees were to wining WWII.

CONGRESSIONAL MEDAL OF HONOR HEROES OF THE PACIFIC

THE BATTLE OF BUNA

I choose not to answer the questions of what, where, when and why on the following battles: of Buna, New Guinea, New Georgia and Savo Island. However, since each battle had Medal of Honors awarded, I have included a very brief statement describing each. This provides me with a reason to look toward a first revision where I can add the details for these battles and correct any mistakes brought to my attention in the original version.

The Battle of Buna was part of the New Guinea campaign in the Pacific Theater. The following troops were awarded the Medal of Honor. (Citations for each are noted in References.)

ELMER J. BURR, First Sergeant U.S. Army born in Neenah, WI. During an attack near Buna, New Guinea, on 24 December 1942, First Sergeant Burr saw an enemy grenade strike near his company commander. Instantly and with heroic self-sacrifice, he threw himself upon it, smothering the explosion with his body. First Sergeant Burr thus gave his life in saving that of his commander.

KENNETH E. GRUENNERT. Sergeant U.S. Army born Helenville, WI Gruennert was second in command of a platoon with a mission to drive through the enemy lines to the beach 600 yards ahead. Within 150 yards of the objective, the platoon encountered two hostile pillboxes. Sergeant Gruennert advanced alone on the first and put it out of action with hand grenades and rifle fire, killing three of the enemy. Seriously wounded in the shoulder, he bandaged his wound under cover of the pillbox, refusing to withdraw to the aid station and leave his men. He then, with undiminished daring and under extremely heavy fire, attacked the second pillbox. As he neared it, he threw grenades, which forced the enemy out where they were easy targets for his platoon. Before the leading elements of his platoon could reach him, Gruennert was shot by enemy snipers.

THE BATTLE FOR NEW GUINEA

The struggle for New Guinea began with the capture of Rabaul at the northeastern tip of New Britain Island by the Japanese. This campaign lasted from early 1942 until the end of the war in August 1945. The following troops were awarded the Medal of Honor during this period. (Citations for each are noted in References.)

GEORGE W. G. BOYCE, JR. Second Lieutenant U.S. Army born in New York City, NY. Second Lieutenant Boyce's troop, having been ordered to the relief of another unit surrounded by superior enemy forces, moved out, and upon gaining contact with the enemy, the two leading platoons deployed and built up a firing line. Second Lieutenant Boyce was ordered to attack with his platoon and make the main effort on the right of the troop. He launched his attack but after a short advance encountered such intense rifle, machine-gun, and mortar fire that the forward movement of his platoon was temporarily halted. A shallow depression offered a route of advance, and he worked his squad up this avenue of approach in order to close with the enemy. He was promptly met by a volley of hand grenades, one falling between him and the men immediately following. Realizing at once that the explosion would kill or wound several of his men, he promptly threw himself upon the grenade and smothered the blast with his own body.

DALE ELDON CHRISTENSEN, Second Lieutenant U.S. Army born in Cameron Township, IA. Second Lieutenant Christensen's platoon engaged in a savage firefight in which much damage was caused by one enemy machine gun effectively placed. Second Lieutenant Christensen ordered his men to remain under cover, crept forward under fire, and, at a range of fifteen yards, put the gun out of action with hand grenades. In another incident, while attacking an enemy position strong in mortars and machine guns, Christensen's platoon was pinned to the ground by intense fire. Ordering his men to remain under cover, Lieutenant Christensen crept forward alone to locate definitely the enemy automatic weapons and the best direction from which to attack. Although his rifle was struck by enemy fire and knocked from his hands, Christensen continued his reconnaissance, located five enemy machine guns, destroyed one machine gun with hand grenades, and rejoined his platoon. He then led his men to the point selected for launching the attack and, calling encouragement, led the charge. This assault was successful and the enemy were driven from their positions with a loss of four mortars, ten machine guns, and many dead left on the field.

On August 4, 1944, near Afua, Dutch New Guinea, Second Lieutenant Christensen was killed in action about two yards from his objective while leading his platoon in an attack on an enemy machine-gun position.

GERALD L. ENDL, Staff Sergeant U.S. Army born in Fort Atkinson, WI. Staff Sergeant Endl was at the head of the leading platoon of his company, advancing along a jungle trail, when enemy troops were encountered and a firefight developed. The enemy attacked in force under heavy rifle, machine-gun, and grenade fire. When his platoon leader was wounded, Sergeant Endl immediately assumed command and deployed his platoon on a firing line at the fork in the trail toward which the enemy attack was directed. The dense jungle terrain greatly restricted vision and movement, and he endeavored to penetrate down the trail toward an open clearing of kunai grass. As he advanced, he detected the enemy, which was supported by at least six light and two heavy machine guns, attempting an enveloping movement around both flanks. Sergeant Endl's commanding officer sent a second platoon to move up on the left flank of the position, but the enemy closed in rapidly, placing US forces in imminent danger of being isolated and annihilated. Twelve members of Endl's platoon were wounded, seven being cut off by the enemy. Realizing that if his platoon were forced farther back, these seven men would be hopelessly trapped and at the mercy of a vicious enemy, Endl resolved to advance at all costs, knowing it meant almost certain death, in an effort to rescue his comrades. In the face of extremely heavy fire, he went forward alone and, for approximately ten minutes, engaged the enemy in a heroic close-range fight, holding them off while his men crawled forward under cover to evacuate the wounded and to withdraw. Courageously refusing to abandon four more wounded men who were lying along the trail, Sergeant Endl brought them back to safety, one by one. As he was carrying the last man in his arms, he was struck by a heavy burst of automatic fire and was killed.

RAY E. EUBANKS, Sergeant U.S. Army born February 6, 1922, in Snow Hill, NC. While moving to the relief of a platoon isolated by the enemy, Eubanks's company encountered a strong enemy position supported by machine-gun, rifle, and mortar fire. Sergeant Eubanks was ordered to make an attack with one squad to neutralize the enemy by fire in order to assist the advance of his company. He maneuvered his squad to within thirty yards of the enemy, where heavy fire checked his advance. Directing his men to maintain their fire, he and two scouts worked their way forward up a shallow depression to within twenty-five yards of the enemy. Directing the scouts to remain in place, Sergeant Eubanks armed himself with an automatic rifle and worked himself forward over terrain swept by intense fire to within fifteen yards of the enemy position, then opened fire with telling effect. The enemy, having located his position, concentrated their fire, with the result that he was wounded and a bullet rendered his rifle useless. In spite of his painful wounds, Sergeant Eubanks immediately charged the enemy and, using his weapon as a club, killed four of the enemy before he was himself again hit and killed.

JOHNNIE DAVID HUTCHINS, Seaman First Class U.S. Navy Reserve born August 4, 1922, in Weimer, TX. As the ship on which Hutchins was stationed approached the enemy-occupied beach under a veritable hail of fire from Japanese shore batteries and aerial bombardment, a hostile torpedo pierced the surf and bore down upon the vessel with deadly accuracy. In the tense split seconds before the helmsman could steer clear of the threatening missile, a bomb struck the pilot house, dislodged him from his station, and left the stricken ship helplessly exposed. Fully aware of the dire peril of the situation, Hutchins, although mortally wounded by the shattering explosion, quickly grasped the wheel and exhausted the last of his strength in maneuvering the vessel clear of the advancing torpedo. Still clinging to the helm, he eventually succumbed to his injuries, his final thoughts concerned only with the safety of his ship, his final efforts expended toward the security of his mission.

NEEL E. KEARBY, Colonel U.S. Army Air Corps born in Wichita Falls, TX. Colonel Kearby volunteered to lead a flight of four fighters to reconnoiter the strongly defended enemy base at Wewak. Having observed enemy installations and reinforcements at four airfields and secured important tactical information, he saw an enemy fighter below him, made a diving attack, and shot it down in flames. His small formation then sighted approximately twelve enemy bombers accompanied by thirty-six fighters. Although his mission had been completed, his fuel was running low, and the numerical odds were twelve to one, he gave the signal to attack. Diving into the midst of the enemy airplanes, Colonel Kearby shot down three in quick succession. Observing one of his comrades with two enemy fighters in pursuit, he destroyed both enemy aircraft. The enemy broke off in large numbers to make a multiple attack on Kearby's airplane, but despite his peril, he made one more pass before seeking cloud protection. Coming into the clear, he called his flight together and led them to a friendly base. Colonel Kearby brought down six enemy aircraft in this action, undertaken with superb daring after his mission was completed.

DONALD R. LOGAUGH, Private U.S. Army born in Freeport, PA. While Private Lobaugh's company was withdrawing from its position on July 21, the enemy attacked and cut off approximately one platoon of American troops. The platoon immediately occupied, organized, and defended a position, which it held throughout the night. Early on July 22, an attempt was made to effect its withdrawal, but during the preparation, the enemy emplaced a machine gun, protected by the fire of rifles and automatic weapons, which blocked the only route over which the platoon could move. Knowing that the route was the key to the enemy position, Private First Class Lobaugh volunteered to attempt to destroy this weapon, even though to reach it, he would be forced to work his way over about 30 yards of ground devoid of cover. When partway across this open space, Private Lobaugh threw a hand grenade but exposed himself in the act and was wounded. Heedless of his wound, he boldly rushed the emplacement, firing as he advanced. The enemy concentrated fire on him, and he was struck repeatedly, but he continued his attack and killed two before he was slain. Private Lobaugh's heroic actions inspired his comrades to press the attack and to drive the enemy from the position.

JUNIOR VAN NOY, Private U.S. Army born in Grace, ID. When wounded late in September, Private Van Noy declined evacuation and continued on duty. On October 17, 1943, he was gunner in charge of a machine-gun post only five yards from the water's edge when the alarm was given that three enemy barges loaded with troops were approaching the beach in the early morning darkness. One landing barge was sunk by Allied fire, but the other two beached ten yards from Private Van Noy's emplacement. Despite his exposed position, Va Noy poured a withering hail of fire into the debarking enemy troops. His loader was wounded by a grenade and evacuated. Private Van Noy, also grievously wounded, remained at his post, ignoring calls of nearby soldiers urging him to withdraw, and continued to fire with deadly accuracy. He expended every round and was found, covered with wounds, dead beside his gun. In this action, Private Van Noy killed at least half of the thirty-nine enemy troops taking part in the landing.

THE BATTLE FOR NEW GEORGIA

The New Georgia Campaign was a series of land and naval battles of the Pacific Theater. The Japanese had captured New Georgia in 1942 and had built an air base at Munda Point. In recapturing these islands, the following troops were awarded the Medal of Honor. (Citations for each are noted in References.)

FRANK J. PETRARCA, Private First Class U.S. Army born in Cleveland, OH. Private First Class Petrarca advanced with the leading troop element to within one hundred yards of the enemy fortifications, where mortar and small-arms fire had caused a number of casualties. Singling out the most seriously wounded, he worked his way to the aid of Private First Class Scott, lying within seventy-five yards of the enemy, whose wounds were so serious that he could not even be moved out of the direct line of fire. Private Petrarca fearlessly administered first aid to Private Scott and two other soldiers and shielded the former until Scott's death. On July 29, 1943, Private Petrarca, during an intense mortar barrage, went to the aid of his sergeant, who had been partly buried in a foxhole under the debris of a shell explosion, dug the sergeant out, restored the sergeant to consciousness, and caused his evacuation. On July 31, 1943, against the warning of a fellow soldier, Private Petrarca went to the aid of a mortar fragment casualty, where his path over the crest of a hill exposed him to enemy observation from only twenty yards' distance. A target for intense knee-mortar and automatic fire, he resolutely worked his way to within two yards of his objective, where he was mortally wounded by hostile mortar fire. Even on the threshold of death, Petrarca continued to display valor, and contempt for the foe; raising himself to his knees, this intrepid soldier shouted defiance at the enemy, made a last attempt to reach his wounded comrade, and fell in glorious death.

ROBERT S. SCOTT, Captain U.S. Army born in Washington, DC. After twenty-seven days of bitter fighting, the enemy held a hilltop salient that commanded the approach to Munda Airstrip. The American troops were exhausted from prolonged battle and heavy casualties, but Lieutenant Scott advanced with the leading platoon of his company to attack the enemy position, urging his men forward in the face of enemy rifle and machine-gun fire. He had pushed forward alone to a point midway across the barren hilltop within seventy-five yards of the enemy when the enemy launched a desperate counterattack, which, if successful, would have gained undisputed possession of the hill. Enemy riflemen charged out on the plateau, firing and throwing grenades as they moved to engage US troops. The company withdrew, but Lieutenant Scott, with only a blasted tree stump for cover, stood his ground against the wild enemy assault. By firing his carbine and throwing the grenades in his possession, he momentarily stopped the enemy advance, using the brief respite to obtain more grenades. Disregarding small-arms fire and exploding grenades aimed at him, and suffering a bullet wound in the left hand and a painful shrapnel wound in the head after his carbine had been shot from his hand, he threw grenade after grenade with devastating accuracy until the beaten enemy withdrew. US troops, inspired to renewed effort by Lieutenant Scott's intrepid stand and incomparable courage, swept across the plateau to capture the hill.

RODGER W. YOUNG, Private U.S. Army born in Tiffin, OH. On July 31, 1943, the infantry company of which Private Young was a member was ordered to make a limited withdrawal from the battle line to adjust the battalion's position for the night. Private Young's platoon was engaged with the enemy in a dense jungle where observation was very limited. The platoon suddenly was pinned down by intense fire from a Japanese machine gun concealed on higher ground only seventy-five yards away. The initial burst wounded Private Young. As the platoon started to obey the order to withdraw, Young called out that he could see the enemy emplacement, whereupon he started creeping toward it. Another burst from the machine gun wounded him a second time. Despite the wounds, he continued his heroic advance, attracting enemy fire and answering with rifle fire. When he was close enough to his objective, he began throwing hand grenades and while doing so was hit again and killed. Private Young's bold action in closing with this Japanese pillbox and thus diverting its fire permitted his platoon to disengage itself without loss and was responsible for several enemy casualties.

THE BATTLE OF SAVO ISLAND

The Battle of Savo Island was a naval battle of the Pacific Campaign. The battle took place in August 1942 and was the first major naval engagement of the Guadalcanal Campaign. It was the first of several battles in the straits later named Ironbottom Sound as a result of so many ships being sunk in this vicinity. The battle has also been cited as the worst defeat in the history of the US Navy. The Japanese sank three US cruisers and one Australian cruiser with only light damages in return. The following men were awarded the Medal of Honor for action during this battle. (Citations for each are noted in References.)

DANIEL JUDSON CALLAGHAN, Rear Admiral U.S. Navy, born July 26, 1982, in San Francisco, CA. Although out-balanced in strength and numbers by a desperate and determined enemy, Rear Admiral Callaghan, with ingenious tactical skill and superb coordination of the units under his command, led his forces into battle against tremendous odds, thereby contributing decisively to the routing of a powerful invasion fleet and to the consequent frustration of a formidable Japanese offensive. While faithfully directing close-range operations in the face of furious bombardment by superior enemy fire power, he was killed on the bridge of his flagship.

BRUCE MCCANDLESS, Commander U.S Navy born August 12, 1911, in Washington, DC. In what is referred to as the Third and Fourth Battles of Savo Island, November 12-13, 1942. In the midst of a violent night engagement, the fire of a determined and desperate enemy seriously wounded Lieutenant Commander McCandless, rendering him unconscious, and killed or wounded the admiral in command, the admiral's staff, the captain of the ship, the navigator, and all other personnel on the navigating and signal bridges. Faced with the lack of superior command upon his recovery, and displaying superb initiative, McCandless promptly assumed command of the ship and ordered her course and gunfire against an overwhelmingly powerful force. With his superiors in other vessels unaware of the loss of their admiral, and challenged by his great responsibility, Lieutenant Commander McCandless boldly continued to engage the enemy and to lead a column of following vessels to a great victory. Largely through McCandless's brilliant seamanship and great courage, his ship, the *San Francisco*, was brought back to port, saved to fight again in the service of her country.

HERBERT EMERY SCHONLAND, Commander U.S. Navy born September 7, 1900, in Portland, ME. In what is referred to as the Third and Fourth Battles of Savo Island, November 12-13, 1942. In the midst of a violent night engagement in which all of his superior officers were killed or wounded, Lieutenant Commander Schonland was fighting valiantly to free the *San Francisco* of large quantities of water flooding the second-deck compartments through numerous shell holes caused by enemy fire. Upon being informed that he was commanding officer, he ascertained that the conning of the ship was being efficiently handled, then directed the officer who had taken over that task to continue while he himself resumed the vitally important work of maintaining the stability of the ship. In water waist deep, he carried on his efforts in darkness illuminated only by hand lanterns until water in flooded compartments had been drained or pumped off and watertight integrity had again been restored to the ship. His great personal valor and gallant devotion to duty at great peril to his own life were instrumental in bringing his ship back to port under her own power, saved to fight again in the service of her country.

HEROES OF THE PACIFIC NOT INCLUDED IN ANY OF THE ABOVE BATTLES

(Citations for each are noted in References.)

RICHARD NOTT ANTRIM, born December 17, 1907, in Peru, IN. Acting instantly on behalf of a naval officer who was subjected to a vicious clubbing by a frenzied Japanese guard venting his insane wrath upon the helpless prisoner, Commander (then Lieutenant) Antrim boldly intervened, attempting to quiet the guard and finally persuading him to discuss the charges against the officer. With the entire Japanese force assembled and making extraordinary preparations for the threatened beating, and with the tension heightened by 2,700 Allied prisoners rapidly closing in, Commander Antrim courageously appealed to the fanatic enemy, risking his own life in a desperate effort to mitigate the punishment. When the officer had been beaten unconscious by fifteen blows of a hawser and was repeatedly kicked by three soldiers to a point beyond which he could not survive, Antrim gallantly stepped forward and indicated to the perplexed guards that he would take the remainder of the punishment, throwing the Japanese completely off-balance in their amazement and eliciting a roar of acclaim from the suddenly inspired Allied prisoners. By his fearless leadership and valiant concern for the welfare of another, Antrim not only saved the life of a fellow officer and stunned the Japanese into sparing his own life but also brought about a new respect for American officers and men and a great improvement in camp living conditions.

JOHN DUNCAN BULKELEY, born August 19, 1911, in New York, NY. The remarkable achievement of Lieutenant Commander Bulkeley's command in damaging or destroying a notable number of Japanese enemy planes, surface combatant, and merchant ships, and in dispersing landing parties and land-based enemy forces during the four months and eight days of operation, without benefit of repairs, overhaul, or maintenance facilities for his squadron, is believed to be without precedent in this type of warfare. His dynamic forcefulness and daring in offensive action, and his brilliantly planned and skillfully executed attacks, supplemented by a unique resourcefulness and ingenuity, characterize him as an outstanding leader of men and a gallant and intrepid seaman.

GEORGE HAM CANNON, born November 5, 1915, in Webster Groves, MO. First Lieutenant Cannon was at his command post when he was mortally wounded by enemy shellfire. He refused to be evacuated from his post until after his men who had been wounded by the same shell were evacuated, and he directed the reorganization of his command post until forcibly removed. As a result of his utter disregard of his own condition, he died from loss of blood.

HORACE S. CARSWELL JR. Major U.S. Airforce born July 18, !916 Fort Worth, TX. Carswell piloted a bomber in a one-plane strike against a Japanese convoy in the South China Sea on the night of October 26, 1944. Taking the enemy force of twelve ships escorted by at least two destroyers by surprise, Carswell made one bombing run at 600 feet, scoring a near miss on one warship and escaping without drawing fire. He circled and, fully realizing that the convoy was thoroughly alerted and would meet his next attack with a barrage of antiaircraft fire, began a second low-level run, which culminated in two direct hits on a large tanker. A hail of steel from Japanese guns riddled Carswell's bomber, knocking out two engines, damaging a third engine, crippling the hydraulic system, puncturing one gasoline tank, ripping uncounted holes in the aircraft, and wounding the copilot, but by magnificent display of flying skill, Major Carswell controlled the plane's plunge toward the sea and carefully forced it into a halting climb in the direction of the Chinese shore. Upon flying over land, where it would have been possible to abandon the staggering bomber, one of the crew discovered that his parachute had been ripped by flak and rendered useless; Major Carswell, hoping to cross mountainous terrain and reach a base, continued onward until the third engine failed. He ordered the crew to bail out while he struggled to maintain altitude and, refusing to save himself, chose to remain with his comrade and attempt a crash landing. He died when the airplane struck a mountainside and burned. With consummate gallantry and intrepidity, Major Carswell gave his life in a supreme effort to save all members of his crew.

HENRY TALMAGE ELROD, Captain U.S. Marine Corps born September 27, 1905, in Rebecca, GA. Engaging vastly superior forces of enemy bombers and warships on December 12, 1941 at Wake Island, Captain Elrod shot down two of a flight of twenty-two hostile planes and, executing repeated bombing and strafing runs at extremely low altitude and close range, succeeded in inflicting deadly damage upon a large Japanese vessel, thereby sinking the first major warship to be destroyed by small-caliber bombs delivered from a fighter-type aircraft. When his plane was disabled by hostile fire and no other ships were operative, Captain Elrod assumed command of one flank of the line set up in defiance of the enemy landing and, conducting a brilliant defense, enabled his men to hold their positions and to repulse intense hostile fusillades to provide covering fire for unarmed ammunition carriers. Capturing an automatic weapon during one enemy rush in force, he gave his own firearm to one of his men and fought on vigorously against the Japanese. Responsible in a large measure for the strength of his sector's gallant resistance, on December 23 a few days later, Captain Elrod led his men with bold aggressiveness until he fell, mortally wounded.

ERNEST EDWIN EVANS, Commander U.S. Navy born August 13, 1908, in Pawnee, OK. The first to lay a smokescreen from his Destroyer (DD 557) and to open fire as an enemy task force vastly superior in number, firepower, and armor rapidly approached, Commander Evans gallantly diverted the powerful blasts of hostile guns from the lightly armed and armored carriers under his protection, launching when the USS *Johnston* came under straddling Japanese shellfire. Undaunted by damage sustained under the terrific volume of fire, he unhesitatingly joined others of his group to provide fire support during subsequent torpedo attacks against the Japanese and, outshooting and outmaneuvering the enemy as he consistently interposed his vessel between the hostile fleet units and US carriers despite the crippling loss of engine power and communications with steering aft, shifted command to the fantail, shouted steering orders through an open hatch to men turning the rudder by hand, and battled furiously until the *Johnston*, burning and shuddering from a mortal blow, lay dead in the water after three hours of fierce combat.

EUGENE BENNETT FLUCKEY. Rear Admiral U.S. Navy born October 5, 1913, in Washington, D.C. Admiral Fluckey was commanding officer of the USS *Barb* during her eleventh war patrol along the east coast of China from December 19, 1944, to February 15, 1945 and sank a large enemy ammunition ship and damaged additional tonnage during a running two-hour night battle on January 8. On January 25, Commander Fluckey, in an exceptional feat of brilliant deduction and bold tracking, located a concentration of more than thirty enemy ships in the lower reaches of Nankuan Chiang (Mamkwan Harbor). Fully aware that a safe retirement would necessitate an hour's run at full speed through the mined and rock-obstructed waters, he bravely ordered, "Battle station—torpedoes!" In a daring penetration of the heavy enemy screen, and riding in five fathoms of water, he launched the *Barb's* last forward torpedoes at a range of 3,000 yards. Quickly bringing the ship's stem tubes to bear, he turned loose four more torpedoes onto the enemy, obtaining eight direct hits on six of the main targets to explode a large ammunition ship and cause inestimable damage by the resultant flying shells and other pyrotechnics. Clearing the treacherous area at high speed, he brought the *Barb* through to safety and four days later sank a large Japanese freighter to complete a record of heroic combat achievement.

DONALD ARTHUR GARY, Lieutenant Junior Grade U.S. Navy born July 23, 1903, in Findlay, OH. Stationed on the third deck when his ship was rocked by a series of violent explosions set off in her own bombs, rockets, and ammunition by an attack, Lieutenant Gary unhesitatingly risked his life to assist several hundred men trapped in a messing compartment filled with smoke and with no apparent egress. As the imperiled men belowdecks became increasingly panic-stricken under the raging fury of incessant explosions, Lieutenant Gary confidently assured them that he would find a means of effecting their release and, groping through the dark, debris-filled corridors, ultimately discovered an escape. Staunchly determined, he struggled back to the messing compartment three times despite menacing flames, flooding water, and the ominous threat of sudden additional explosions, on each occasion calmly leading his men through the blanketing smoke, until the last one had been saved. Selfless in his concern for his ship and his fellows, he constantly rallied others about him, repeatedly organized and led firefighting parties into the blazing inferno on the flight deck, and, when fire rooms one and two were found to be inoperable, entered the third fire room and directed the raising of steam in one boiler in the face of extreme difficulty and hazard—an inspiring and courageous leader.

NATHAN GREEN GORDON, Lieutenant U.S. Navy born September 4, 1916, in Morrilton, AR. Gordon was commander of a Catalina patrol plane rescuing personnel of the US Army 5th Air Force shot down in combat over Kavieng Harbor in the Bismarck Sea on February 15, 1944. On air alert in the vicinity of Vitu Islands, Lieutenant [then Lieutenant (junior grade)] Gordon unhesitatingly responded to a report of the crash and flew boldly into the harbor, defying close-range fire from enemy shore guns to make three separate landings in full view of the Japanese and pick up nine men, several of them injured. With his cumbersome flying boat dangerously overloaded, he made a brilliant takeoff despite heavy swells and almost total absence of wind and set a course for base, only to receive the report of another group stranded in a rubber life raft 600 yards from the enemy shore. Promptly turning back, he again risked his life to set his plane down under direct fire of the heaviest defenses of Kavieng and take aboard six more survivors, coolly making his fourth dexterous takeoff with fifteen rescued officers and men. By his exceptional daring, personal valor, and incomparable airmanship under the most perilous conditions, Lieutenant Gordon prevented certain death or capture of American airmen by the Japanese.

OWEN FRANCIS PATRICK HAMMERBERG, Private U.S. Army born May 31, 1920, in Daggett, MI. Hammerberg was a diver engaged in rescue operations at West Loch. Two fellow divers were hopelessly trapped in a cave-in of steel wreckage while tunneling with jet nozzles under an LST sunk in forty feet of water and twenty feet of mud. Hammerberg unhesitatingly went overboard in a valiant attempt to affect their rescue despite the certain hazard of additional cave-ins and the risk of fouling his lifeline on jagged pieces of steel imbedded in the shifting mud. Washing a passage through the original excavation, Hammerberg reached the first of the trapped men, freed him from the wreckage, and, working desperately in pitch-black darkness, finally effected the man's release from fouled lines, thereby enabling him to reach the surface. Wearied but undaunted after several hours of arduous labor, Hammerberg resolved to continue his struggle to wash through the oozing submarine and subterranean mud in a determined effort to save the second diver. Venturing still farther under the buried hulk, he held tenaciously to his purpose, reaching a place immediately above the other man just as another cave-in occurred and a heavy piece of steel pinned him crosswise over his shipmate in a position that protected the man beneath from further injury while placing the full brunt of terrific pressure on Hammerberg. Although he succumbed in agony eighteen hours after he had gone to the aid of his fellow divers, Hammerberg, by his cool judgment, unfaltering professional skill, and consistent disregard of all personal danger in the face of tremendous odds, contributed effectively to the saving of his two comrades.

DAVID MCCAMPBELL, Lieutenant U.S. Navy born January 16, 1910, in Bessemer, AL. Commander McCampbell, during combat against Japanese aerial forces in the First and Second Battles of the Philippine Sea, was an inspiring leader fighting boldly in the face of terrific odds. He led his fighter planes against a force of eighty Japanese carrier-based aircraft bearing down on the American fleet on June 19, 1944. Striking fiercely in valiant defense of the US surface force, he personally destroyed seven hostile planes during this single engagement in which the outnumbering attack force was utterly routed and virtually annihilated.

During a major fleet engagement with the enemy on October 24, Commander McCampbell, assisted by only one plane, intercepted and daringly attacked a formation of sixty hostile land-based craft approaching our forces. Fighting desperately but with superb skill against such overwhelming airpower, he shot down nine Japanese planes and, completely disorganizing the enemy group, forced the remainder to abandon the attack before a single enemy aircraft could reach the fleet. His great personal valor and indomitable spirit of aggression under extremely perilous combat conditions reflect the highest credit upon Commander McCampbell and the US Naval Service.

JOSEPH TIMOTHY O'CALLAHAN, Commander (Chaplain Corps) U.S. Navy Reserves born May 14, 1904, in Boston,

MA. O'Callahan was chaplain on board the USS *Franklin* when that vessel was fiercely attacked by enemy Japanese aircraft during offensive operations near Kobe, Japan, on March 19, 1945. A valiant and forceful leader, calmly braving the perilous barriers of flame and twisted metal to aid his men and his ship, Lieutenant Commander O'Callahan groped his way through smoke-filled corridors to the open flight deck and into the midst of violently exploding bombs, shells, rockets, and other armament. With the ship rocked by incessant explosions, with debris and fragments raining down and fires raging in ever-increasing fury, he ministered to the wounded and dying, comforting and encouraging men of all faiths; organized and led firefighting crews into the blazing inferno on the flight deck; directed the jettisoning of live ammunition and the flooding of the magazine; and manned a hose to cool hot armed bombs rolling dangerously on the listing deck, continuing his efforts despite searing, suffocating smoke that forced men to fall back gasping and that imperiled others who replaced them. Serving with courage, fortitude, and deep spiritual strength, Lieutenant Commander O'Callahan inspired the gallant officers and men of the *Franklin* to fight heroically and with profound faith in the face of almost certain death and to return their stricken ship to port.

EDWARD HENRY O'HARE, Lieutenant U.S. Navy born March 13, 1914, in St. Louis, MO. As section leader and pilot of Fighting Squadron Three on February 20, 1942, having lost the assistance of his teammates, Lieutenant O'Hare interposed his plane between his ship and an advancing enemy formation of nine attacking twin-engine heavy bombers. Without hesitation, alone and unaided, he repeatedly attacked this enemy formation at close range in the face of intense combined machine-gun and cannon fire. Despite this concentrated opposition, Lieutenant O'Hare, by his gallant and courageous action and his extremely skillful marksmanship in making the most of every shot of his limited amount of ammunition, shot down five enemy bombers and severely damaged a sixth before they reached the bomb-release point. As a result of his gallant action—one of the most daring, if not *the* most daring, single action in the history of combat aviation—he undoubtedly saved his carrier from serious damage.

OSCAR VERNER PETERSON, Chief Watertender U.S. Navy born August 27, 1899, in Prentice, WI. During an attack on the USS *Neosho* by Japanese aerial forces on May 7, 1942, lacking assistance because of injuries to the other members of his repair party, and severely wounded himself, Peterson, with no concern for his own life, closed the bulkhead stop valves and in so doing received additional burns that resulted in his death.

ARTHUR MURRAY PRESTON, Lieutenant U.S. Navy born November 1, 1913, in Washington, DC. Preston was commander of Motor Torpedo Boat Squadron 33, which effected the rescue of a Navy pilot shot down in Wasile Bay, Halmahera Island, fewer than 200 yards from a strongly defended Japanese dock and supply area on September 16, 1944. Volunteering for a perilous mission unsuccessfully attempted by the pilot's squadron mates and a PBY plane, Lieutenant Commander (then Lieutenant) Preston led PT-489 and PT-363 through sixty miles of restricted, heavily mined waters. After being twice turned back while running the gauntlet of fire from powerful coastal defense guns guarding the eleven-mile strait at the entrance to the bay, he was again turned back by furious fire in the immediate area of the downed airman. Aided by an aircraft smokescreen, Lieutenant Preston finally succeeded in reaching his objective and, under vicious fire delivered at 150-yard range, took the pilot aboard and cleared the area, sinking a small hostile cargo vessel with 40 mm fire during retirement. Increasingly vulnerable when covering aircraft were forced to leave because of insufficient fuel, Preston raced PT boats 489 and 363 at high speed for twenty minutes through shell-splashed water and across minefields to safety. Under continuous fire for two and a half hours, Preston successfully achieved a mission considered suicidal in its tremendous hazards and brought his boats through without personnel casualties and with only superficial damage from shrapnel.

ALBERT HAROLD ROOKS, Captain U.S. Navy born December 29, 1891, in Colton, WA. Rooks was commanding officer of the USS *Houston* during February 4–27, 1942, while in action with superior Japanese enemy aerial and surface forces. While proceeding to attack an enemy amphibious expedition as a unit in a mixed force, *Houston* was heavily attacked by bombers. After evading four attacks, she was heavily hit in a fifth attack, lost sixty killed, and had one turret wholly disabled. Captain Rooks made his ship again seaworthy and sailed within three days to escort an important reinforcing convoy from Darwin to Koepang, Timor, Netherlands East Indies. While it was so engaged, another powerful air attack developed that, by *Houston's* marked efficiency, was fought off without much damage to the convoy. The commanding general of all forces in the area thereupon canceled the movement and Captain Rooks escorted the convoy back to Darwin. Later, while in a considerable American–British–Dutch force engaged with an overwhelming force of Japanese surface ships, *Houston* with HMS *Exeter* carried the brunt of the battle, and her fire alone heavily damaged one and possibly two heavy cruisers. Although the ship was heavily damaged in the actions, Captain Rooks succeeded in disengaging his ship when the flag officer commanding broke off the action and got her safely away from the vicinity, whereas half of the cruisers were lost.

CLYDE THOMASON, Sergeant U.S. Marine Corps Reserve born May 23, 1914, in Atlanta, GA. During the Marine Raider expedition against the Japanese-held island of

Makin on August 17–18, 1942, leading the advance element of the assault echelon, Sergeant Thomason disposed his men with keen judgment and discrimination and, by his exemplary leadership and great personal valor, exhorted them to similar fearless efforts. On one occasion, he dauntlessly walked up to a house that concealed an enemy Japanese sniper, forced in the door, and shot the man before he could resist. Later in the action, while leading an assault on an enemy position, Sergeant Thomason gallantly gave his life in the service of his country.

GEORGE WATSON. Private U.S. Army born (Date of birth unknown), 1915, in Birmingham, Alabama Private Watson received the Medal of Honor for extraordinary heroism in action on March 8, 1943. Private Watson was on board a ship that was attacked and hit by enemy bombers. When the ship was abandoned, Private Watson, instead of seeking to save himself, remained in the water, assisting several soldiers who could not swim to reach the safety of the raft. This heroic action, which subsequently cost him his life, resulted in the saving of several of his comrades. Weakened by his exertions, Watson was dragged down by the suction of the sinking ship and was drowned.

ACE FIGHTER PILOTS

The following pilots fought air battles all over the Pacific Campaign. They were not associated with only one individual campaign but as individuals were heroes in every respect. For their actions in battle, they were awarded the Medal of Honor. (Citations for each are noted in References.)

GREGORY BOYINGTON. Colonel U.S. Marine Corps born December 4, 1917, in Coeur d'Alene, Idaho Colonel Boyington was in action against Japanese forces in the central Solomons area from September 12, 1943, to January 3, 1944. Consistently outnumbered throughout successive hazardous flights over heavily defended hostile territory, Major Boyington struck at the enemy with daring and courageous persistence, leading his squadron into combat with devastating results to Japanese shipping, shore installations, and aerial forces. Resolute in his efforts to inflict crippling damage on the enemy, Major Boyington led a formation of twenty-four fighters over Kahili on October 17, and, persistently circling the airdrome where sixty hostile aircraft were grounded, boldly challenged the Japanese to send up planes. Under his brilliant command, American fighters shot down twenty enemy craft in the ensuing action without the loss of a single ship. A superb airman and determined fighter against overwhelming odds, Major Boyington personally destroyed twenty-six of the many Japanese planes shot down by his squadron and by his forceful leadership developed the combat readiness in his command that was a distinctive factor in the Allied aerial achievements in this vitally strategic area.

JEFFERSON J. DEBLANC. Captain U.S. Marine Corps Reserve born February 15, 1921, in Lockport, LA. DeBlanc was involved in aerial operations against Japanese forces off Kolombangara Island in the Solomon's group on January 31, 1943. Taking off with his section as escort for a strike force of dive bombers and torpedo planes ordered to attack Japanese surface vessels, First Lieutenant DeBlanc led his flight directly to the target area, where, at 14,000 feet, the American strike force encountered a large number of Japanese Zeros protecting the enemy's surface craft. In company with the other fighters, First Lieutenant DeBlanc instantly engaged the hostile planes and aggressively deterred their repeated attempts to drive off American bombers, persevering in his efforts to protect the diving planes and waging fierce combat until, picking up a call for assistance from the dive bombers under attack by enemy float planes at 1,000 feet, he broke off his engagement with the Zeros, plunged into the formation of float planes, and disrupted the savage attack, enabling American dive bombers and torpedo planes to complete their runs on the Japanese surface disposition and to withdraw without further incident.

Although his escort mission was fulfilled upon the safe retirement of the bombers, First Lieutenant DeBlanc courageously remained on the scene despite a rapidly diminishing fuel supply and, boldly challenging the enemy's superior number of float planes, fought a valiant battle against terrific odds, seizing the tactical advantage and striking repeatedly to destroy three of the hostile aircraft and to disperse the remainder. Prepared to maneuver his damaged plane back to base, he had climbed aloft and set his course when he discovered two Zeros closing in behind. Undaunted, he opened fire and blasted both Zeros from the sky in short, bitterly fought action that resulted in such hopeless damage to his plane that he was forced to bail out at a perilously low altitude atop the trees on enemy-held Kolombangara.

THOMAS BUCHANAN MCGUIRE, JR., Major U.S. Marine Corps born August 1, 1920, in Ridgewood, NJ. After service in the United States and Alaska, McGuire was ordered in March 1943, to the 49th Fighter Group of the 5th United States Air Force, then operating in the South West Pacific Area and in particular providing an early air screen for Darwin and Northern Australia. Subsequently, he was transferred to the 475th Fighter Group, 13th Air Force, where he won promotion to major. He was already a leading ace with a record of thirty-one Japanese planes shot down when he volunteered on December 5, 1944, to lead a squadron of P-38s on a bomber escort mission over Mabalacar Airdrome on Luzon, Philippines. He shot down three of twenty Japanese Zero fighters that attacked his squadron. The next day, on a similar mission over Clark Field, near Manila, he exposed himself to draw fire away from a crippled bomber and shot down three of the four fighters that were attacking it. Another score on his way home that day brought his total to thirty-eight. On January 7, 1945, while leading a flight of four P-38s over Los Negros Island, he crashed when he attempted a highly dangerous maneuver to aid a comrade who was losing an encounter with a Japanese Zero. He was posthumously awarded the Medal of Honor in March 1946, for his actions on December 25–26, 1944, and January 7, 1945. His score of thirty-eight enemy kills made him the second leading American fighter pilot of WWII, following Major Richard Bong.

JAMES SWETT. First Lieutenant U.S. Marine Corps Reserve born June 15, 1920, in Seattle WA. In a daring flight to intercept a wave of 150 Japanese planes, First Lieutenant Swett unhesitatingly hurled his four-plane division into action against a formation of fifteen enemy bombers and during his dive personally exploded three hostile planes in midair with accurate and deadly fire. Although separated from his division while clearing the heavy concentration of antiaircraft fire, he boldly attacked six enemy bombers, engaged the first four in turn, and, unaided, shot them down in flames. Exhausting his ammunition as he closed on the fifth Japanese bomber, he relentlessly drove his attack against terrific opposition, which partially disabled his engine, shattered the windscreen, and slashed his face. In spite of this, he brought his battered plane down with skillful precision in the water off Tulagi without further injury. This superb airmanship and tenacious fighting spirit enabled First Lieutenant Swett to destroyed eight enemy bombers in a single flight.

KENNETH A. WALSH, First Lieutenant U.S. Marine Corps born November 24, 1916, in Brooklyn, NY. Walsh was a pilot in Marine Fighting Squadron 124 in aerial combat against Japanese forces in the Solomon Islands area. Determined to thwart the enemy's attempt to bomb Allied ground forces and shipping at Vella Lavella on August 15, 1943, First Lieutenant Walsh repeatedly dived his plane into an enemy formation outnumbering his own division six to one and, although his plane was hit numerous times, shot down two Japanese dive bombers and one fighter.

After developing engine trouble on August 30, during a vital escort mission, First Lieutenant Walsh landed his mechanically disabled plane at Munda, quickly replaced it with another, and proceeded to rejoin his flight over Kahili. Separated from his escort group when he encountered approximately fifty Japanese Zeros, he unhesitatingly attacked, striking with relentless fury in his lone battle against a powerful force. He destroyed four hostile fighters before cannon shellfire forced him to make a dead-stick landing off Vella Lavella, where he was later picked up.

Another poem," Tribute to the WWII Generation," by Timothy Churchill applies to all those all who served in WWII at home or abroad, in every branch of service.

Tribute to the WWII Generation

A generation, tapped by fate,
To bear the nation's pain,
Was destined to become the core,
Of courage, loss, and gain,

A generation born to strife,
Whose time was fraught with fear,
With drought and dust across the land,
And stark depression near.

The hardships brought on fortitude,
To guard our "freedom" star,
American courage, faced the test,
To fight a worldwide war.

Our nation's very heart was sore
We faced our "longest day,"
Defend our shores, our liberty,
Or die along the way.

That generation gained its strength
Through brotherhood, and pride,
With love of country, patriots came,
Five hundred thousand died.

With gratitude and honor due,
For all they lost, and gave,
A generation making safe,
Our own "home of the brave."

PART VI: SUMMARY OF WORLD WAR II

THE COST

WWII was the most destructive conflict in history. It cost more money, damaged more property, killed more people, and caused more far-reaching changes than any other war in history. Many children on the home front began their early years with a missing father. Production, except for the war effort, was halted. Food restrictions were installed. Life changed for most people.

At the time of the Pearl Harbor attack, ninety-six ships were anchored in the harbor. During the attack, eighteen, including eight battleships, were sunk or seriously damaged. Three hundred and fifty aircraft were destroyed or damaged.

It is difficult to list accurate casualities figures from WWII as countries reported differently. Further, resources used different numbers. I attempted to be as accurate as the resources allowed.

Nevertheless, think about how many artists, inventors, problem solvers, world leaders, ...the world lost when nearly 100 million people died as a result of WWII. What would our world today look like had they lived?

Table 21 provides a summary of casualties for the major players in the Pacific Theater and indicates the nearly three-to-one wounded-to-killed ratio for the United States and the nearly eighteen-to-one killed-to-wounded ratio for the Japanese.

Table 21. Estimated Asia and the Pacific Theater casualties

	USA	JAPAN	CHINA	AUSTRALIA
Killed/Missing	111,606	1,270,000	2,500,000*	26,976
Wounded	253,142	140,000	1,762,006	180,864
POWs	21,580	41,440		21,726

*China also had an approximate 7,500,000 civilian deaths

Table 22 provides a summary of killed and wounded in the Pacific Theater for the major Allied countries in the war. I am convinced that the United States' higher ratio of wounded to killed is the result of our better application of medical support on the battlefield. A big thanks to our Army medics and Navy corpsmen!

Table 22. Estimated total allied troop casualties during World War II

TROOPS	KILLED	WOUNDED
USA	291,557	670,846
USSR	6,115,000	14,013,000
Canada	42,042	53,145
United Kingdom	357,116	369,267

Table 23 shows the worldwide troop casualties of World War II.

Table 23. Estimated total allied troop and civilian casualties during World War II

Battle Deaths	20,858,000
Battle Wounded	27,372,900
Civilian Deaths	48,231,700
TOTAL	96,462,600*

*Other sources report 70-85,000,000

OTHER FACTS

- Though the *Enola Gay* became well known for dropping the first atomic bomb on Hiroshima, few people know the name of the plane that dropped the bomb on Nagasaki. It was *Bock's Car*, named after the plane's commander, Frederick Bock. (Enola Gay was the name of the mother of Paul Tibbets, the pilot of Hiroshima plane.)

Atomic bomb explosion over Hiroshima (Courtesy U.S. Navy Photograph – Public Domain)

The bomb will never go off, and I speak as an expert in explosives — **Admiral William D. Leahy (advising President Truman on the atom bomb project, 1945)**

- The *Enola Gay* raced away from Hiroshima after dropping the bomb, which exploded at 1890 feet above ground, but the shockwave from the explosion caught up with the plane and shook it like a near miss from flak. The mushroom cloud boiled up to 45,000 feet high and beyond, and the city below disappeared under a blanket of smoke and fire.
- The Japanese launched 9,000 "wind ship weapons", of paper and rubberized-silk balloons that carried incendiary and antipersonnel bombs to the United States. More than 1,000 balloons hit their target; they reached as far east as Michigan. Only six deaths resulted from a balloon bomb, including five children and a pregnant woman on a picnic in Oregon.
- The Japanese kamikaze (divine wind) tactic was suggested on October 19, 1944, by Vice Admiral Onishi in an attempt to balance the technological advantage of the invading American forces. Through the numbers are disputed, it is estimated that approximately 2,800 kamikaze pilots died. They sank 34 and damaged 368 US ships, and killed 4,900 and wounded 4,800 sailors.
- The United States Air Force, a part of the Army during WWII, became a separate branch of the military after the war.

- In 1941, a private earned $21 per month, increased to $50 per month in 1942.
- During WWII, 650,000 jeeps were built. American factories also produced 300,000 military aircraft, 89,000 tanks, three million machine guns, and seven million rifles.
- If it had become necessary to drop a third atomic bomb on Japan, Tokyo would have been the city hit.
- During World War I, Japan had fought on the side of Britain, France, and the United States and felt cheated by its failure to gain much territory when the peace treaty was composed. Additionally, in the 1920s, the Japanese government came under the control of fanatical nationalists and eventually sided with the Germans.
- Author Ian Fleming based his character 007 on the Yugoslavian-born spy Dusko Popov. Popov spoke at least five languages and came up with his own formula for invisible ink. He obtained information that the Japanese were planning an air strike on Pearl Harbor, but the FBI did not act on his warning. Popov later lived in the United States in a penthouse and created a reputation as a playboy. He wrote an account of his activities in his novel *Spy, Counterspy* in 1974.
- From 1942, the Marines in the Pacific used the Navajo language as their secret code. Around

400 Navajo Indians were trained to use the code. The Japanese never cracked the code.
- While my brother Norman did not serve in the Pacific Theater during WWII he was awarded the Bronze Star for bravery in action in the European Theater. The citation is below.

Norman L. Young 35 675 468 Private, Calvary Troop "C", 93rd Cavalry Reconnaissance Squadron, Mechanized, for meritorious achievement in connection with military operations against an enemy of the United States on April 17, 1945, near Mettmann, Germany. Private Young, Radio electrician, voluntarily exposed himself to enemy fire to drive his one-quarter ton truck up and down the column, disseminating vital information to the various platoons. Through his coolness under fire and initiative the unit commander was able to maintain constant contact with his men despite the failure of radio. His exemplary conduct is worthy of the highest praise. He entered military service from Danville, Kentucky in 1942.

Signed John Milikin
Major General U.S. Army
Commanding

(Norman passed away on April 6, 2015)

PART VIII: SHIPMATE REUNIONS—COMMENTARY ON FIVE REUNIONS, WITH POETRY BY TIMOTHY CHURCHILL

CANTON, OHIO (1997)

After my first retirement in 1985, I searched each year to discover if my ship was having a reunion. Finally, I wrote to the Navy in Washington, DC, and received a prompt response with a contact for the tenth reunion, in Canton, Ohio. It was really exciting to meet shipmates like Chet Maki, Bob Tagatz, Tim Churchill, Doug Webb, and, best of all, Naval Officer Melvin Badger, who was the officer in charge for the beach party on Saipan and Tinian. It was great to talk to all the shipmates, but especially Lieutenant Badger because we rehashed our time on the beach during the invasions. He told me that he had recommended all of the members of the beach party for the Silver Star for what we went through on Saipan and Tinian but it was turned down.

I missed only a couple of reunions during the next eleven years, and that was because my wife became ill with Alzheimer's, but I was able to host three reunions in Kentucky during that period.

LEXINGTON, KENTUCKY (2005)

The reunion in 2005 was staged at the Campbell House in Lexington and included a day at the races (Keeneland), a bus tour to a horse farm, dinner at Boone Tavern in Berea, and a pig roast on my farm. This was the second of three such reunions I hosted over the years.

The Bluegrass Land Again

Once more in old Kentucky,
The horse and bluegrass state,
Where *The Bell* crew
got together,
Before time gets too late.

In the year two, aught,
aught, five,
On Ralph Young's orchard farm,
The pig roast brought
us running,
And the sunshine
made us warm.

We lived again the olden days,
Young sailors brave, and bold,
We fought and won the
World War Two,
Our normal lives on "hold."

We scattered to the
four winds then,
Each going his own way,
But once each year,
the faithful few,
Join up to cheer the day.

We reminisce, and honor those,
Who sailed on to distant seas,
They were men who
shared our world,
Our "shipmates," if you please.

So, some are gone,
and some remain,
But we shall meet once more,
If not on land we
fought to save,
Then on some "other" shore.

Tim Churchill told me that he got on the wrong elevator in Denver, Colorado, after his discharge from the Navy and ended up accidentally in an Army recruiting office, where he negotiated a commission as an Army officer and was shipped to Germany, where he met and fell in love with Helga, who has been his wife ever since. Helga is a beautiful lady, and they make a great pair.

GOLD CANYON, ARIZONA (2007)

One of the most enjoyable reunions was in 2007 with Max and Marlene Miller in Arizona. The reunion was built around their beautiful and spacious home, and it took in about all of the sights in the area, which Tim describes in his poem "Thanks for the Memories." I remember this reunion well because it was a stopover for Janice and me on our three-month honeymoon trip to Thailand, China, and other areas in Southeast Asia.

Thanks for the Memories

Thanks to Max and
Marlene Miller,
From "shipmates,"
friends, and wives;
From sons and daughters of the crew,
You've enriched all our lives.

You hosted our reunion there,
In Arizona land,
And gave us memories to last,
Until the last command.

We will remember
moonlit nights,
And trips to outer scenes,
And all the camaraderie
With what that really means.

Our trips along Apache Trail,
Saguaro Lake so blue,
The "Rockin' R" with
western swing,
No end of things to do.

As we salute *J. Franklin Bell*,
With reverent
thoughts of those,
Who served with us in
World War Two,
Now resting in repose.

As World War Two
vets fade away,
From many to so few,
Then those of us,
who yet survive,
Can meet, as comrades do.

And somewhere past
the great beyond,
When Bos'n sounds his call,
We muster on the
Quarter Deck,
To answer, one and all.
"Thanks for the Memories"

DANVILLE, KENTUCKY (2008)

Timothy Churchill almost always had a reason for his poetry. It could be a Veterans Day parade when the organizers of parade requested a poem, or a USS *J. Franklin Bell* reunion.

To understand the meaning of many of his poems, you would have to know some of the events that occurred. For example, in his poem "Reunion in Danville," you have to know that shipmate Tom Lyons, who owned a travel business in Texas, flew into Louisville rather than Lexington, where I was waiting to pick up him and his daughter Joy. I was waiting at the American Airline baggage carousel when I answered my cell phone to hear Tom, "Where are you, Ralph Young?" I said, "Waiting at the American Airlines baggage claim," and Tom said, "That is impossible, because I am at American Airlines and you are nowhere in sight." When asked what airport, he was in, his answer was "Louis-ville." I said, "Wait right there, Tom. I will see you in about ninety minutes."

Another part of the poem relates to the fact that shipmate Bob Tagatz was without a doubt the luckiest guy at all our reunions. (I might add that in my ninety years here on Earth I have also noticed that the luckiest people always seem to be the most talented.) Whether it was gambling at the casinos or winning the raffles, Tagatz seemed to always win, so when it came to horse racing and none of us could keep up with shipmate Tony Tralla, Tim just had to rub it in for Tagatz.

Then when Tagatz led the parade of cars past the turn to my place and all ended up in Crab Orchard, Kentucky, twenty miles from my home, Tim could not let him off without another jab to his pride.

Reunion in Danville

The "twenty-oh-eighter" in Danville,
A reunion for the books,
Was fraught with fun and memories,
And even some "mistooks."

Just think of old Tom Lyons,
(The travel agent guy),
Like "Wrongway" Corrigan of old,
He never learned to fly.

Tom meant to go to Lexington;
From there he had a ride,
But he said "I'm in Louis-ville,"
"Where did Lex-ton hide?"

But Ralph came to the rescue,
And really saved the day;
Hosting all of us in Dan-ville,
He was generous that way.

The racehorse club in Keeneland,
Was fun for each and all,
And Tralla really took the cake,
(As Tagatz took a fall.)

But Tagatz made a great comeback,
To lead the trip to Ralph's;
He led us past the right highway,
(He knows his Norths and Souths.)

The joy ride with Doug and Faye,
To "Crab Tree Orchard" town,
Provided added thrills for Tim;
(Doug never lets me down.)
So everything was peachy keen.

Forgotten Warriors by D. Ralph Young with poetry by Timothy D. Churchill

TYLER, TEXAS (2009)

The reunion in 2009, hosted by the Lyons, was memorable for more than one reason. This reunion turned out to be the twenty-first and final reunion. At the Executive Committee Meeting of the association, I objected to reimbursing the Lyons for the cost of using an event planner, my objection being that those of us who had volunteered for all previous reunions had agreed to do the planning and so had the Lyons. Having hosted three reunions myself, I had spent hundreds of unreimbursed dollars. By vote of the committee, we rejected paying the $1500 cost, though, I have reason to believe that Tagatz came to the rescue for the Lyons. In any event, this was, next to Max and Marlene Miller's, the best of all the reunions. It was well planned, with a lot of enjoyable activities and with a beautiful photo book being sent to everyone after the reunion was over. Since Tom had flown into Louisville instead of Lexington on my previous reunion, I told him I was flying in to Houston, Texas and giving him a call for pickup. In the end, we are still shipmates and best of friends.

The Old Bell Crew and Tyler Too

Deep in the heart of Tyler town,
Down Eastern Texas way,
The boys of the "Bell" met one more time,
To rehash yesterday.

Remember the war and shared events,
And what we did back then,
When we were young, and fighting mad,
With World War Two to win.

In Tyler we had quite a show,
Museums by the score,
And dinner on the lake front,
Margaritas by the shore.

Thanks to Tom and Bill and Joy,
Our hosts for this go 'round,
The "get together" warmed our hearts,
With ties forever bound.

The laughter, and recounted tales,
May not have all been new,
But every version, new or old,
Still rings as being true.

So hoist a toast to old sea dogs,
And reminisce with me,
While shipmates gather memories,
To cast beyond the sea.

PART IX: CONCLUSION AND FINAL THOUGHTS

I am puzzled by the fact that our elected presidents and congressional members are so attracted to Normandy but seldom visit the American Cemetery in the Philippines. I say this because we have 7,819 more casualties and 20 more Medal of Honor winners in the American Cemetery than we have at Normandy. I can only conclude that being close to Paris is more desirable than being close to Manila. This tells me the visits are not so much about honoring veterans but more about honoring self.

I have heard all kind of excuses as to why the European Theater is more popular, including that we the people of the United States migrated from Europe; the battles on Luzon and Okinawa occurred when people in the United States were getting ready to celebrate the victory in Europe; and the death of FDR took the headlines when those final Pacific battles were coming to a conclusion. The fact remains that out of 72,000,000 casualties in WWII, 50 percent were in the Pacific Theater. In my opinion, Midway should be treated like a Normandy and celebrated each year. What those Marine and Navy pilots did for this country at Midway should never *ever* be forgotten.

This is my third and, in all probability, last book to write. I keep thinking how much easier it would have been if I could still have my secretary of many years, Peggy Drummond. In previous books, I had thought that I should not mention one of my past employees unless I mentioned them all, but I am embarrassed for not mentioning previously what a wonderful and efficient secretary Peggy was. She always seemed to be a step ahead of my thoughts and did a beautiful job of caring for our clients and me when we were in town. Sorry, Peggy. I consider you and your husband Robert two of my very best friends.

Among my thoughts is the war in Iraq. I find it hard to believe that no one seems to figure how ISIS got its start in Iraq and occupied so much of Anbar Province so quickly. Maybe the belief that the surge was effective is because all the people involved, in the Bush Administration, seem to think that it was the surge in troops that brought Anbar Province under control when the real success was the surge in money. The money is what caused the "Awaking Consul of Sunni tribes "of Anbar Province to come into existence. We became successful in Anbar Province only when we put all the tribal chiefs and their clans on the government payroll, and ISIS became powerful only after the Shiite government dropped the mostly Sunni clans of Anbar Province from the payroll about 2013. It seems to me that the cheapest plan would be to put all the clans back on the payroll and start over again on weaning them off one clan at a time. However, the religious animosity between the Shiite and Sunni tribes may be impossible to bridge peacefully.

D. Ralph Young at Surprise 90th Birthday Celebration Cruise (Courtesy Chad Young)

Janice, my wife, loves cruises and as a result we have been on several. I keep wondering if the cruises are because she likes them or just to see if I have the sea legs that I brag about from my years in the Navy. In any event I have to write about what occurred on March 4, 2015, when I turned ninety. Janice, said, "I would like to take you on a short cruise—just the two of us—to celebrate." It sounded like a great ideal. A couple of days before the cruise, I said to Janice, "If you tell anyone on this cruise that I am ninety, I am going to jump overboard."

We arrived at dock to board the ship. After we checked in, a lady with the cruise line came, saying, "Follow me."

As we walked through the door to enter the customs area, there stood twenty-six of my family and friends yelling, "Happy birthday!" These included my daughter

Marsha from Melbourne, Australia, my son David and wife Penny from Kentucky, and several grandchildren, plus about all of Janice's family, including her ninety-two-year-old mother, Helen, from Dayton; her sisters, Sharon from Boston and Sondi from Dayton; her brother Jim, from Dayton. Her nieces Allie from San Francisco and Kristin from Connecticut also joined the group. I mention these to give an idea of how much distance several had to travel.

In addition to spouses, other nieces and nephews, and brother- and sister-in-law's was Janice's son Ben, the biggest surprise of all. He sure looked handsome in coat and tie. I think there were about 3,000 passengers on board, and I am convinced that before we left the ship, every one of them knew it was my ninetieth birthday, because all twenty-six friends and family plus Janice wore big buttons that said HAPPY 90th BIRTHDAY with my picture showing through-out the duration of the cruise. Needless to say, I had to reconsider my threat about jumping overboard.

One last nagging thought that I cannot hold within is on "enhanced interrogation". It gives a black eye to the beautiful and wonderful country that we of the greatest generation fought and died to defend. I know that I speak for a majority of World War II veterans when I say, "We would never believe it would happen in the USA."

Senate, Intelligence Committee Chairwoman Dianne Feinstein described the action as "a stain on US history" To make even more terrible and disgusting is the Bush Administration and President Bush himself says, waterboarding is not torture. They completely disregard that the individual is made to think he is drowning resulting in panic, struggling which causes their body to go into spasm with possible brain and psychological damage. There were many other tactics used such as, sleep deprivation up to 180 hours, or crammed into a box just big enough for the body and left for hours with loud music blaring.

Former CIA lawyer John Rizzo authorized the program. He defended the decision by saying, capturing and interrogating terrorists was better than killing through drone strikes. I have news for him, they are both wrong and totally un-American. Killing innocence people in an effort to target one terrorist is just as bad as torture. My guess is that, we will live to regret this policy, when the terrorist drones start flying over the USA.

APPENDIX A: REFERENCES

1. **Tables**: All references for tables came from: Scheile. US Casual Statistics of American Battles (www.US/Battle Info.ASP); Wikipedia, the free encyclopedia (www.wikipedia.org) or World War II Death toll of all nations (www.world/chronicle.org). (Since discrepancies existed in final numbers the author used numbers from these sources in the order listed – that is, if numbers were missing from the first source, the second source was used and so forth.
2. **Medal of Honor Citations**: All references for Medal of Honor Citations came from: US Government Citations; Wikipedia, the free encyclopedia (www.wikipedia.org); or the Medal of Honor Society (www.medalofhonor.org); http://www.worldwar2history.info/II/Medal-of-Honor/Guam.html; Congressional Medal of Honor Society (www.cmohs.org). Since different sources were used not all information is consistently stated.
3. **Maps**: References for maps came from: (www.worldatlas.org); University of Kentucky Cardiology Lab (Jacqueline Goins, (www.uky.edu); Wikipedia, the free encyclopedia (www.wikipedia.org);); GNU Free Documentation License-Wikipedia; or (www.historyplace.com
4. **Pictures**: References for pictures are cited with each picture – Official U. S. Navy photograph (p://us navy photographs/publicdomain.gov

5. **Poetry**: All poetry was written by Timothy J. Churchill over the past 75 years.
6. *Naval History,* "Peleliu: The Forgotten Battle," by Maj. Henry Donigan (September 1994)
7. *The Power of a Mother's Prayer* by D. Ralph Young Tate, May, 2014.
8. *The Girls of Atomic City* by Denise Kiernan (2013)

APPENDIX B: ORIGINAL CREW ASSIGNED TO USS *J. FRANKLIN BELL*, APRIL 2, 1942

Aaron, Hugh

Acord, Donald J.

Adams, John M.

Adams, Silvester

Albersman, Joseph B.

Alexander, Burdatt

Algeo, Edwin H.

Alix, James D.

Allen, Clifford D.

Andrews Raymond

Agualo, Franciso G.

Arguello, Roman

Arnetl, Floyd Y. Jr.

Baglione, Phillip F.

Bahan, Julius M.

Bailey, George B.

Baldwin, Joseph C.

Baugus, Melvin E.

Benson, Raymond E.

Berckhamer, Charles. C.

Bignell, Ernest H. L.

Blackman, Raymond L.

Blount, Ralph D.

Bluhm, Alfred R.

Boetticher Oscar G

Bold, Robert J.

Boynton, William P.

Bradley, O'Dell

Braud, John E. Jr.

Bray, Marvin John Jr

Breton, Leonard

Breton, Leonard

Bridge, David D.

Brigham, Samuel Jr.

Brinkham, Bernard J.

Brock, William E.

Browne, Robert K

Bryan, Daniel

Bunn, Kenneth R.

Burns, Ward R.

Burros, Andrew

Campbell, Morgan "JP"

Cannon, Henry W.

Capshaw, Ross L

Carr, Edward C.

Carter, David

Cartwright, Jessie H

Ceraso Frank T.

Chan James

Chaney, Wesley G.

Choate, William M

Christian, Dale R.

Ciprian, Michael

Ciscell, Harold L.

Clement, Edward

Clifton, John R.

Cliver, John R.

Clow, Leslie G.

Colley, John C.

Collins, Archiebald

Compton, Earl H.

Conner, James T.

Corbecky, Domino W.

Corboy, Jerome F.

CornwallL, Ted J.

Cottrell, George

Cowan, Robert C.

Cox, Joseph

Cranfield, L. B.

Crawford, Richard

Creekmore, Bernard T.

Curry, Julius G. Jr.

Curtiss, Everett M.

Dahna, Alfred D.

Daill, Garland F.

Danielson, Ronald R.

Davenport, Lloyd W.

Davis, Charles E. Jr.

Davis, Samuel

Davis, William R.

Dean, William E.

Decker, Theo

DeFreest, Donald F.

Dehart, Marvin A.

Denson, Augustus M.

DeVerra, Genaro

Devlin, William G.

DeWitt, Francis W.

DeWitt, Warren H.

Dewitt, Warren J.

Dietl, Walter J.

Digges, Gilbert

Dinwiddie, James H.

Dinwiddie, Ralph H.

Dungoa, Juan Q.

Durham, Paul A.

Edquist, Herbert E.

Eggleston, Arthur G.

Elkins, Robert E.

Ellis, Francis E.

English, Herbert

Entzminger, Ulysses F.

Ervin, Harrison H.

Evangelista, Eulallo

Evans, Irving

Evans, John E.

Ewing, Sanford I.

Farnsworth, Normand

Foster, James A.

Freitas, Henry R.

Frost, Dwight W.
Furman, Donald E.
Gahwiler, Raymond R. Rm
Gallaway, Cecil E.
Gerllca, Joseph F.
Giaimo, John J.
Gillett, Howard L.
Galloway, Lawrence H.
Gamble, William F.
Gamblin, Melville A.
Gardner, John E.
Garland, Oscar
Garnett, Nathaniel
Garzione, Thomas
Gear, Robert M.
George, Robert G.
Gerllca, Joseph F.
Giaimo, John J.
Gillett, Howard L.

Glynn, Robert J.
Goff, William A.
Gooch, William P.
Goodman, Dan J.
Gordon, Ray M.
Green, John H.
Greenleaf, Fred S.
Griffith, John Joseph
Grindell, Charles E.
Grissom, Firm D.
Groves, Wallace L.
Gunning, John J.
Hacker, Richard L.
Hackler, Lonnie L.
Hajducko, Michael
Hall, Harman W.
Hall, Laird D.
Hall, William J.
Halloran, Thomas R.

Hamilton, Bruce F.
Hamilton, Jack G.
Hammock, James C.
Hancock, John H.
Hankins, Charles L.
Hansen, Carl
Hardacre, Richard E.
Harrigan, Martin D.
Harris, George B.
Harrison, William A.
Hart, Robert W.
Hartman, Harvey A.
Hawker, Everett J.
Hawkins, Bill
Hay, Colbert T.
Headly, Milton F.
Henry, William H.
Herbert, Anthony M.
Herriman, Richard F.

Hess, Gerald H.
Hills, Burch M.
Hinkle, Thomas F.
Hinners, Norman E.
Hiter, Charles
Hodge, James E.
Hoehn, Donald J.
Hoffman, Frederick
Hoffman, Robert D.
Holmes, Julius A.
Holshouser, Jesse A.
Honsinger, Emerson G.
Hood, Delbert B.
Hooten, Roland W.
Hoover, Harold V.
Hopkins, Wallace R.
Houch, John D.
Hovland, Luther J.
Hudak, Steve

Hudson, John R.	Johnson, Merlin E.
Hughes, William E.	Johnson, Royal E.
Highey, Eugene LeRoy	Jones, Olin P.
Hunnicutt, Robert B.	Jones, Robert
Hutton, Richard L.	Jones, William C.
Ivie, Edward V.	Jordon, Buck
Jackson, Claude L.	Jorgensen, Henry
Jackson, Ernest	Juranek, Eugene O.
Jaeger, Ralph G.	Kane, Robert W.
James, John R.	Kantorowitz, Edward J.
Jansen, Edwin Leroy	Karstens, Robert V.
Jesus, Juan B.	Katz, Jacob
Jinks, Martin T.	Kaye, Stanley J.
Joachim, Harry R.	Kearns, John J.
Johnsen, Henry	Keith, Joseph F.
Johnson, Bezel M.	Kern John B.
Johnson, Howard S.	Kibley, Oliver E.
Johnson, Ike L. Jr.	King, James O.
Johnson, Leonard	Kinser, Jesse J.

Kirby, Clarence E.

Kirby, William P.

Kirkham, Burns S.

Klingeman, Donald W.

Kohleffel, Raymond L.

Kotter, Donald T.

Krepps. Charles

Kreiger, Donald F.

Kubala, Thaddeus X.

Kuechmeister, Frank E.

Kuhl, Robert C.

Kurraseh, George F.

Kurmadas, Leo J.

Kurtz, August

Lagaman, Savido

Lambert, Henry K.

Landaz, Fidel

Lanius, Aubrey R.

Lanquein, Leo L.

Larson, William W. L.

Laster, Earl H. Jr.

Laupp, Graham M.

Lay, Robert L.

Leath, James C.

Lee, James G.

Lenard, Herbert C.

Lenarski, Stanley J.

Lesh, Clyde R.

Lester, Ian V.

Lewis, Howard N.

Leyde, Carl B.

Liles, Barnnie R.

Linday John H.

Lineberry, Loren L.

Lohrman, Joseph D.

Lomat, Venancio (n)

Lowitz, Carl A.

Lupton, Vincent D.

Mabayak, Jose
Maki, Chester L.
Manderson, James T.
Marino, Ralph T.
Martin, James H. Jr.
Martin, Max E.
Martin, Walter
Matson, Keith C.
Mathews, William P. Jr.
Mattson, Harold H.
May, Louis
McBride, Donald F.
McCabe, James P.
McCahen, Walter D.
McCorkle, James W.
McDonald, William P.
McIlrath, Jesse D.
McKellop, James A.
McKinney, Frank B.

McMaster, Mack E.
McNamee, Earl M.
McNatt, Robert H.
McQuarrie, Alfred A.
McShea, Bernard
Mead, Jack W.
Messinger, Elmer E.
Meyer, Clifford R.
Miles, Aubrey A.
Miller, Carroll S.
Miller, Charles C.
Miller, Clyde W.
Miller, John Jr.
Miller, Douglas R.
Milner, Aubray A.
Mitchell, William V.
Mize, Robert C.
Mooney, James J.
Moore, Albert F.

Moore, Loen C.

Moore, Milton M.

Morano, Patsy

Murel, Nicholas

Myers, Howard E.

Myers, Ray

Nash, Robert H.

Nava, Juan L.

Nerim, Alvin A.

Nesany, Bruce B.

Neville, John J.

Obelles, Robert R.

O'Brien, Jack R.

O'Connor, James E.

Odaware, Phillip L.

Olcott, Byron R.

Oldack, Edwin

Oliver, Robert J.

Oppenheimer, Benjamin

Osbourne, Francis M.

Ott, William C.

Owen, Gerald R.

Paarman, Eugene M.

Palker, James L.

Palmer, Harold R.

Palmer, Sharwood H.

Parsons, Quentin

Patrick, Earl S.

Patten, Myrne R.

Paxton, Freeman E.

Peacock, Darrel Y.

Pearman, Max B.

Peck, William E.

Peloquin, Ferdinand C.

Peters, Rodger E.

Peterson, Leroy

Philbrick, Russell A.

Phillips, Patrick

Pierce, Joseph C.
Pilkington, Albert X.
Pokatello, John
Poland, Jack
Pollitt, Robert E.
Pomeroy, Daniel E.
Powell, Theodore S.
Priest, Bill E.
Pulaski, Elmer R.
Pulis, Lorin H.
Ramborger, William O.
Ramey, James H.
Ramsey, Collier
Rawn, Robert D.
Reading, Thomas A.
Reed, Ernest D.
Reed, Thomas H.
Reichlin, Joseph J.
Renner, Clarance H.

Reno, Robert J.
Reyes, Aroenic
Richardson, Frank E.
Richmand, Roy F.
Riley, William J.
Roberts, Curry A. Jr.
Roberts, Leo A.
Robinson, Darvin E.
Rodgers, Alphonso
Roley, William R.
Rolfe, Donald R.
Romaniak, Frank
Romero, Robert "E"
Rose, Victor
Rowe, Phil M.
Ryan, Francis P.
Sablan, Antonio L.
Sablln, Juan T.
Salatka, Edward A.

Salter, George W.
Sanford, Billie P.
Sargent, Harvey E.
Sauer, Carl J.
Saunders, Charlie
Sayles, Edward P.
Scaley, Harold A.
Schadee, Richard W.
Schaffneer, Robert J.
Schenk, Edgar O.
Scherber, Eugene E.
Schrader, Donnell E.
Scott, George A. Jr,
Scott. Lloyd E.
Scott, Wilbur
Searles, Roy W.
Sehrier, Joseph M.
Selak, Frank
Severson, Russell M.

Shank, Charles R.
Sheets, Michael L.
Shepard, William M.
Silakowski, Michael J.
Silvers, Harold C.
Simas, Williams
Simmons, Roy D.
Skeley, Harold A.
Slater, Harry S.
Slaughter, Roy A. Jr.
Slayton, Zachary T.
Smith, Charles J.
Smith, Earl C. Jr.
Souza, John S.
Spalding, Louis R.
Spivey, Roy L.
Squires, Robert P.
Stabenow, Glenn C.
Stanchfield, William B.

Stanfield, James E.	Taylor, William E.
Stanley, John B.	Thomas, George A.
Stapleton, James A.	Thompson, Dallas L.
Staron, Frank W.	Thompson, J. D.
Starr, Willard D.	Thompson, Richard K.
Steinhoff, Wilbur C.	Thourman, Eddie
Stephenson, Thomas M.	Tipton, Harold N.
Stettler, Carl E.	Tirlot, Eugene D.
Stimmler, Hugo M.	Todd, Paul A.
Stock, Francis A.	Tourtelotte, Chester L.
Stoneburner, John R.	Townsend, Carl Alvin
Stoner, Harley J.	Tralla, Wade A.
Stophel, Robert E.	Trice, James
Strait, Russell W.	Turner, Ottis
Strawn, Warren A.	Van Court, Louis T.
Strickland, Roy A.	Van Decar, James W.
Stutzman, Warren L.	Van Wager, Robert
Swaney, Marlo	Vaughn, James H.
Tagatz, Robert C.	Vincent, Howard R.

Visich, John
Wade, James P.
Wahlborg, Clyde G.
Wanbaugh, Calvin C.
Warnock, George G.
Washington, Charles L.
Watkins, William G.
Weaver, James R.
Weber, Fred
Wells, Harold E.
Wells, Lawrence A.

Wentzel, Glenn I.
Werth, Kenneth L.
West, Archie A.
Wilson, Robert W.
Winters, William F.
Wise, Franklin N.
Wood, Jack B.
Wood, Jack J.
Woods, Morris W.
Worshek, Harry L
Wylie, Donald L

APPENDIX C: SURVIVING USS *J. FRANKLIN BELL* SHIPMATES AND/OR SPOUSES IN 2009

Allen, Mrs. Beverly

Arnold, Clayton (Sami)

Badger, Mrs. Genie

Ballard, C.D.

Barney, Winston

Benett, William

Biddle, Casey

Brigham, Edward

Brodt, William

Carlton, Robert F.

Carpenter, Robert L.

Chapman, Jack. O.

Chiarmonte, Joseph F. Jr.

Christian, Lawrence D.

Churchill, Timothy D.

Clark, Charles

Coombs, Mrs. Faye

Crammond, Clyde

Crawford, Charles J.

Crecco, John I.

Curtin, Peter

Curtis, Mrs. Marjorie

Damin, Earl L.

Dauntless, Mrs. Jean

Davenport, Mrs. Marilyn

Davis, Ms. Janet

DeWitt, Warren

Dimiceli, Frank V.

Draper, Bill C.

Draper, Mrs. Mary

Dubose, Perry

Elkins, Mrs. Eleanor

Evans, Mrs. Emma

Fahey, Frank R.

Finley, Mrs. Marge
Flanagan, Joe
Fleming, Donald
Fratt, Mrs. Margaret H.
Freitas, Mrs. Peggy
Fresler, Felix M. Jr.
Gallagher, Mrs. Joyce
Garland, Oscar
Garvin, Bob
Gasslander, Dennis
Geginhimer, Mrs. Laura
Germano, Frank
Giaimo, John
Gilley, Mrs. Doris
Giron, Joe
Glasgow, Colin F.
Graham, Bill E.
Hall, Mrs. Margaret
Harrigan, Mrs. Dorothy A.

Harrison, Mrs. William
Hart, Robert
Hawker, E. Jack
Hayes, Mrs. Betty
Heck, Mr. Caro
Henleben, Edwin
Henniker, George
Higgins, Homes
Hill, Robert P.
Hinners, Mrs. Norman
Hoehn, Donald
Hooker, Mrs. Joy
Hores, Roger W.
Houck, Mrs. Alza Ann
Huey, Mrs. Dorothy
Hughes, William E. Sr.
Jackson, Mrs. Ann
Jefferies, Mrs. Doris
Jette, Louis

Johnson, Royal
Jones, Floyd L.
Jones, Olin P.
Jarstens, Robert
Kelly, Joe
Kelley, Oliver
King, Bill
Kirby, Mrs. Beth
Kobel, Chester
Koenning, Mrs. Myrtle
Kohleffel, Mrs. Dorothy
Kopyscinski, Steve
Kuhl, Robert C.
Lamb, Mrs. Goldie
Leavitt, L. D.
Leon, Ruben
Lewis, Mrs. Alberta
Ligocki, Paul
Lyons, Pat

Lyons, Tom W.
Maki, Chester L.
Makosh, Fred
Markel, Charles
Marshall, Vernon L.
Matson, Keith
Matthews, W. P.
McBee, James C.
McBride, Donald F.
McCorkle, James
McCormick, Ralph
McDonald, Richard E.
McDonald, Ms. Laurie
McDonald, William P.
McGee, William E.
McGraw, Arthur A.
McIlvaine, Mrs. Edward J.
Meeks, Mrs. Fran
Miles, M. W.

Miller, John	Pilkington, Albert E.
Miller, Thomas M.	Pokatello, John
Mitchell, George	Pollock, Frank D.
Mize, Mrs. Charles W.	Priest, Mrs. Joan
Moore, Mrs. Janie	Prince, Mrs. Mildred
Morby, Harold	Pritchett, Charles M.
Morgan, George	Pulaski, Mrs. Elaine
Morrow, Donald	Rains, Mrs. Lynn
Moss, E. W. "Pete"	Ramborger, Mrs. Fae
Murel, Nicholas	Raschke, John F.
Northcult, Mrs. Tabitha	Reichlin, Moe
Otwell, Noel	Rigsby, Marvin E.
Palmer, James E.	Roberts, Ms. Sharon
Palmer, Potter C.	Robertson, Douglas
Parson, Quentin	Robinson, Mrs. Betty
Patterson, George	Rolfe, Mrs. Betty
Peterson, Mrs. Jo Ann	Rollins, Mrs. Mary Jo
Philbrick, Mrs. Tally	Romero, Robert
Phillips, Jack A.	Romero, Mrs. Regina

Rossington, Bill
Rothlisberger, Ralph
Rowe, Phil M.
Rush, Floyd D.
Ryan, Francis
Schaffner, Robert
Schimanski, Howard
Schrader, Mrs. Marie
Schultz, Leslie
Scott, Wilbur
Selack, Frank
Sellers, Lenn
Shank, Mrs. Odean
Shannon, Ray
Smith, Earl C.
Somson, Charles A.
Stapleton, James
Steele, Philmore
Stoker, Ms. Barbara

Stroud, Robert R.
Swann, Ernest
Tadlock, George
Tagatz, Robert
Tapp, Mrs. Nella
Thomas, Mrs. Jean
Thomas, Richard Jr.
Thompson, James F.
Toledo, Manuel
Trainor, Donald
Tralla, W. Anthony
Varney, Edward F.
Wade Mrs. Beverly R.
Watts, Mrs. Ernestine
Webb, Douglass G.
Welch, Mrs. Dorothy
Wells, Ms. Susan
Welsh, Louis
Wheeler, Albert H.

Wheeler, Leon J.

Williams, Arthur

Williams, Dick

Williams, James

Williams, Marlon

Wood, Mrs. Janet

Wyatt, James W.

Wyres, Mrs. Ruth

Yoder, Mrs. Mary

Young, Ralph

Young, Mrs. Ula

Zander, Alois W.

Zurick, Mike

APPENDIX D: DECEASED SHIPMATES AS OF 2009

USS J FRANKLIN BELL
ROLL OF HONOR

Accord, Donald
Allen, George M.
Anderson, Carl
Arehart, Mark

Badger, Melvin L.
Barger, Charles
Baugus, Melvin E.
Bean, Joe
Berry, M. R.
Beyer, Libert A.
★Biddle, Wayne D.
Boss, Dick
Bourne, Charles
Bourne, John

Boyle, Charles
Bradburn, Bill
Braden, John
Breece, John L.
Brett, George T.
Bridges, Jack
Brigandi, Anthony
Brosnahan, Robert

Churchill, L. L.
Collier, Harold
Compton, Eugene
Coombs, R. V.
Corbecky, Dominic
Cornwell, Theodore
Curtis, Everett M.
Dallman, Richard
Dauntless, Everett
Davenport, Lloyd
De Witt, Francis
Diddle, BM 1C
Draper, Bill

Edquist, Herbert
Eiland, Jesse
Elkins, Robert
Evans, Louis

Faith, Warren
Farland, John
Flurer, Ray D.
  09/22/09

Fratt, Russell
Freed, Tom
Freitas, Hank
Gallagher, Robert
Geginheimer, Roland
Gibbs, William G.
Gillette, H.
Gilley, Neal
Goff, Bill
Groves, Wallace
Gutierrez, Gabe

Hall, Merle
Halsell, Perry
Hancock, John
Hanson, Carl
Harrigan, Marty
Harrison, William
Hayducko, Michael
Hayes, Guy
Headley, Milton
Heck, Elmer
Henderson, Ray
Herrell, E. E.
Hinners, Norman
Hixon, Walter
Holland, Claude L.
Hoopengardner, D.
Hosier, Walter W.
Houck, John D.
Hoyt, Robert D.
Hudson, John
Huey, David
Hunnicut, Robin B.

Jackson, Claude
Jefferies, Cosmos
Johnson, Leonard
Johnson, Wilbert E.
Jones, Paul
Jones, William
Jorden, Buck

Judd, Ralph A.
Kantorowitz, Edward
Kerns, Jack
Kinser, Jesse J.
Kirby, Casher
Kirby, Frank L.
Klinge, Arthur
Koenning, Harold
Kohleffel, Raymond
Koski, Arden R.
Kubala, Tex

Lahart, Jack
Lamb, Charles W.
Lees, Robert T.
Lester, Van V.
Levey, Donald V.
Lewis, James
Lewis, John
Liggett, Leonard
Lowitz, Carl A.

Manderson, James
Mattson, Hal
McDonald, Dr. R.P.
Mc Ivane, Edward
Mc Natt, Robert
McQuarrie, Alfred
McQuarrie, Dr. Chas.
McQuillen, Nelson
Meeks, Forrest L.
Messinger, Elmer
Mize, Charles W.
Mone, Russel W.
Moore, Robert
Morrison, Thomas
Murphy, James

Napier, John
Neville, John
Nichols, Leo. S.
Olsen, William

Olson, Ralph

Patten, Myrne
★Philbrick, Russell
★Pipkin, Louis
Plummer, Garvin
Priest, Bill
Prince, Buford L.
Pulaski, Elmer
Pulis, L. H.

Rackley, John
Rains, Robert S.
Ramborger, Wm.
Rawn, Robert
Reed, Thomas
Reimus, A. J.
Riffe, Orville
Riley, Richard
★Roberts, Bruce
Roberts, Marvin
Robertson, Edward
Rolfe, Donald R.
Rollins, Floyd D.
★Romero, Paul
Rosander, John
Ross, George L.
Rowley, R. W.
Russo, Louis

Salatka, Edward
Scherber, Gene
Schrader, Donnell
Schulstad, Ralph
Sens, Edward
Shank, Charles R.
Sharum, Lee
Shirley, Robert E.
Simpson, Don
Simpson, Thomas
Slaughter, Roy
Smith, Billy

Spangenberg, Walt
Spinato, Samuel
Sproat, George
Stophel, Robert
Sturla, Norman Red

Tapp, William
Thomas, Myron
Thompson, Robert
Tourelotte, Chester
Trippet, Paul

VanWagner, Robert
Vermillion, Waldo
Volkman, Henry A.
Wade, James P.
Walroth, James
Watson, Delbert
Watts, Huelin
Webber, Fred
Welch, John
Welsh, Maurice S.
Wierhake, Clark
Wisser, Edwin
White, George
Wisniewski, Ed
★Wood, Jack
Worsted, Charles
★Wyres, Eugene D.

Yoder, Willis E.
Young, Robert E.
Zimmerman, E.

★-Reported since 10/08.

APPENDIX E: USS J. FRANKLIN BELL ASSOCIATION MEMBERS AS OF 2009

Name	Spouse
Badger, Melvin	Mrs. Genie
Barney, Winston M.	
Biddle, Casey	
Brigham, Edward	
Brodt, William	Ocie
Carlton, Robert F.	
Caton, Ms. Kay Rains	
Chapman, Jack O.	Norma
Chiarmonte, Joseph F. Jr.	
Churchill, Timothy D.	Helga
Crammond, Clyde	Ruth
Crawford, Charles J.	
Curtin, Peter	Emily
Davenport,	Mrs. Marilyn
DuBose, Perry	Marge

Name	Spouse
Fahey, Frank R.	Rita A.
Glasgow, Colin F.	Mae
Hart, Robert	Shirley
Hill, Robert P.	Priscilla
Hooker, Mrs. Joy	Bill
Jones, Floyd L.	Jean
King, Bill	Nellie
Kobel, Chester	Shirley
Lyons, Tom W.	
Makosh, Fred	
Markel, Charles	
McBride, Donald F.	Inda
McCormick, Ralph	Hazel
McDonald, Richard E.	
McGee, William E.	Maxine
McGraw, Arthur A.	Morgen
Meeks, Mrs. Fran	

Name	Spouse
Miller, Thomas M.	Marlene
Morrow, Donald	
Northcutt, Mrs. Tabitha	
Pilkington, Albert E.	Geraldine
Pollock, Frank D.	
Rains, Mrs. Lynn	
Roberts, Ms. Sharon	
Rolfe, Mrs. Betty	
Rossington, Bill	
Rowe, Phil M.	Tommie L.
Schaffner, Robert	
Shannon, Ray	
Smith, George S.	*Agnes*
Steele, Philmore	
Tagatz, Robert	*Dorothy*
Thompson, James F.	
Trainor, Donald L.	

Name	Spouse
Tralla, W. Anthony	
Wade, Mrs. Beverly R.	
Walker, Ms. Susan	
Weaver, James R.	
Webb, Douglass G.	Faye
Williams, Arthur	
Young, Ralph	Janice
Zander, Alos W.	

APPENDIX F: LISTING OF PICTURES, MAPS AND TABLES

PHOTOGRAPHS

Richard Kraus at Eighteen 5

D. Ralph Young at eighteen, on board the USS
    J. Franklin Bell 5

A Navy launch approaches the blazing USS
    West Virginia to rescue a sailor 11

The Battle Ship USS Pennsylvania 12

Ford Island taken by the Japanese during the
    surprise attack 12

The Memorial for the USS Arizona 15

The Bell camouflaged to avoid detection by
    the enemy 229

Shipmates at tenth reunion in Canton, Ohio 231

Attendance at last reunion in 2009 in Tyler, Texas . . 231

The USS *J. Franklin Bell* overshooting the pier
    in San Francisco 239

Coast Guardsman and Marine on the island
    of Guam 252

Coast Guardsmen watching as depth charges
    explode. 253

A Group of Chinese and their coast guardsmen. . . . 254

D Ralph Young on Bora Bora 258

Atomic bomb explosion over Hiroshima. 300

D Ralph Young surprise 90th birthday cruise 312

MAPS

The routes taken by the Japanese for their
  attack on Pearl Harbor and return to Japan 10

The Japanese Empire in early 1942. 17

The Battle inThe Aleutian Islands campaign
  for Adak, Attu and Kiska 34

The Battle for The Solomon Islands. 41

The Battle for Guadalcanal, in the Solomon Islands . 44

The Battle for Bougainville Island 53

The Battle of the Coral Sea 59

The Battle of Midway. 64

The Battle for The Gilbert Islands on the island
  of Tarawa 73

The Battle for Kwajalein. 82

The Battle for Eniwetok 87

Paths taken by the naval forces during the
  Battle of the Philippine Sea 90

The Battle of Saipan 94

The Battle for Tinian 103

The Battle for Guam 109

The Battle for Leyte in the Philippines 115

The Battle for Luzon 133

The Battle for Peleliu 168

The Battle for Iwo Jima. 175

The Battle of Okinawa 203

TABLES

Table 1. Comparison of Average Casualty rates for ground Combat Units xv

Table 2. Pearl Harbor Casualtities 18

Table 3. Aleutian Islands casualties 39

Table 4. Solomon Islands casualties 43

Table 5. Guadalcanal casualties 47

Table 6. Bougainville casualties 55

Table 7. Coral Sea casualties 61

Table 8. Midway casualties 71

Table 9. Tarawa casualties 78

Table 10. Kwajalein and Roi Namur casualties 84

Table 11. Eniwetok casualties 88

Table 12. Philippine Sea casualties 93

Table 13. Saipan casualties. 99

Table 14. Tinian casualties 106

Table 15. Guam casualties (first and second battles) 111

Table 16. Leyte casualties. 119

Table 17. Luzon casualties 137

Table 18. Peleliu casualties 170

Table 19. Iwo Jima casualties. 179

Table 20. Okinawa casualties. 206

Table 21. Estimated Asia and the Pacific Theater casualties 298

Table 22. Estimated total allied troop casualties during World War II 298

Table 23. Estimated total allied troops and civilian casualties during World War II. 299

APPENDIX G: POETRY BY TIMOTHY D. CHURCHILL

The American Veteran xvi

A Celebration of Our Forces. 3

The Day the Music Died 14

Another Shipmate Gone. 37

Deathly Encounters 120

The Spirit of the *J. Franklin Bell* 230

Farewell Salute to the *Bell* 240

Tribute to the WWII Generation 296

The Bluegrass Land Again. 305

Thanks for the Memories. 306

Reunion in Danville. 308

The Old Bell Crew and Tyler Too 310

CPSIA information can be obtained
at www.ICGtesting.com
Printed in the USA
FFOW02n2129230917
40203FF

9 781457 545917